A.D. **9**                    **30**                    **70**

# Contents

# Introduction

What is History? Many answers have been given to this question. To most people it is undoubtedly the record of past events. But a moment's reflection will show that it is not a record of everything that has happened, whether the subject be the history of mankind as a whole, or of a nation, a city, a religion or institution. History, as it is recorded by chroniclers or presented by historians, inevitably involves the selection of certain events as being especially significant among all that happened within a specific area of the past. And selection also implies criteria of interpretation by which events are considered significant. In other words, out of the complex of past happenings certain events are chosen as being "historical." This process of selection and interpretation is a very complicated one, and it has been going on ever since man first began to record his past—about the beginning of the third millennium B.C.

Selecting an "historical" event also involves a process of abstraction and concretion that is fundamentally artificial, yet instinctive to man and a basic factor of his rationality. It presupposes that the passage of time is made up of a series of "events," each distinct and identifiable. But, on analysis, this presupposition is very difficult to justify. What we call "Time" is essentially mysterious; it is one of the main categories of our consciousness, and we cannot get outside it and assess it objectively. Time presents itself to us primarily in the ever-changing pattern of our experience; if we were not conscious of such change, it is difficult to see how we should be aware of Time. But, although our apprehension of temporal change is continuous when we are conscious, some phenomena affect us more than others and we naturally endow them with especial significance; we abstract from a continuous sequence some specific section, and isolate it as a decisive "event." The section which we thus choose may extend over a period of some years as, for example, the French Revolution is designated a decisive event in French history; but generally our instinct is to select some more sharply defined happening that we can invest with definite significance as, for example, the storming of the Bastille on July 14, 1789 is said to constitute the beginning of the French Revolution—in other words, as being a "milestone" in French history.

The great German historian Leopold von Ranke (1795-1886) defined the historian's task as being that of describing the past "as it really happened" (*wie es eigentlich gewesen*). His definition will doubtless always stand as the ideal of scientifically objective history, and as a warning against the writing of history as propaganda or apologia for some nationalist, political or religious end. But it has come to be realized that this represents an ideal that can never be wholly achieved. As already noted, History inevitably implies selection and interpretation of the facts considered to be relevant. Both activities ultimately depend upon human minds, which are conditioned by many factors such as education, religion and nationality, quite apart from personal interests and consciously conceived aims. Throughout all ancient Hebrew historiography, for instance, runs the basic conviction that Time is a linear process in which the providence of Yahweh, the god of Israel, was being progressively revealed as History on behalf of his chosen people, the "children of Israel". By contrast, according to both the Hindu and Buddhist views, the empirical world is not reality but an illusory process of phenomena that moves unceasingly in repetitive cycles, so History can have no ultimate significance.

Nevertheless, even though von Ranke's ideal of History is beyond practical attainment, and all our records of the past contain an irreducible factor of personal evaluation, the conviction remains deep-rooted that History is important and worthy of study.

It is so regarded partly because it attests that man is an effective agent in the working-out of his destiny. For, even though the Marxist view of History as the inevitable fulfillment of fundamental economic laws is now widely recognized as logical, a realistic assessment of the evidence warns us against accepting our past and present as merely the result of economic predestination. We have all seen enough during the six decades of this century to be convinced that imponderable factors, as well as economic ones, operate to prevent the future pattern of History being forecast, as astronomers can forecast the future position of the planets. Thus, although it might have been predicted that a second world war would have resulted from the European situation after World War I, no one could have foreseen the part that Adolf Hitler was to play in the 1920s, or even in the first years of the 1930s. Several events of World War II, where History turned on the personal equation, might well have produced vastly different consequences for all concerned: what would have resulted if the Battle of Britain in 1940 had been won by Nazi Germany, or the Battle of Stalingrad had gone the other way in 1942–43, or the first atomic bomb had been completed in Germany instead of America? All these events, seen in retrospect, can rightly be called milestones of History.

Any philosophical definition of historical fact or of History itself must surely admit that some happenings in the story of man have been more critical or decisive for his destiny than others. Hence, a sequential study of such milestones of History will provide, as it were, a synoptic chart of the past of our race, rather as anatomical charts show the synapses or nerve centers of the human body. By linking each milestone with essays to show the connection of each historical synapse with those before and after, an account of human culture and civilization should emerge that is both dramatic and instructive, recording some of the factors that have shaped our situation today.

This volume of the series deals with a sequence of sixteen milestones, ranging in time from c. 3000 B.C. to A.D. 70. Limitation of space has inevitably precluded many that would have merited inclusion in a larger volume; but reference will be made to these in the linking essays. The selection of the first milestone constituted a problem, because recorded History started about the same time in Egypt and Sumer—indeed, a famous Sumerologist, Professor S. N. Kramer, has written a book entitled *History Begins at Sumer*, thus advocating the priority of the civilization in which he specializes. A good case can, indeed, be made out for the chronological primacy of Sumer; but, whereas the Sumerians had established small city-states in Lower Mesopotamia by the end of the fourth millennium B.C., it was in Egypt that the first national state, with a centralized government, was set up about 3000 B.C. From then on, the cultural achievement of Egypt equaled, if it did not excel, that of Sumer. However, the establishment of these first civilized states in the Valley of the Nile and the plain between the Tigris and Euphrates was preceded by millennia of gradual cultural development of the human race. And, although no written records exist to inform us of decisive milestones, some of the basic discoveries made during that long, remote period laid the foundations for the later achievements of civilization.

The earliest skeletal remains of *homo sapiens* revealed by archeology, together with relics of his culture, date from about thirty thousand years ago. From this evidence it is clear that certain fundamental discoveries had already been made. The use of fire can, indeed, be traced back to 300,000 B.C.; indications of its use were found in the rock shelters at Chou K'ou Tien, which had been inhabited by the so-called "Peking Man", a remote hominian precursor of *homo sapiens*. How this ability, never achieved by the other animals, was first acquired by the sub-men who preceded the first ancestors of our race is unknown; but it was basic to man's conquest of his natural environment. The ability to make tools and weapons has, similarly, a long unknown ancestry. Although some animals are accustomed to employ materials for purposes beyond the range of their own physical endowment (e.g., the dam-building of beavers), man alone has had the talent continuously to improve his tools and weapons, giving him an increasing mastery over animals stronger and swifter than himself. During the Old Stone Age, man also became an artist, as the painted caves in France, Spain and elsewhere impressively show. This art seems to have been inspired not by aesthetic ideas but by magical beliefs. Indeed, many other Palaeolithic practices show that already man was aware of problems, both natural and supernatural, which he sought to solve by religio-magical means. Thus he felt that the dead needed special tending: he carefully buried them with food, tools and ornaments, suggesting belief in some kind of *post-mortem* existence. He carved figurines representing women, with the maternal attributes grossly exaggerated and the faces left blank; and at Laussel, in the Dordogne area of France, he has left behind one such figure that, from its position, suggests a cult-object, deifying the Mother as the source of fertility and life.

Man in the Old Stone Age was a food-gatherer, who obtained his food chiefly by hunting. During the New Stone Age (*c.* 8000 B.C.), he became a food-producer. Agriculture began, although how and where remains unknown to us. But what has aptly been called the "Neolithic Revolution" laid the foundations of civilization. With the development of agriculture went the domestication of animals, and the in-vention of pottery and weaving. Soon the first agrarian settlements were founded, with stone-built houses and defenses: at Jericho and Çatal Hüyük in Anatolia, they date back to the seventh millenium B.C. A fertility religion also developed, centered on a mother goddess and the virility of the bull. The complexity of this Neolithic culture presupposes the elaboration of language as a means of communication. How and when language first began is beyond our knowing, but such complex undertakings as cave art suggest that it must surely have existed in some form in the Palaeolithic era.

Through these long and dim corridors of Time, before human thought and action began to be recorded in writing, there were doubtless many occasions which were truly milestones in the evolution of man. Who sowed the first seed corn, made the first earthen pot, worked the first metal, sailed the first boat, wrought the first wheel, must remain forever unknown. Yet these acts, involving new concepts and the technical skill to translate them into practical realities, initiated the long technological development which made possible all later achievements of civilized living. Hence we must recognize that, though their exact date is unknown, there were many great milestones in the story of man long before History, as such, began.

S. G. F. BRANDON

# Gift of the Nile

*On the long road to civilization, the emergence of the national state—particularly in the context of the world in which we live—is of paramount importance. Although other countries, and in particular Mesopotamia, the modern Iraq, developed some of the arts of civilization earlier, Egypt was the first country to draw itself together with a national identity. The documents that survive from the period are few, and therefore it is all the more remarkable that we know as much as we do about the unification of Upper and Lower Egypt. The invention of writing occurred in Egypt shortly before the event, but there is no written history on which to rely. However, the significance of the event is plain for all to see. Under successive dynasties of pharaohs the country prospered and its civilization flourished. The brilliance of the Egyptian achievement and its continuity have inspired and influenced mankind profoundly.*

If you travel south from Cairo, along the west bank of the Nile, you will see on your left a narrow strip of bright green vegetation, sometimes shadowed by palm groves and ending suddenly in the broad, slow-moving, mud-brown river. On your right the vegetation ends abruptly, and beyond it the Western Desert begins, a ridge of golden, wind-blown sand, with here and there eroded rocks that look as if they had been baked and split by the fierce sun.

The road swings to the right and climbs the desert ridge, and suddenly you see before you a mighty pyramid built in steps, surrounded by a high wall enclosing a large courtyard; and not only this, but many other pyramids rising out of a plateau of billowing sand that stretches endlessly to the west, as sterile and hostile as it was in the days of the pharaohs. You have arrived at the five-thousand-year-old cemetery of Saqqara, burial place of generations of kings, noblemen and high officials for more than a thousand years.

The Step Pyramid, built for the Pharaoh Djoser (c. 2800 B.C.) is the oldest large stone monument in the world, but it is far from being the oldest tomb at Saqqara. A little to the north of it are the ruins of a series of large mud-brick structures called *mastabas*—the Arabic word for bench. One of these, prosaically known to archaeologists as Tomb 3357, once contained the funerary equipment, and probably the body, of the first pharaoh of the First Dynasty, a ruler who preceded Djoser by at least four hundred years. His tomb or cenotaph—it is not certain which—has been variously dated as somewhere between 3200 and 3000 B.C. One of his names (for the pharaohs bore several) was Hor-Aha, and he was the first pharaoh to rule over a united Egypt.

Hor-Aha's reign, and that of his predecessor, Narmer, mark a momentous turning point in history, the point at which Egypt, until then an agglomeration of petty states loosely federated into two kingdoms, became one truly united state under one divine ruler, the pharaoh. The conquest was probably achieved mainly by Narmer, who came from southern or Upper Egypt, but the unification was advanced by Hor-Aha, one of whose names was Min or Men. It is significant that the historians of Greek classical times, who had access to Egyptian temple records long since destroyed, state that the founder of Egypt was *Menes*, which seems to be the classical Greek form of Men or Min. There is still some controversy among Egyptologists as to whether Menes was Hor-Aha or Narmer. Perhaps the two kings had become fused in folk memory as one man. What *is* certain is that Hor-Aha was the first pharaoh of the First Dynasty and that he ruled at some time between 3200 and 3000 B.C., after the conquests of his predecessor, Narmer, had laid the foundations of unification. It is important to remember that we are dealing with a period before the beginnings of written history, and the invention of writing seems to have occurred in Egypt only shortly before Narmer's conquest. The documents that have survived are thus few and rudimentary, and a great deal of speculation is involved.

Narmer's original capital was probably Hierakonpolis in the south. Unlike Lower (i.e. northern) Egypt, which consisted mainly of the flat, highly fertile Nile Delta, Upper (i.e. southern) Egypt covered more rugged land and probably bred a hardier race of people. Already by about 3200 B.C. the inhabitants of both Upper and Lower Egypt were at a fairly advanced state of civilization. They could make copper as well as stone weapons. They could write. They were capable of producing works of art such as the Slate Palette of Narmer and the famous ivory Mace-head of Hierakonpolis, both of which are carved with scenes apparently depicting Narmer's conquest of Lower Egypt.

The Slate Palette of Narmer found at Hierakonpolis is one of the most important historical

Seated statue of Pharaoh Djoser, from a chapel adjoining the Step Pyramid, his tomb.

*Opposite* The Step Pyramid of Saqqara is the oldest stone monument in the world. It dates from *c.* 2800 B.C. and was built to house the dead Pharaoh Djoser.

*Right* Pre-dynastic pottery group of mother and child.

*Below* One of the stone mace-heads from Hierakonpolis, now in the Ashmolean Museum in Oxford. It depicts King Narmer during the celebration of his jubilee festival.

documents discovered in Egypt. On one side there is a scene showing Narmer walking in procession, preceded by his attendants; on the same panel are rows of decapitated corpses of his enemies. Another section on the same side of the palette shows the pharaoh, in the form of a bull, demolishing an enemy fortress. On the reverse side, Narmer is shown in an attitude typical of that adopted by later pharaohs, with one hand grasping the hair of a kneeling captive, the other holding a club. Beneath this the king's enemies are shown in flight. The date of the palette is between 3200 and 3000 B.C. and the primitive hieroglyphs on the stone spell out the name Nar-Mer.

The Mace-head of Narmer is equally important. It shows Narmer seated on a throne and wearing the "Red Crown" of Lower Egypt. Above him hovers the vulture-goddess Nekhbet of Hierakonpolis; before him march the standard-bearers of his conquering army. There is also a little figure of a woman seated beneath a palanquin. This figure is believed to represent a princess of the conquered kingdom of Lower Egypt whom Narmer subsequently married—probably Queen Nit-hotep, whose lavish tomb was discovered at Nagadeh. The primitive hieroglyphic signs clearly depict the name Nar-Mer (within a rectangular structure called the *serekh*, probably representing the panelled façade of his palace) and various numerals that indicate 120,000 men, 400,000 oxen and 1,422,000 goats captured in war.

That Narmer was a mighty conqueror is without doubt; yet no large monuments of his period have yet been found north of Tarkhan, and his queen was buried at Nagadeh. A somewhat insignificant tomb, No. B10, at Abydos, also in the south, has been identified as his. But since the kings of this and later periods had two tombs, one in the south and another in the north (symbolizing their dominion over the two kingdoms of Upper and Lower Egypt), it is possible that the real tomb of Narmer still awaits discovery.

Hor-Aha, Narmer's successor and the first ruler of a united Egypt, bore a name that means "fighting hawk." This was his *Horus* name, as ruler of Upper Egypt, but to symbolize his rule over Lower Egypt, he used the *Nebti* name of Men (or Min) signifying "Established." The co-relation of these two names was proved when an ivory plaque bearing them both was discovered in the tomb of Queen Nit-hotep. This ivory label also depicts a most important scene commemorating the unification of the two lands.

Hor-Aha fought successful campaigns against the Nubians beyond the First Cataract, and no doubt had to engage in other frontier wars, but, by right of both conquest and inheritance, he was the first ruler of a united Egypt. His greatest achievement was the foundation of a new capital, called by the Greeks Memphis, near the point at which the two main branches of the Nile divide, a little south of modern Cairo. This site was carefully chosen as the natural frontier between north and south. In order to create it Hor-Aha had to divert the course of the Nile (as Herodotus tells us) and drain the land in order to construct a huge dike.

Hor-Aha made a wise choice of site for his capital. The first Neolithic invaders of Egypt, attracted by the beneficent Nile with its annual gift of rich fertilizing mud and the abundance of wild game near its banks, had arrived some 2,000 years before Hor-Aha's time. Unlike their wandering hunter ancestors, these Neolithic people could settle permanently in one place. But they and their descendants lived in a conglomeration of petty tribal states scattered over both Lower and Upper Egypt, and it was chiefly by siting Memphis at a point that gave him control over an area from the Delta to the First Cataract, six hundred miles up the Nile, that Hor-Aha and his successors were able to create and maintain a unified Egypt.

Saqqara was the cemetery of Memphis, and if one stands on the edge of the plateau, one can see beyond the river and amid the palm groves on the east bank a cluster of mud-brick dwellings which is all that remains of what was once the richest and most powerful city on earth. It stretched some ten miles along the east bank of the Nile as far as modern Cairo and beyond. There lay the royal palace and the villas of the nobles and high officials of Pharaoh; there rose the temples of their gods, many-columned and magnificent. All were built of mud-brick, because at this time (*c.* 3200 B.C.) the

*Left* The Slate Palette of Narmer, showing the Pharaoh (who wears the White Crown of Upper Egypt) seizing a kneeling captive.

*Below* Detail from the reverse side of the Palette of Narmer. The pharaoh is walking in procession, wearing the Red Crown of Lower Egypt, preceded by his standard-bearers. Before them are rows of decapitated enemies.

*Above* Detail of the Hunter's Palette, now in the British Museum; it shows Egyptians hunting lion, gazelle, ostrich, and other desert creatures.

*Below left* Gray-white marble bowl, probably Pre-dynastic.

*Below right* Bedjmes the shipbuilder, Third Dynasty; red granite statue now in the British Museum.

Egyptians had not yet learned the art of building monumentally in stone. We know what these buildings looked like because they are crudely represented on the ivory tablets and slate palettes found in the tombs of the First and Second Dynasties. Further, when in the Third Dynasty (*c.* 2800 B.C.) the Egyptians raised their first great stone building, the Step Pyramid of Djoser and its surrounding walls, courtyards and temples, they reproduced in stone the type of architecture they had previously used for mud-brick and timber.

It is a curious fact that this type of architecture, with its characteristic "panelled façades" also occurs in ancient Sumer, in Lower Mesopotamia, at a somewhat earlier date. Moreover, some of the Egyptian hieroglyphics of this period seem to have been derived from Sumer. These similarities have led certain Egyptologists, notably Professor Walter Emery, Professor of Egyptology at University College, London, to put forward the theory that the founders of Egyptian civilization and the unifiers of Egypt were a foreign race, originating perhaps in Lower Mesopotamia, whose cultural influences spread both eastward to Sumer and westward to Egypt. Only further archaeological investigation can prove or disprove this theory. The majority of scholars continue to assume that the earliest rulers of ancient Egypt sprang from a native stock, though they were almost certainly influenced by the civilization that had arisen in Lower Mesopotamia.

It is unlikely that in Narmer's own time and that of his immediate successors the effect of the unification was widely felt. Sumer, the only comparable civilization, was very remote from Egypt and there appears to have been only a slight contact, though an important one—that is, unless one accepts Professor Emery's theory. Nevertheless, objects found in tombs and made during and after Hor-Aha's time prove that between approximately 3200 and 2800 B.C. Egyptian civilization was developing at a rapid rate. Magnificent stone

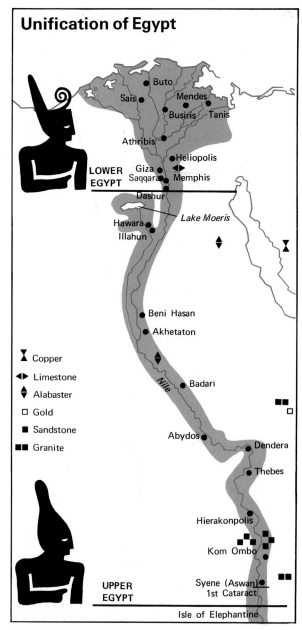

# Unification of Egypt

LOWER EGYPT

Buto
Sais
Mendes
Busiris
Tanis
Athribis
Heliopolis
Giza
Saqqara
Memphis
Dashur
Lake Moeris
Hawara
Illahun
Beni Hasan
Akhetaton
Badari
Abydos
Dendera
Thebes
Hierakonpolis
Kom Ombo
Syene (Aswan)
1st Cataract

UPPER EGYPT

Isle of Elephantine

Nile

⚒ Copper
◄► Limestone
◆ Alabaster
☐ Gold
■ Sandstone
■■ Granite

*Left* Seated figure of a scribe, showing how a roll of papyrus was held in the left hand and gradually unrolled in use.

*Below* Egyptian hiero-glyphs. The signs are colored, and outlined in black ink.

vases show the skill of the Egyptians in stone carving, a skill that was eventually to reveal itself in the building of the pyramids, tombs, and temples of hewn stone. Carpentry, gold work and copper work make it clear that even at this remote period, before the first pyramid was built, Egypt was on the threshold of a long period of cultural expansion.

For the first few centuries after Hor-Aha (or Menes) the emphasis was on internal unification and the creation of an immense monolithic state. The tribal divisions became *nomes* (provinces), each with its own chief city. Agriculture flourished as the Egyptians learned how to control the flooding of their great river to produce an increasing abundance of food and provide for an increasing population. A large standing army was created. An elaborate hierarchy of officials controlled the kingdom. Expeditions were sent south into Nubia, partly for expansion and partly for trade, and also into Libya, in the Western Desert.

Writing, one of man's greatest inventions, developed swiftly and soon became very sophisticated. Scribal schools were set up, adjacent to the temples, and a new class of literate priests and their followers provided a body of tax collectors, civil servants and other officials who ran the economy of the newly united kingdom. In about 2700 B.C. the Pharaoh Khufu (or Cheops, to give him his Greek cognomen) built a monument of stone—the Great Pyramid—so enormous that it has been said to contain enough stone to reach two-thirds of the way round the world at the Equator. Similar pyramids were erected by Khufu's successors, notably at Saqqara, Abusir, and Dahshur, all intended to preserve for eternity the bodies of their royal builders.

After a period of civil war and internal disruption, the causes of which are unknown, the country revived under a new dynasty of pharaohs, those of the so-called Middle Kingdom (2100–1700 B.C.).

The tradition of national unity established by Narmer and Hor-Aha, however, was so strong that in the end a new dynasty of pharaohs, the Eighteenth, succeeded in driving out the invaders and creating the New Kingdom (1570–1085 B.C.), the first three centuries of which marked the most illustrious period of Egyptian power and influence. This was the period of imperial expansion that eventually led to Egyptian armies penetrating not only into Lebanon, Palestine and Syria but even as far as what is now northern Iraq. Egyptian colonies were set up along the Mediterranean coast and at strategic points in the hinterland, each under its governor.

In later years the innate conservatism of the Egyptians hindered their development in comparison with other peoples. For example, they learned to use the horse and chariot in warfare only after the Hyksos had beaten them with this weapon in about 1720 B.C. They continued to depend on bronze weapons when iron was rapidly coming into use in other lands, and even in Ptolemaic times (from the fourth century B.C.) they continued to follow their ancient customs—although the hieroglyphic inscriptions on temple walls reveal many errors, indications that the engravers had little or no knowledge of the early writings and had become mere copyists. This may be taken as symbolic of Egyptian culture as a whole. Great and splendid though it was in its prime, every generation tended to follow an accepted pattern laid down by their remote ancestors. Even when, in the first century B.C., Egypt became a province of the Roman Empire, the Caesars were represented on temple walls in the traditional dress, and performing the traditional ceremonies, of pharaohs just like Narmer and Hor-Aha. And to the very end of their civilization, which survived down to Greek and Roman times, they preserved the fiction of the Two Kingdoms of the South and North that had existed before the conquests of Narmer and Hor-Aha. The pharaoh was always known as "The King of Upper and Lower Egypt."

Yet the debt owed to Egypt by western Asia and eastern Europe is immense. The ancient Greeks, probably the most intelligent race that has ever lived, acknowledged this debt freely. From the time when their merchants began setting up trading posts in Egypt in the seventh and sixth centuries B.C. they were fascinated by Egypt, as one can tell from the pages of Herodotus and Diodorus. Archaic Greek art was clearly influenced by Egyptian sculpture, which at its best has few equals anywhere in the world. The Greeks copied Egyptian medicine and surgery and in many other fields of knowledge looked upon the Egyptian priests as their mentors. As one Egyptian said to an inquiring Greek, "You Greeks are like children, everlastingly asking questions." One may be sure that they would not have asked questions had they not expected useful and illuminating replies.

Narmer and his successors, by bringing the

Wooden panel carved in relief with the figure of Hesy-ra, one of Pharaoh Djoser's officials (c. 2000 B.C.). This is one of the earliest, and one of the finest, Egyptian sculptures in wood.

The rising power of the *nomarchs*—governors of the *nomes* or provinces—was held in check, but disruptive forces threatened the central authority and weakened the power of the pharaohs. A group of tribes from western Asia, known to later historians as the Hyksos or "Shepherd Kings," seized the opportunity to occupy parts of Lower Egypt. Their leaders set themselves up as pharaohs, so that at one period there were two pharaohs, a Hyksos interloper ruling from Avaris, in the Delta, and a native Egyptian pharaoh ruling from Thebes in Upper Egypt.

resources of the whole country under the control of one ruler, had achieved something of immense importance. For Egypt was one of the most fertile lands in the world and potentially one of the richest. From these beginnings great cities were to spring up, armies would be levied and trained, trade would expand, the arts and crafts would develop, and more and more power would be centered on the divine figure of the pharaoh, who claimed to be the "Son of Re," god of the sun and creator and maintainer of all living things. The unification laid the foundations of a civilized and powerful Egypt with a military and cultural influence extending far beyond its borders.

LEONARD COTTRELL

*Above* Wooden model of bakers and brewers.

*Below* Wooden model of men and oxen ploughing. Models such as these were frequently placed in Egyptian tombs, as part of the provisions made for the needs of the dead person in the after-life, which was thought to be very similar to life in this world.

The ancient Egyptians can be said to have been the first ancient people to create a national state. Another ancient people, however, can claim priority over the Egyptians in the invention of some of the arts of civilization and in the development of urban life. These were the inhabitants of ancient Mesopotamia, now called Iraq, the land through which the Tigris and Euphrates, the Twin Rivers, flow. The southern part of this land the inhabitants called Sumer. Excavations have shown that at a time when the Egyptians were still simple fishermen living in wattle and daub huts, using flint tools and storing their grain in baskets, there were people living in the valley of the Euphrates who already lived a life of some sophistication, in walled towns which (since this is a relative term only) we may call cities. They had built imposing towers and temples of mudbrick, ornamented with mosaic and fresco, and had achieved considerable technological mastery in stone-cutting, metallurgy and the potter's craft. The most remarkable evidence of this urban culture comes from Warka, about two hundred miles from the present

Urnanshe of Lagash with his family

head of the Persian Gulf, which was the site of ancient Uruk—the Biblical Erech. But similar remains, dating to the middle of the fourth millennium B.C., have been found at Ur, Nippur, Eridu and Lagash, and many other sites in Sumer, and also farther north at Mari, on the Euphrates near its junction with the Khabur, and at Tell Brak on its headwaters.

## Life in Sumer

Agriculture and dairy farming were the bases of life in Sumer. The alluvium brought down by the rivers is very fertile and the productivity of the land remarkable; barley and wheat were the staple

crops, and the date palm and vine were cultivated. Fish abounded, and was an important source of food; so also were sheep and goats, of which there were many varieties. But the rivers, whose annual flood brought life to the fields of the Sumerians, were also a constant threat to their safety. Tradition preserved the memory of a disastrous flood which had once all but wiped out mankind; the hero Ziusudra, who escaped in a boat of bitumen and reeds built at the behest of the god Enki, the water-god, was the prototype of Noah.

Bronze model of mule-drawn chariot

## The invention of writing

One of the greatest advances in the history of man was the invention, about 3500 B.C., of a system of writing. The earliest clay tablets are simple accounts—lists of objects, persons or animals, each depicted by a line drawing, or "pictogram," followed by a series of numerical signs or numbers. They are little more, in fact, than tallies, inscribed on small square cushions of clay. Gradually, however, the picture writing was stylized and the lines, jabbed for

Predynastic pictographic tablet

speed with the slanting edge of a reed stylus, became wedge-shaped, or cuneiform. This writing system evolved to such an extent that abstract ideas could be expressed.

## Sumerian origins

The Sumerian language is quite different in structure and vocabulary from any other known language of the ancient world, and attempts to derive the Sumerians from an original home in the Caucasus mountains, or from the Iranian plateau, on linguistic grounds have so far failed. Nor does

Ziggurat; Babylonian seal

archaeology give us much help. It has been suggested that the curious temple-tower characteristic of Sumerian cities—the ziggurat, as it was called—is evidence that the Sumerians once worshiped their gods on the tops of mountains. Perhaps many strands were interwoven to make the fabric of their civilization. There may have been a Semitic element in the population of Mesopotamia from early times—certainly in the north at Mari, for the princes of Mari bore Semitic names, though they wore the sheepskin skirts and leather cloaks of the Sumerians and shared the same material civilization. And it was a Semite, a man called Sharrukin, or Sargon, who became cupbearer to the King of Kish (near Hillah) and finally seized power in that city. In a series of brilliant campaigns, Sargon wrested the hegemony of Sumer from the leading city of the time, Umma, establishing his new capital at Agade in Akkad, not far from Kish, in about 2370 B.C. Henceforward he was to rule as King of Sumer and Akkad. His successors claimed the title "King of the Four Quarters (of the World)." Both he and his grandson, Naram-Sin, led armies into North Syria and Anatolia, sources of copper, lead, silver and gold; they hewed conifers in the Amanus mountains and floated the logs down the Euphrates to build their palaces. For the first time Mesopotamia was united under a single, strong administration and the Akkadian kings dominated the whole of western Asia. The ships of the merchants of Agade sailed southwards from the port of Ur, down the Persian Gulf to Tilmun,

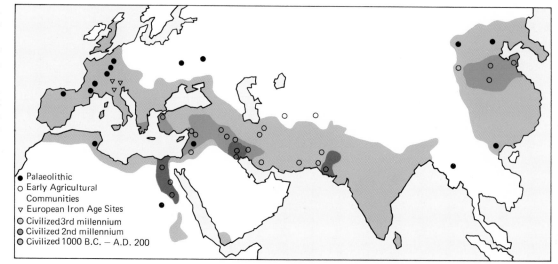

- ● Palaeolithic
- ○ Early Agricultural Communities
- ▽ European Iron Age Sites
- ◎ Civilized 3rd millennium
- ● Civilized 2nd millennium
- ◉ Civilized 1000 B.C. — A.D. 200

Early centers of culture

Sargon of Akkad

which is thought to be the island of Bahrein, and further south to the lands of Magan and Melukhkha. Magan, which may be the Makran coast of Persia, perhaps included also the coast of Oman on the other side of the Straits, a land rich in copper and stone. For

Akkadian ship

Magan furnished the Sumerians with the hard black stone for their statues, copper ore, and lumps of lapis lazuli, the valuable blue stone used in inlay and jewelry, which came many hundreds of miles from the mines in Afghanistan. Melukhkha lay even farther away: many scholars believe this is the Sumerian name for India.

## Indus Valley Civilization

In the northwest corner of the continent of India at this time a great civilization had grown up in the basin of the Indus River. Its two chief cities, called today Mohenjo-Daro and Harappa, lay some five hundred miles apart. Each was a masterpiece of town-planning, with rectangular blocks of houses divided one from the other by a crisscross of streets broad enough to take the solid-wheeled ox-carts. Houses and public buildings were of burnt brick—a necessity in a

land of monsoon rain, whereas unbaked brick sufficed in Sumer—and there was an elaborate and skillfully planned drainage system to carry away both sewage and rainwater. More will be said of this Indus Valley Civilization, or Harappan Culture, as it is sometimes called, in a later chapter; suffice it here to say that ample evidence has recently been discovered of the existence at this time of Indian ports and trading stations in the Gulf of Cambay and on the Pakistan coast north of Karachi, and even on the south coast of Makran itself. Seals and other objects of Indus Valley workmanship found by excavators on Mesopotamian sites of the Akkadian period are evidence of contact between Sumer and the Indus

Bullock cart from Mohenjo-Daro

Valley, and some scholars are inclined to think that the civilization of Mohenjo-Daro and Harappa was either directly based on, or else inspired by, that of Sumer at an earlier period. There are, however, many essential differences between the two and the pictographic script of the Indus Valley owes nothing, so far as we can see (the language is unknown, for it is as yet undeciphered), to the cuneiform of Mesopotamia or its pictographic prototype. Moreover, the animals on the beautifully cut steatite seals are entirely those of the Indian fauna—the buffalo, the elephant and the rhinocerus, none of which was known in Sumer. While it cannot be denied that there was contact, either direct or indirect, between the two areas—perhaps over a long period, till the time of the First Dynasty of Babylon—the inspiration behind the civilization of the Indus Valley has yet to be traced.

## Defeat of Naram-Sin

In Mesopotamia, Sumerian was gradually replaced in official documents by Semitic Akkadian, though Sumerian was retained in the temples. The administration of the

Figures from the Standard of Ur

kingdom was centralized and the old citizen army of the Sumerian states was replaced by a professional body trained in mountain warfare. The need for such an army was a real one, for enemies now began to press in upon the kingdom of Agade. Naram-Sin himself met with defeat from a coalition of mountain chieftains in the north of his realm, and though his successors managed for a time to stave off disaster, in about 2200 B.C. the Gutians, invaders from the Zagros mountains to the northeast of Iraq, captured Agade and took over the country.

In the south of the country, however, the old Sumerian cities seem to have been little affected by Gutian rule, and it was in these ancient centers of civilization, Uruk and Ur, that the people finally combined forces to drive out the invaders. Under the able rule of the Third Dynasty of Ur, the country was reunited and prosperity returned. Elam was made subject, and a profitable trade with the interior of Iran was thereby secured. Ships sailed again down the Persian Gulf, and among

Festival scene from Khafajah

the treasures they brought back were carved ivory figures and pearls. This was the golden age of Sumerian civilization. Temples were rebuilt on a grander scale than ever before, among them the great ziggurat at Ur, which became a landmark for miles around. Literature flourished under royal patronage, and a system of law was codified.

The significance of Sumerian culture lies not only in its antiquity and intrinsic achievement, but in that it was adopted, and adapted, by the Akkadians and their successors, the Babylonians and Assyrians. They adopted the pantheon of Sumerian gods and adjusted it to accommodate their own gods of desert and sky. They took over Sumerian script, adapting it to their own language, and kept Sumerian as the language of liturgy.

Thus after the collapse of the Ur dynasty, the ancient traditions continued. After a period of confusion, the city-states regrouped under new leaders: these were the Amorites, a Semitic people from the west who moved into the cities of Mesopotamia and gradually took control of many of them. Babylon was the seat of one of these Amorite dynasties, and Hammurabi its king.

An able warrior as well as a capable administrator, Hammurabi inherited from his Amorite predecessors a modest kingdom centered around the small town called Babil, or Babylon. Early in his reign he achieved some success, but he had to wait thirty years for his great victories. If one considers the significance of his reign in terms of human achievement, Hammurabi's name is connected with one remarkable document. This document, and its far-reaching significance, is to be the subject of the next chapter.

# The First Law Code

*As the political state evolved, the problem of its administration evolved too. The territory ruled over by Hammurabi of Babylon was composed not simply of two adjacent areas with similar characteristics—as in Narmer's Egypt—but of former independent states with very different traditions. Hammurabi had extended his territory by conquest, but as overlord he proved a conscientious ruler, dedicated to reform, and possibly the greatest tribute paid to him by his subjects was the comment, preserved in the chronicles of the country : "He established justice in the land." Inscribed on a stone, the memorial of his justice was providentially preserved for all time, despite its being carried off to Susa by an Elamite king early in the twelfth century B.C. Regardless of the fact that Hammurabi's immediate successors were unable to hold on to the territory he had won, his legacy to mankind constitutes a momentous milestone in the progress of human achievement.*

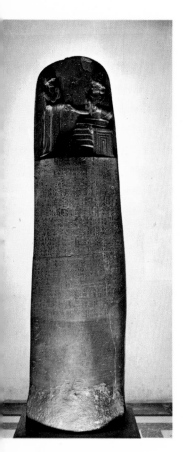

*Above* The black basalt stele on which the Code of Hammurabi is inscribed. The lower part was erased by a Elamite king who captured the stele about 1200 B.C.

*Opposite* Relief on the stele of Hammurabi. The king is standing before a divinity, who is probably Shamash, the sun god, regarded as the law-giver.

Sometime toward the end of his reign, the great Babylonian king Hammurabi (*c.* 1792–1750 B.C.) inscribed a code of "laws" on a tall stele of hard stone. It was neither the first nor the last document of its type in Mesopotamia: at least half a dozen similar codes are known, of which the oldest dates from the end of the third millennium. But none of them so deserves to be considered the classic of its kind: no other is so broad in its scope and of such intellectual and literary perfection.

The Code of Hammurabi, in fact, provides both a brief history of, and a triumphant monument to, his reign. It is only toward the end of his life that a monarch feels the need to draw up an honors list of his successes and to give a summary of his experience and wisdom in order to inspire emulation as well as admiration. We know that the Babylonian empire as it appears in this code existed only during the great king's final years: in the prologue to the code, Hammurabi mentions victories that he did not win until the thirty-fifth or even the thirty-eighth year of his forty-year reign. It is because that reign marks one of the culminating points in the history of ancient Mesopotamia, a civilization that lasted for at least three or four thousand years, that the code is so important as documentary evidence.

In the 1,500 years before Hammurabi's reign, the "Land Between the Two Rivers" and above all the southern part of that territory, between present-day Baghdad and the Persian Gulf, had become the location of what one can call, compared with other minor prehistoric cultures, the oldest civilization in the world. Mesopotamian society was based on the systematic exploitation of land: the soil was cultivated intensively, and its natural productivity, already considerable, was increased by the establishment of a great system of canals that ensured effective irrigation. In those areas that had not been taken for agriculture or the cultivation of palm trees, stock raising flourished, chiefly sheep and goats but also donkeys, cattle, pigs and other livestock. This work was carried out by the greater part of the population, both urban and rural. Its administration led to the establishment of a body of highly specialized civil servants, who preferred to live in the city near the palace and the temples; for it was there that the real rulers, the gods and their representative the king, had their headquarters.

The earth and all its produce belonged to the gods, as did the workers, who were their servants. Hence the harvest and the crops and the produce from herds (notably wool and skins) were brought for sale to the temples and stored in their warehouses. Once enough had been redistributed to meet the requirements of all citizens, according to their social standing, the rest was used as capital and as credit for huge commercial enterprises.

Since earliest times trade had been conducted with all the surrounding countries, and even farther afield—from the Lebanon and Asia Minor to Persia, both along the coast and in the mountainous interior, and as far as the western borders of India. Trade was vital to Mesopotamia because although it had a surplus of grain and animal products, it completely lacked certain raw materials that were necessary for civilized life. The soil provided only clay, bitumen and reeds; there was no timber whatever, no stone and no metal, although technicians had developed since at least the fourth millennium a technique of bronze work. Imported materials were worked by a host of skilled, often highly artistic craftsmen, who provided not only tools for farmers and stock breeders but also furnishings and works of art for the temples and palaces. These finished goods often found their way abroad as exports. One can see from this how well organized, how active and expanding the Mesopotamian economy was, and how systematized and orderly was its society.

The vast amount of accountancy that such

*Above* A letter from King Hammurabi to an official, instructing him to procure the ransom of a soldier with money from the treasury of the temple in the soldier's home town. The Code of Hammurabi includes detailed instructions as to who shall provide ransom money, according to the circumstances.

*Right* The Code of Hammurabi did not cover all the subjects that would now be dealt with in a code of law; its principal features are summarized in this diagram.

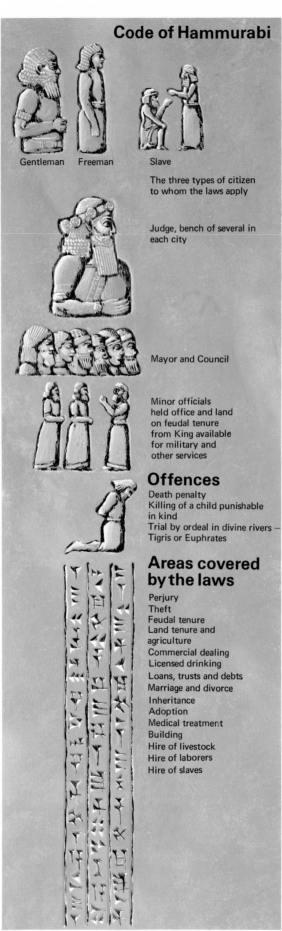

## Code of Hammurabi

Gentleman  Freeman  Slave

The three types of citizen to whom the laws apply

Judge, bench of several in each city

Mayor and Council

Minor officials held office and land on feudal tenure from King available for military and other services

## Offences

Death penalty
Killing of a child punishable in kind
Trial by ordeal in divine rivers – Tigris or Euphrates

## Areas covered by the laws

Perjury
Theft
Feudal tenure
Land tenure and agriculture
Commercial dealing
Licensed drinking
Loans, trusts and debts
Marriage and divorce
Inheritance
Adoption
Medical treatment
Building
Hire of livestock
Hire of laborers
Hire of slaves

operations entailed had been considerably simplified about 2800 B.C. by what was virtually a stroke of genius: the invention of a system of writing. The system was still very complicated and was to remain so for a long period. Only specialists could understand and operate it, but they were to create the environment for the development of a truly intellectual culture. This writing was first used exclusively for keeping the accountancy records of the temples, but it was soon simplified and made more flexible and was then used for the compilation of dictionaries of signs and words, comprising all the symbols. Next it was used to record the deeds and exploits of kings, religious rites, and myths that the philosophers and theologians of the time had constructed to explain the great eternal problems of human existence and destiny. Finally it was used to express a certain number of scientific ideas and theories, the result of persistent observation and a profound desire to see the universe as orderly according to a particular perspective: divination, mathematics, medicine and jurisprudence.

This high degree of civilization, already established by the third millennium, was the product of a mixed population, of which the major elements and the most easy for us to identify were Semites and Sumerians. The former belonged to an ineradicable race of semi-nomadic shepherds who since the dawn of history have lived on the fringes of the great Syrian and Arabian deserts, and of whom a certain number have always been attracted by town life and have settled there. The Sumerians, whose provenance is unknown but who probably arrived from the east or the southeast by the fourth millennium at the latest, seem to have severed all ties with their former home and their kinsmen: in Mesopotamia they never received that infusion of new blood that has perpetually nourished and strengthened the Semitic part of the population. Consequently, while in the first half of Mesopotamian history, up to the end of the third millennium, the Sumerians appear to be the active, inventive and creative force in the development of civilization and at first more important in the political field, they were to find themselves gradually supplanted by the Semites.

Politically, the country was divided into a certain number of small states, each grouped around a city, with a majority of Semites in the north. These city-states sometimes allied with each other, sometimes fought against each other and were sometimes combined into larger kingdoms by the predominance of one or other among them. By the third millennium it was the Semites who seemed to have the advantage of the biggest alliances: first, at an early stage, around the city of Kish; and second, toward 2350 B.C. and for the following century and a half, around the city of Agade. At the beginning of the second millennium another Semitic dynasty, which seems to have been dominated by immigrants from the west, made Babylon their seat of power for three centuries

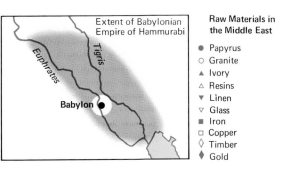

Babylon

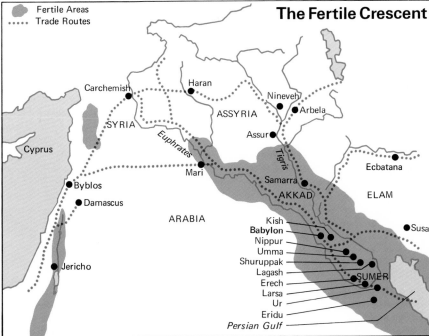

Fertile Areas
Trade Routes

## The Fertile Crescent

Carchemish
Haran
Nineveh
ASSYRIA
Arbela
SYRIA
Assur
Cyprus
Euphrates
Tigris
Ecbatana
Mari
Samarra
AKKAD
ELAM
Byblos
Damascus
ARABIA
Kish
Babylon
Susa
Nippur
Umma
Shuruppak
Jericho
Lagash
SUMER
Erech
Larsa
Ur
Eridu
Persian Gulf

(about 1900–1600 B.C.). This gave the greatest of their kings the opportunity to create a third Semitic empire, displacing the Sumerians—who were this time completely absorbed and wiped forever off the map—and giving a special brilliance to the ancient civilization that had continued to expand and thrive for almost 2,000 years. This king was Hammurabi, whose "code" thus marked an achievement and a peak of civilization never before attained.

Hammurabi's impressive work—some 3,500 lines of cuneiform characters—is divided into three parts. There is a central section written in straightforward, clear, unadorned prose. This section is framed by a prologue of three hundred lines and an epilogue of five hundred, which are sublime and lyrical in tone, with a choice of words and turns of phrase more like poetry.

It is from the central part that the monument derives its name of "code," which was bestowed upon it by its first decipherers. This section consists of a series of regulations—282 in all—that cover many secular activities. Some of these regulations concern crimes and their punishment:

If a man has brought an accusation of murder against another without being able to produce proof—the accuser shall be put to death.

Others are related to administrative problems, such as the proper conduct of business affairs:

If a man of business has entrusted to a shopkeeper either grain or wool or oil or any other merchandise to sell retail—once the sale has taken place and the purchase money has been accounted for, then the shopkeeper shall transmit it to the businessman, but shall receive from him a sealed document in evidence of the sum which has been remitted.

A listing of the subjects covered shows the range of these regulations. They concern false witness, theft, royal fiefs (lands allotted by the sovereign to members of his entourage, on condition that they share with him the produce), husbandry, town planning, commerce, deposits and pledges, marriage, divorce, second wives, the joint responsibility of husbands and wives for debts, preparations for marriage, the disposal of assets after the death of a spouse or parent, certain particular cases like the marriage of widows or priestesses, adoption, wet-nursing, assault and injuries, regulations for certain occupations, both professional and menial, and slavery.

Not all aspects of communal life appear in this list: for instance there is no reference to taxation.

Furthermore, when one looks at the code more

*Left* The stele of Naram Sin, King of Agade, who is shown standing before a mountain, his feet resting on slain enemies, while soldiers ascend a wooded path.

*Right* Map of Mesopotamia, showing the principal towns of the kingdom of Hammurabi and its natural resources.

*Above* The remains of the prisons of Hammurabi, excavated at Babylon.

*Above right* Gudea, the Ensi or ruler of Lagash, under whom the city of Lagash became the leading cultural center of Sumer
The Sumerians were the earliest rulers of the civilization of Mesopotamia, and were displaced finally by the Semitic dynasty of Babylon under King Hammurabi.

closely the various paragraphs are all so concerned with specific and individual cases that it is impossible to describe them as "laws" in the proper sense of the word—that is to say, truly abstract and universal propositions. For example in the first paragraph quoted earlier, the question of false accusation on a capital charge relates only to murder, whereas there are numerous other possible examples like treason and sacrilege which should have been included for consideration. And in the second paragraph quoted, the need for scrupulous and documented accounts should surely extend to many business dealings other than the specific one between the man of business and his agent.

It is therefore a mistake to refer to a "code," at any rate if we mean to use the word in its true sense of a compilation of the entire legislation of a country and of a period. We are dealing rather with a collection of judgments originally pronounced to resolve actual cases, and subsequently classified into a sort of treatise on jurisprudence, illustrated by examples. We must realize that the ancient Mesopotamians were as yet incapable of formulating abstract and truly universal principles, i.e. laws. They chose to instruct in methods of ordering society by formulating examples from a

sufficiently large and typical selection of actual cases—in the way that we still teach our children grammar and arithmetic. The Code of Hammurabi is, then, both a manual on the art of judgment and a treatise on jurisprudence.

The prologue and epilogue enable us to understand better the significance that its author intended this imposing work to have. In the prologue Hammurabi confides to us his concept of himself and his role: he portrays himself as appointed by the gods to exercise royal power over his people, and he flatters himself that he has accomplished this great duty to perfection:

When Anu the Sublime, King of the gods together with Enlil, Lord of the sky and of the earth, the master of destiny of peoples, had bestowed upon Marduk, the eldest son of Enki, supreme power over all peoples and had enabled him to prevail over all the other gods, when they had pronounced the majestic name of Babylon and decreed the extension of its power over the whole universe and the establishment of an eternal kingdom based on foundations as immovable as those of the sky and the earth, then Anu and Enlil also pronounced my own name, Hammurabi, devout prince and worshiper of the gods, so that I might bring order to my people and so that I might free them from evil and wicked men, that

I should defend the weak from the oppression of the mighty, and that I might rise like the sun over men and cast my light over the whole country.

In order to prove his success, the sovereign then enumerates his great achievements, in both foreign affairs and internal politics. The list of the former is shorter and less detailed: it recalls how one after the other he had subdued and united in a vast empire centered on Babylon all the formerly autonomous cities that had made up Mesopotamia.

However, in Hammurabi's own eyes his most important achievement, the one most noble and the most welcome to the gods, was as an administrator who had kept his country in order and hence in a state of well-being and prosperity. This is why he lists the 282 articles, which were not only to immortalize his decisions and wise maxims, but also to demonstrate his real knowledge of law and his genuine gift of judgment.

Then, after this lengthy catalogue, the sovereign insists in the epilogue on the high ideals he has of kingship, and the zeal he has devoted to his divine mission. He presents himself as a model king and hands down his conduct, his experience and his knowledge as a source of instruction and inspiration for every sovereign worthy of the name who might come after him:

If any of my successors possesses the necessary understanding to keep the country in order, then let him pay attention to what I have engraved on my stele, for this will explain to him the course and the conduct to pursue by reminding him of the judgments which I have made for my people and the decisions which I have given them. In this way he will succeed in keeping his subjects in order, give them judgments and decisions, eradicate evil and wicked men from their midst and so achieve the well-being of the people! Yes, it is me, Hammurabi, the just king, upon whom the god Shamash has bestowed the understanding of justice!

After the end of the Hammurabi dynasty the political balance was profoundly altered: henceforth the struggle for supremacy was between the Semites of the south of the country, around Babylon, and those of the north, first around Assur and then around Nineveh. They were to contend for power for at least a thousand years to come, until Mesopotamia passed under the domination first of Persia (539 B.C.) and then of Greece (330 B.C.). About 1200 B.C. the Elamite king Shutruknahhunte, who had come to conquer and destroy Babylon, carried off the stele on which the code was inscribed to his capital, Susa, as a trophy of war. Here archaeologists found it 3,000 years later, broken in three pieces and partly damaged. As a work of literature and learning, however, this same code was to last right up to the end of the history of ancient Mesopotamia, continually studied, reread and recopied as one of the immortal classics of literary and intellectual achievement produced by this ancient civilization.

The Code of Hammurabi not only translates into clear language, with a precision of detail and

Two seals of the third millennium B.C. showing shepherds and their flocks (*above*) and river transport (*left*).

Two seals of the third millennium B.C. showing agricultural workers (*above*) and a hunting scene (*left*).

*Above* Six plaques showing figures from Mesopotamian life: a carpenter, a man with a goat, a woman suckling a child, a harpist, an itinerant showman with monkeys, and a married couple.

*Opposite* The golden head of a bull, decorating the front of a lyre from Ur.

an often remarkable exactitude, the principal institutions, the structure of the hierarchy and society, the administrative machinery and the economic mechanism of the great civilization of ancient Mesopotamia. It also conveys Mesopotamia's quintessential spirit: the supreme importance of the gods and their decisions to everything that happens here below; the nobility and importance of the monarchy; the ideals of order and justice that must govern society and inspire the ruling class; and a preoccupation with scientific analysis, order and clarity.

For all these reasons, the code is a significant milestone in that ancient heritage built up over thousands of years by our far-off ancestors on the banks of the Euphrates and the Tigris, a heritage that fed two sources of our own civilization, Israel and Greece.

JEAN BOTTÉRO

28

The Babylonian kings who followed Hammurabi were unable to hold the wide territories that he had won. New enemies challenged the supremacy of Babylon in

Boundary stone from Khafajan

Mesopotamia; the south broke away and a new kingdom came into being, the dynasty of the Sea Land, with its center in the marshy region around the head of the Persian Gulf. The Babylonian army was more than once defeated by the Cassites, a mountain people from the region now known as Kurdistan, of whom we shall say more later. In the northwest, the Mari region regained independence. From the encircling highlands, barbarian newcomers were

Map of Babylon, c. 600 B.C.

pouring into the semicircle of river valleys and urban settlements known as the Fertile Crescent. The ethnic map of the Near East was undergoing the first of a series of violent changes, perhaps the most far-reaching of all in its effects on the history of man.

## Cosmic order

A motif that recurs in the mythology of many ancient peoples is that of the emergence of order from disorder, of cosmos out of chaos. This is the theme of the creation legends of Mesopotamia and of Egypt. The concept of cosmic order, which the gods bring about and which mankind is concerned to maintain, is present in many ancient literatures. It implied the taming of the forces of nature, storm and fire and flood, and the defense of civilization against dangers from without. These dangers were ever-present, for throughout the whole of the ancient period and for many centuries afterwards, the areas of civilization were islands in a vast ocean of barbarism. To appreciate society and to understand its history, we must know something of this great hinterland of barbarian peoples, for their periodic incursions often constituted milestones of deep historical importance.

The civilized world of the ancient Near East was surrounded on all sides by barbarian lands that seemed to stretch to infinity. Of their peoples, only a fraction on the borderlands was known. South and west of Egypt extended the whole continent of Africa. But Egypt, owing to her geographical isolation, was not greatly troubled by the invasion of other African peoples. The situation was very different for the peoples of Western Asia. Northwards and eastwards lay the vast steppeland of Central Asia. The population of this huge expanse, though relatively sparse to the land over which they ranged, constituted an ever-present threat to the agricultural peoples of the more favored territories around the Fertile Crescent.

As a result of archeological research, particularly in the U.S.S.R., a certain amount is now becoming known about the inhabitants of this vast and hitherto little-known territory. It would appear that in Siberia and Mongolia a Palaeolithic economy, based on hunting, continued long after the rise of civilization in Western Asia. With the development of agriculture in areas that bordered on the steppeland, a mixed economy evolved, embracing both the growing of crops and the herding of animals; since they did not practice irrigation, and water was scarce, they

Copper bison from Lake Van

grew and harvested cereal crops after the season of rain and then moved on with their herds, seeking pasture over a wide range. This pattern of existence may be described as nomadic. At Tripolye, near Kiev, however, and at other sites in the Ukraine and eastern Rumania, remains of the settlements of stone-using agriculturalists have been found, dating to the third millennium B.C. They were not nomads, for they lived in large houses built of timber and clay, and had domesticated goats, cattle and dogs. The bones of horses also have been found in their settlements, and this is possibly the earliest evidence of the domestication of this friend of man.

## A new weapon

Now in the Mari letters, and other documents of about the same date, there occur some names which are neither Sumerian nor Semitic. These names betray the presence of a new element in the population. The horse, too, makes its first appearance in the Near East, as a rare and precious gift sent by ruler to ruler. Usually two horses are mentioned, and it is evident that they were used in pairs as draft animals, to draw a new and revolutionary form of vehicle: the light war chariot. The Sumerians had used chariots to

Woman taming animals; Sumerian bowl

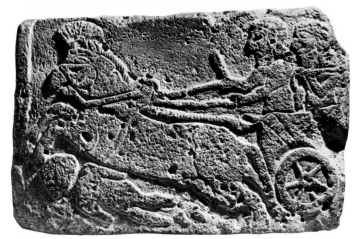
War chariot from Tell Halaf

## Hittite civilization

Babylonian model divining liver

great effect in battle, but they were heavy, clumsy affairs with solid wooden wheels, pulled by teams of the wild sort of asses, known as onagers, which are now extinct but once roamed the Syrian desert. From pictures of these Sumerian chariots in action, it can be seen that they must have thundered forward in a straight line, like a kind of tank, carrying two or three warriors with spears leveled, mowing down the enemy and spreading panic. The new chariots were quite different: very light, with spoked wheels, and built for speed. The military effectiveness of horse-drawn chariotry was quickly appreciated by those who suffered its onslaught, and it soon became an essential weapon of offense in every western Asiatic army. Its introduction is to be attributed to the newcomers, whom we know as the Hurrians, the Cassites and the Hittites.

### The Hittites

The Hittites were the first to settle. Originally nomads with no knowledge of writing, they arrived in Anatolia at the end of the third millennium or the beginning of the second, and by about 1900 B.C. had begun to overrun eastern Turkey and to impose their rule on the native Hattians. During the following century they spread northwards, and about 1650 B.C. made the hilltop fortress of Hattusas (modern Boghazköi), in the bend of the river Halys, their capital. By this time they had adopted the cuneiform script of Mesopotamia and the first historical texts date from this period (known as the Hittite Old Kingdom).

The language of the Hittites of Hattusas is one of the Indo-European group of languages; that is to say, that though very different from Greek and Latin, the Germanic languages, and Sanskrit, it is basically akin to all these. Compare for instance the Hittite word *kuis* ("who") with Latin *quis*; *watar*, which in Hittite means water; and *mekkis* ("great"), which is like the Greek *megas*. The case endings of nouns and the inflection of verbs are also similar to those in various Indo-European languages. The Hittites, too, were great horse-breeders: it is interesting to find among the tablets from Boghazköi a treatise on the training of horses which is ascribed to a Hurrian expert in such matters, and which uses technical terms most nearly paralleled by Sanskrit.

Neither the Hurrians nor the Cassites were Indo-Europeans, judging by the remnant of their languages that is left to us; but by the sixteenth century, if not earlier, they were led by an aristocracy who spoke Indo-European languages, worshiped Aryan gods and were experts in the arts of warfare and the chase. In Babylonia the Cassites moved in to occupy the capital, Babylon, after an unexpected raid launched by the Hittite king Murshil, in 1530 B.C., in which the last of Hammurabi's successors perished. At about the same time, confederate Hurrian kingdoms were set up in North Syria and in the region now called the Jezira, between the Tigris and Euphrates. The greatest of these kingdoms was Mitanni, whose capital on the river Khabur has not yet been excavated. For a time, the kings of Mitanni were overlords of wide territories from Asia Minor to the foothills of Persia, and reckoned themselves the equals of any of the great powers of western Asia.

Few Hurrian texts have yet been discovered, and it is probable that the Hurrians, like the Cassites, adopted the civilization of the country in which they found themselves and gradually lost their individuality. At any rate, it is difficult to pick out elements in their culture which are specifically Hurrian or specifically Cassite. With the Hittites we have more evidence. From the material remains of their civilization and from the many thousands of tablets on which their royal records, their prayers and liturgies, their treaties, contracts and laws are written, we can form a fairly complete picture of their national character and a good deal about their way of life. The basis of the economy was agriculture; corn, wine and oil were staple products. Barley and

Hittite king protected by a god

wheat grew in the valleys, and fruit on the hill slopes. The mountains were rich in minerals; copper, silver and lead were mined and also a little iron, probably the first to be smelted (in early Egypt the only iron known was in meteoric lumps hammered into shape). The

medium of exchange was silver and a fixed tariff of prices, in terms of weight of silver, was laid down from time to time by the government.

The king's authority was absolute. He was the leader in war, high priest and lawgiver. Though he was not regarded as a god in his lifetime, as the Egyptian Pharaoh was, he was deified at death and offerings were made to the divine spirits of dead kings. Members of the royal family enjoyed special privileges: the queen in particular was often prominent in affairs of state. An elaborate and strict protocol governed court life. The nobles held land in fief from the king and were bound to him by the obligation of military and other service. In the old kingdom, an assembly of nobles advised the king and had some say in the appointment of his successor, but later these functions were no longer exercised and the king himself administered justice through his officers. Such laws as survive show that the Hittites had a well-developed legal system and a strong sense of justice. Great care was taken to sift all the evidence in a case, and penalties for crime were devised to compensate the injured party as well as to punish the wrongdoer.

Hittite figures on rock relief

# The Eruption of Santorin

## 1450 B.C.

*By 2000 B.C. Crete, and its outpost the island of Santorin, was the home of a remarkable, flourishing civilization. Known as Minoan, after the legendary King Minos, this civilization ranks with Mesopotamia and Egypt as one of the great centers of human development and progress. The Cretans were great seafarers and traders, and they soon carried their civilization to other islands of the Aegean and to the Greek mainland. Archaeology has shown us that about the year 1700 palaces in Knossos and Phaistos, the two chief towns of Crete, were destroyed by fire. They were rebuilt, however, and a bright new chapter seemed to open up for Crete. Then suddenly an even greater disaster overtook Cretan civilization, on a scale unknown since. The whole of Santorin exploded, with devastating effects for the surrounding area. From that day Crete never recovered.*

The legend of Atlantis—a tale, first told by Plato, of a great center of civilization suddenly and violently destroyed by the sea—has inspired generations of scholars to speculate on the possible historical reality of a lost continent. Some have subscribed to the theory that Atlantis may have been the Aegean island of Santorin, a flourishing outpost of Europe's earliest civilization, the one that took root in Crete during the third millennium B.C. For early in the fifteenth century B.C., Santorin and Crete were hit by a series of natural disasters on a scale that has never been repeated in the civilized world. Archaeological exploration will no doubt continue to reveal more about this cataclysmic series of events; meanwhile, we know enough to show how remarkable was the civilization these islanders had created.

The first inhabitants of Crete are believed to have reached its shores some eight thousand years ago. These earliest settlers were peasant farmers, who arrived in ships, bringing with them some of their animals and their seed-corn. Their tools were of stone, and they had not yet learned to work metal. Most likely they came to Crete from the east, either from the neighboring coasts of Anatolia or from farther afield in Cilicia or Syria.

The settlers continued to have some contact with the outside world. For making sharp-edged knife blades they used obsidian, a volcanic glass that they could have obtained from Melos in the Cyclades Islands, some ninety miles north of Crete. Some of their obsidian, however, seems to have been brought from the distant region of Kayseri in central Anatolia. In the course of time stone vases from Egypt and copper tools from other areas also began to reach Crete.

At the beginning of the third millennium B.C. new groups of immigrants from the east appear to have settled on the island. These may have been refugees escaping from the great political disturbances of the time. For it was about then that

the Nile valley was united by conquest under the rule of one king, Hor-Aha, to inaugurate the First Dynasty of Egypt. One of the earliest kings of Egypt's new dynasty extended his conquests into southern Palestine, and styles of pottery appearing in Crete suggest that refugees may have come to the island from that area.

Along with new styles of pottery, the art of metallurgy—making tools and weapons of copper and eventually of tin-bronze—seems to have been introduced to Crete at this time. In the centuries that followed, while the great pyramids were being erected in Egypt, other groups of immigrants found their way to Crete from the east. Some may have been fleeing the barbarous invaders who overran Syria and Palestine about the middle of the third millennium.

Brought to Crete by refugees, or by traders, ideas and arts such as those of stone vase-making, seal-engraving and writing, soon became established on the island. By the end of the third millennium the island had become the seat of a high civilization, the first on European soil, with cities and large palaces apparently belonging to rulers who were able to concentrate power and wealth in their hands.

This new civilization, while deriving much from Egypt, and even more perhaps from Syria and Mesopotamia, was something very different; and in turn it influenced the older cultures. The spiral designs that became fashionable in Egypt from about two thousand B.C. onwards, during the Middle Kingdom, may have been inspired by the spiral decoration on imported Cretan textiles. No such textiles have survived; but fine painted pottery from Crete, some of it with spiral decoration, has been found in Egypt, and many Egyptian objects—beads, scarabs, stone vases and ivories—reached Crete.

The Cretans were evidently seafarers and traders. Many of their most important towns were

Patterns of spirals are found on many Cretan artifacts of the Bronze Age, and may have been the origin of the spiral patterns that became popular in Egypt *c.* 2000 B.C. This limestone amphora, from Knossos, dates from *c.* 1400 B.C., and is thus probably a little later than the Santorin eruption.

*Opposite* Part of the crater on the island of Nea Kameni, in the Santorin lagoon. The first of the Kameni islands (Palaea Kameni) was formed by volcanic activity in the second century B.C., and subsequent activity has created Nea Kameni. These islands, on which the volcano is still active today, represent the aftermath of the great eruption of the fifteenth century B.C.

on the coast where sandy beaches allowed the small ships of those days to be hauled ashore. Pictures of these ships on seal stones show them with single mast and square sail supplemented by oars or paddles.

In about 1700 B.C. the two largest palaces in Crete, at Knossos in the north and at Phaistos near the south coast, were destroyed by fire—whether by accident or as a result of earthquake or war is uncertain. Crete at this time appears to have been divided into several independent states, which probably indulged in intermittent warfare among themselves. The destruction of the palaces may also have been caused by foreign enemies, but if so, there is no evidence that they remained on the island.

After this destruction, the palaces at Knossos and Phaistos were rebuilt with even greater magnificence and splendor to inaugurate what was to be the most flourishing period of the Bronze Age civilization of Crete. Noble paintings in fresco now adorned the walls of the palaces and great houses. The arts of metal-working, gem-engraving, ivory-carving and faience-molding reached their highest perfection, although the art of pottery declined, probably because vases of metal—copper, gold and silver—were now in general use in the palaces and houses of the great.

This vigorous and attractive civilization soon began to spread beyond the shores of Crete, to the northern islands of the Aegean, and to large areas of the Greek mainland. Evidence of Cretan culture can be seen in the unplundered royal shaft graves at Mycenae, the chief city of the mainland. The earlier graves, which may date back to the seventeenth century B.C., contain some vases and other objects imported from Crete, while in the later graves, of the sixteenth and fifteenth centuries B.C., nearly all the vases, weapons and jewelry are of Cretan manufacture. Of course, it is hard to tell whether these were imports, or whether they are the work of Cretan artists employed at Mycenae or native artists trained in a Cretan style.

The spread of Cretan civilization to the mainland of Greece was perhaps largely the result of peaceful intercourse and admiring imitation. But there may have been a harsher side. In that imperialistic age it is only too likely that the rulers of Crete attempted to extort tribute from the princes of the mainland just as the contemporary pharaohs of Egypt did from the petty chieftains of Syria and Palestine.

Later Greek legends hint that there was a time when parts of mainland Greece were tributary to the kings of Knossos in Crete. Some of the most intriguing of these legends concern Minos, king and legislator of Crete, and the labyrinth at Knossos built to house his wife's monstrous offspring, the Minotaur. It seems possible that the legends concerning Minos' maritime conquests, even as far as Sicily, are based on considerable Cretan expansion in the Mediterranean and on

Among the civilized arts of Crete was the making of faience figurines, and this statuette of a snake goddess, found in the palace at Knossos, is a notable example.
The tiered skirt, wide belt and bared breasts are typical of the court fashion of the period.

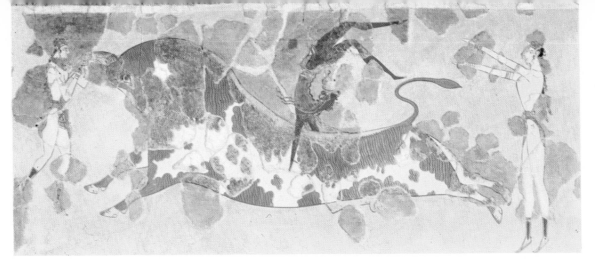

The famous bull games or dances of Minoan Crete are depicted in this fresco from the palace of Knossos. The religious significance of these games, if they had any, is unknown. Some have doubted whether the acrobatic feats shown were, in fact, ever accomplished.

kings who checked the piratical expeditions of their Aegean contemporaries.

Crete seems to have become heavily populated during this period from the seventeenth to the fifteenth centuries B.C. Everywhere throughout the island today there are traces of towns, villages and hamlets, even of isolated villas and farms, dating to those centuries. There may even have been a danger of overpopulation, the classic remedy for which, in later Greek times at least, was overseas colonization. Later Greek tradition recalls colonies of Cretans in the islands of the Cyclades, and archaeologists have identified a number of these, probably founded in the course of the sixteenth century B.C.

One of the islands settled by Cretan colonists was Santorin, the ancient Thera, seventy miles north of Crete and the nearest of the Cyclades to the "homeland." Santorin is a volcano island; but at the time the Cretans settled there its volcano seems to have been long quiescent.

Crete and the Cyclades are much subject to earthquakes and tectonic disturbances of every kind—several times in each century some part of the main island suffers in this way. About 1550 B.C. or a bit later, an earthquake of unusual severity struck Knossos and many of the towns and settlements in the east of Crete. But the damage was soon repaired and the palace at Knossos and the houses there and elsewhere were restored.

Not long afterwards, however, early in the fifteenth century B.C., Crete was ravaged by another major earthquake. The destruction caused by this can also be traced at Knossos and the settlements of eastern Crete. This second earthquake may have been connected with a catastrophe

This scene, painted on the side of a stone sarcophagus from Hagia Triada in Crete, is thought to represent a funeral of the Minoan period. It dates from the fourteenth century B.C., but the styles of clothing are also typical of the period before the Santorin eruption.

on Santorin. For the volcano there, so long inactive, erupted about this time and buried the island's Cretan colonies. Most of the colonists, however, seem to have had time to escape, taking with them their most precious belongings. Excavations have revealed the houses of the colonists wonderfully preserved—as at Pompeii—below the debris of the volcano. Yet only one or two skeletons of human victims have been found, and there is little in the destroyed houses other than clay vases that were expendable.

Some time after this catastrophe—it may have been several years later—a few of the colonists appear to have come back to Santorin. Traces of new houses have been found above the debris of the eruption.

The third and final act in this drama of natural disasters was yet to come. The eruption on Santorin was merely the prelude to a cataclysm of a magnitude that has never been exceeded. A generation or so later, about the middle of the fifteenth century B.C., the whole island of Santorin exploded.

The only comparable natural disaster in history is the explosion in 1883 of the volcano island of Krakatoa in the Sunda Strait between Java and Sumatra, Indonesia. The sound of Krakatoa's eruption was heard as far away as Australia, the Philippines and Japan. The debris of stones and ash shot to a height estimated as seventeen miles or more; on islands in the neighborhood of Krakatoa the deposit of debris was thick enough to cover entire tropical forests, while finer dust, suspended in the atmosphere, eventually spread over the greater part of the surface of the globe. At Jakarta, a hundred miles away, day was turned into night, as debris darkened the sky for days. But the aftermath of the explosion was even more destructive. The great hollow crater left by the escape of debris collapsed and most of Krakatoa disappeared into this void. Where a cone 1,400 feet above sea level had once risen was now a gulf more than one thousand feet deep. Into this gulf the sea poured, causing immense tidal waves, between fifty and one hundred feet high. The waves swept over towns and settlements along the adjacent coasts, killing more than thirty-six thousand people.

The explosion of Santorin about 1450 B.C. is judged to have been on a very much greater scale than that of Krakatoa. The north coast of Crete, only seventy miles away across the open sea, was thickly studded with populous towns and settlements; these coastal settlements and many of those in the more protected interior of the island, must have been wrecked by the blast of the explosion. Some time afterwards the vast empty crater left by the escape of the debris collapsed. The island of Santorin, which had been more or less circular in shape, rising to a high cone in the center, became the jagged group of two islands that it is today. As in the case of Krakatoa, the sea swept into the deep void, causing huge tidal waves, probably as

*Above* In the palace of Knossos foodstuffs—in particular oil and wine—were stored in giant jars called *pithoi* and in large storage pits in the floor. Many of these jars have been unearthed intact.

*Right* The alabaster throne of the rulers of Crete, in the throne room of the palace of Knossos. The frescoes on the wall behind are modern reconstructions carried out by Sir Arthur Evans.

*Above* The landscape of eastern Crete, showing in the distance the palace of Kato Zakro where traces of the Santorin disaster have been found.

much as a hundred and fifty feet high. When they bore down upon the north coast of Crete, such waves would have flattened all that the explosion had left standing. Meanwhile the debris from the eruption, hanging in the air, must have enveloped Crete in darkness for days on end, and poisonous fumes and vapors would have added to the suffering and terror of the survivors.

Many of the Cretan settlements destroyed at this time have been excavated. But at only one of them, Amnisos on the coast north of Knossos, has evidence of the tidal waves been noted, in the form of a layer of pumice stones over the ruins. Debris from the explosion has been identified in the wreckage of a palace at Zakro on the east coast. But the Zakro palace, and many of the buildings destroyed at this time elsewhere in Crete, had also been ravaged by fire. Moreover, although many fine vases of clay, stone and faience, bronze tools and inscribed clay tablets were recovered at Zakro, there was virtually no trace there of precious metals and none whatsoever of victims of the disaster. Here and elsewhere in Crete it looks as if people had some warning of catastrophe, and time enough to escape into the open with their most valued

*Above* The lagoon of Santorin, where the sea has filled the crater of the volcano.
*Right* Diagram showing the stages of the Santorin eruption.

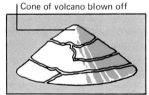

Cone of volcano blown off

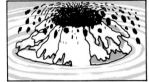

Eruption causes tidal wave which hits Greece and Crete

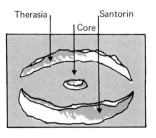

Therasia                    Santorin
                    Core

A lion hunt depicted on a bronze sword inlaid with gold, from Mycenae, on the mainland of Greece. The Mycenaean Greeks may have conquered Crete after the eruption in the fifteenth century B.C.

possessions and household effects.

It has been suggested that the explosion of Santorin was triggered by an earthquake with its center in the seabed off the north coast of Crete. Earthquakes often begin with warning shocks, and result in fires spreading from hearths or lamps in houses. The initial destruction of the palace at Zakro, and of the other towns and settlements in Crete, may have been due to an earthquake and the fires it caused—followed by the explosion of Santorin and by the resulting tidal waves.

The material damage produced by this series of disasters was clearly immense. Most of the chief centers in the populous north and east of Crete had been totally destroyed, and those elsewhere had been wrecked. The eastern end of Crete seems to have been altogether uninhabited for a considerable period after the cataclysm. Because of the direction of prevailing winds, the deposit of debris must have been thicker there than elsewhere in Crete, and, laden as it was with poisonous chloride, would have killed vegetation and made life impossible for man and beast.

The towns in the east of Crete were eventually resettled, but the palaces there were never rebuilt. After the cataclysm, Knossos seems to have become the capital of a centralized bureaucratic state controlling most if not all of Crete. This may

have coincided with a change of dynasty at Knossos, perhaps with rulers who were strangers, either from another part of Crete or from abroad. It is possible that conquerors from the Greek mainland took advantage of the chaos and confusion that overwhelmed Crete after the cataclysm to gain control of Knossos. But the mainland too must have been seriously affected by the disaster, and the archaeological evidence for a subsequent conquest of Crete from abroad is ambiguous.

The palace of Knossos was destroyed yet again by fire, probably early in the fourteenth century B.C. But at this time it was not rebuilt. The inscribed clay tablets found in its ruins have been deciphered and tentatively identified as an early form of Greek. If the language of the tablets really is Greek, then it is highly probable that Greeks from the mainland won control of Knossos and ruled there after the Santorin catastrophe, but this decipherment is contested.

The explosion of Santorin may therefore have led to great political changes, but there is no certainty as to their character. The cataclysm happened to coincide with a marked decline in the quality of Cretan civilization. There is evidence of much wealth and splendor in Crete during the century or so between the cataclysm and the final

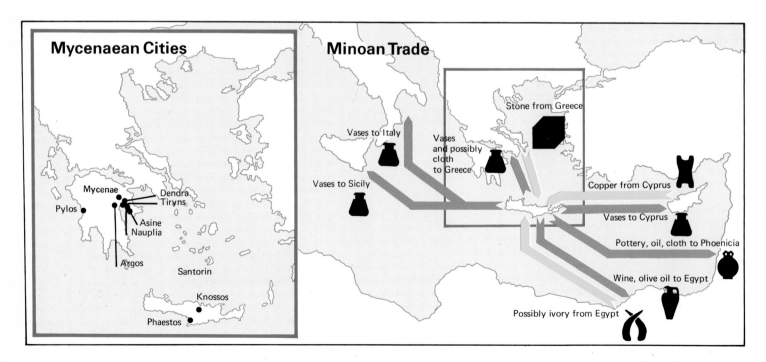

## Mycenaean Cities

Mycenae
Dendra
Tiryns
Pylos
Asine
Nauplia
Argos
Santorin
Knossos
Phaestos

## Minoan Trade

Stone from Greece
Vases to Italy
Vases and possibly cloth to Greece
Vases to Sicily
Copper from Cyprus
Vases to Cyprus
Pottery, oil, cloth to Phoenicia
Wine, olive oil to Egypt
Possibly ivory from Egypt

destruction of the palace at Knossos, but a deterioration is noticeable in taste and workmanship—except that employed in making tools and weapons.

The explosion of Santorin did not cause this decline, which seems to have begun much earlier. And the decline was accelerated after the final destruction of the palace at Knossos, a destruction that seems to have been the work of enemies. Afterwards, Crete, plundered and impoverished, may have become part of an empire ruled from Mycenae on the Greek mainland.

Towards the end of the thirteenth century B.C. Mycenae and the other chief centers of the Greek mainland were in turn destroyed by people moving into Greece from the north. Refugees from the devastated areas made their way overseas, and some of them came to Crete. After an interval, they were followed by other invaders, who occupied the fertile central parts of the island including the region around Knossos. Many of the previous inhabitants escaped abroad or took refuge in the mountains. Finally, at the very end of the Bronze Age, in the eleventh century B.C., the Dorian Greeks arrived to settle in Crete. With the coming of the Dorians the old Bronze Age civilization of Crete at last came to an end.

And for three thousand years—or until archaeologists began probing Crete's ruins late in the nineteenth century—only such vague legends as that of the lost continent of Atlantis survived to remind man of Europe's earliest civilization.

M. S. F. HOOD

When Heinrich Schliemann discovered this gold mask at Mycenae he thought he had discovered the mask of Agamemnon, leader of the Greeks in the Trojan Wars, but it is now known to be at least three hundred years earlier.

We have seen that after the fall of Babylon in 1530 B.C. and the collapse of the Amorite kingdoms of the Euphrates area and North Syria, new peoples of different races entered the area and a new pattern of settlement developed. In the sixteenth and fifteenth centuries, the focus of our interest leaves the valley of the Two Rivers and is concentrated rather on Syria and Palestine, and in particular on the new kingdoms which, with a population now partly Semitic (or "Canaanite," the Biblical writers' term) and partly Hurrian, and often with an Indo-European aristocracy, were emerging as political entities. Their history is bound up with that of the rulers of Egypt, which now for the first time becomes an imperial power with widespread influence and far-reaching commerce.

## Egypt in the Lebanon

The coastal plain of the Levant, later known as Phoenicia, and the Syrian hinterland as far as the Beqa', that is to say, the valley dividing the mountain ranges of Lebanon and Anti-Lebanon, had for some centuries past been in contact with the civilization of the Nile Valley. Originally, Egyptian influence had been confined to Byblos, a well-favored port north of the modern city of Beirut, and the forested slopes behind; from here, since the earliest historic period and perhaps even earlier, the Egyptians had brought the long timbers of pine and cedar they needed for shipbuilding, which were conspicuously lacking in the valley of the Nile. Their interest

Egyptian soldiers marching

had spread during the Middle Kingdom to include other parts of the Lebanon with which they established a trading relationship; in Palestine they may even have achieved some kind of military domination during the Twelfth Dynasty.

Egyptian influence had declined, however, as soon as the strong hand of the Twelfth Dynasty Pharaohs was withdrawn. Egyptian armies no longer marched north and, when the centralized control of the Pharaoh at last broke down and the country was split into principalities, even the sea link with Byblos was broken. The forts that had guarded the eastern frontier ceased to be effective. Bedouin bands infiltrated across the border, the trickle became a stream, and the small kingdom set up in the eastern Delta by these desert sheikhs (or Hyksos, the "shepherd kings" of

Greek tradition) grew in size till the Hyksos bid fair to take over the whole country. For something over a century, between approximately 1720 and 1600 B.C., the valley of the Nile was parceled out between Asiatic Hyksos in the north, native Egyptians in Upper Egypt and Nubian princes to the south, beyond the first cataract of the Nile. It took an almost superhuman effort for a family of local grandees in the Theban area, rallying patriotic support, to drive out the foreigners and restore unified control over the whole country. On the crest of a wave of military success, these first Phar-

Defeat of Nubians

aohs of the Eighteenth Dynasty went on to win back Nubia (which in the Twelfth Dynasty they had controlled as far as the second cataract), and to carry their arms farther into Africa. At the same

time, they started northwards on the military road that was to lead them to the conquest of Syria and Palestine and to bring them face to face with the armies of both the Hurrians and, at length, the Hittites.

The confrontation was not, it seems, immediate. Tuthmosis I appears to have marched unimpeded to the Euphrates but after he withdrew, most of North Syria and even eastern Cilicia came under the overlordship of the Mitannian kings. The greatest of these, Shaushatar, controlled Assyria too and his authority reached as far as Kirkuk, east of the Tigris. But fifty years after Tuthmosis' surprising foray, the challenge was renewed and this time the Egyptian army found its way barred. The Mitannians had rallied to their aid the rulers of many of the small city-states of Syria, many of them now ruled by

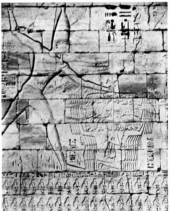

Tuthmosis III smiting Asiatics

Hurrians, and Tuthmosis III, the greatest of Egypt's warrior kings, had to fight every inch of the way. In a series of seventeen campaigns from 1480 to 1454 B.C., he again and again fought in Retenu (the Egyptian name for Syria/Palestine), capturing cities, devastating the countryside, punishing rebel towns that threw out their garrisons and at least once putting to flight the main force of the Mitannian army. By the end of his reign he had driven Shaushatar from North Syria and set his frontier at the Euphrates.

## Colonial administration

Tuthmosis III must be credited, too, with the organization of a rudimentary colonial administration. Native rulers were left in charge of their own city-states, but as vassals bound by solemn oaths

Shipbuilding in Egypt

of fealty to their overlord the Pharaoh. They were bound to pay a heavy war indemnity and to furnish annual tribute assessed in kind: large quantities of copper, gold and other metals, cattle and flocks and agricultural produce, honey, wine and oil. Their sons were taken to Egypt to serve as hostages for their good behavior and also to be given an Egyptian education to fit them for rule when their turn came. The daughters of vassals entered the Pharaoh's harem. Egyptian garrisons were left at strategic points, fortresses were built and Syrian harbors, supplied by local labor, served as supply bases.

## Heyday of empire

This was a time of great prosperity for Egypt. In the heyday of the Egyptian empire, during the reigns of Amenophis II, his son Tuthmosis IV and his grandson Amenophis III, sometimes called the Magnificent, wealth poured into the coffers of Egypt. The gold mines of Nubia were exploited to the full and caravans brought to Pharaoh's treasury the exotic products of the Sudan—ivory and ebony, panther skins, frankincense and myrrh. Tribute poured in from Retenu, and valuable presents were sent by the rulers of the Near East, the Cassite kings of Babylonia, the Assyrians, the Mitannians (now bound in friendship to Egypt by a treaty of alliance), the rulers of Cyprus and of Crete and the Aegean islands. In the tombs at Thebes of great officials—the grand viziers, the treasurers and viceroys whose duty and privilege it was to receive foreign envoys and accept their gifts—many paintings are preserved, some-

Asiatics bring tribute to Pharaoh

times still in their original bright colors, depicting these ceremonial occasions. Here the ruler of Tunip can be seen, carrying on his arm his little son who is to be brought up in Egypt; with him are Syrians,

Goddess pregnant with Akhenaton

their brightly patterned tunics contrasting with the flowing white garments of the Egyptians. Here too are Mitannians—portly, bearded figures with voluminous robes wound round their bodies; and men in Mycenaean dress, identified as from "the isles in the midst of the Great Green (sea)," with bull's head drinking cups and other Aegean vessels familiar from the excavations of Heinrich Schliemann, Sir Arthur Evans and others in Crete and on the mainland of Greece. In some tombs, of the age of Tuthmosis III, the *Keftiu* or Cretans depicted with hair curling over their foreheads, bare chests and short loincloths, are certainly to be identified with the Minoans whose story was told in the previous chapter; they too we must imagine, came to marvel at the magnificence of Pharaoh and to gaze in awe at his huge temples and vast palaces, glittering with gold and precious stones, so different in concept and style from their own cool, frescoed halls.

## The apostate Pharaoh

At the height of the empire's prosperity, a sudden internal crisis developed, which was to distract Egypt's attention for a time and to rule out all possibility of further conquest abroad. It was a strange crisis, one of the most curious episodes in the history of the ancient world, and we do not yet completely understand its cause or its effects. It arose from the personality of one individual—the son and heir of Amenophis III, who bore the same name, and who succeeded his father in about 1380 B.C. Around the figure of this king controversy has raged. Was he genius or madman? Was his religious reform prompted by mono-

theistic zeal, poetic inspiration or political astuteness? In opposition to the powerful and wealthy priesthood of the state cult of the god Amun, Amenophis IV restored the ancient cult of the sun-god, but gave it new expression in the form of the solar disc whose rays, ending in little hands, shed blessing and light upon the king and queen. He insisted that the worship of this sun-god, the Aton, should be exclusive and other cults were either proscribe or neglected. He changed his name to Akhenaton, "pleasing to Aton," and moved to a new capital at Tell el Amarna, which he named "The Horizon of Aton." Here he and his wife Nefertiti, whose beauty is familiar even to those who know nothing of

Akhenaton with Aton, the Sun Disk

her history, were able to worship their new god and live a life of domestic bliss (or so the relief sculptures in the tombs at Amarna would have us believe) with their

six daughters. In the hymns which were written in praise of the Aton, and which many people think he himself composed, there is great emphasis on truth and beauty, and on the universal nature of the sun's domain:

> Thou appearest in beauty on
>     the horizon of heaven,
> O living Aton, the beginning
>     of life!
> When thou risest on the
>     eastern horizon
> Thou fillest the earth with thy
>     beauty.
> Thou art gracious, great,
>     glistening, high over every
>         land,
> Thy rays encompass the earth
>     to the bounds of all that
>         thou hast made . . .

The phraseology of this hymn has been compared with one of the Biblical psalms (104), and Akhenaton's reforms have been regarded by some as foreshadowing and perhaps indirectly influencing the monotheism of the people of Israel. However this may be, he did not succeed in winning over the people of Egypt and after his death, the priests of Amun were again able to assert their influence. The young king Tutankhamen, who had been born into the Aton faith as Tutankhaton, changed his name and, while still a child, returned to Thebes, restored the neglected temples and reinstated Amun as the state god. Within a few years of Akhenaton's death, his memory was execrated and his capital razed. We shall see later how the authority of Egypt abroad suffered during this unhappy interlude, and how the Ramesside kings restored the prestige of Egypt in Syria.

Tutankhamen hunting

# The Aryan Invasion of India 1400 B.C.

*Some four thousand years ago in India, around the Indus Valley at Mohenjo-daro and farther north at Harappa, a civilization flourished rivaling those of Egypt and Mesopotamia. Streets were laid out at right angles, brick houses existed, and an elaborate drainage system was installed. Writing had also been invented. Pottery was produced, and there were certainly trading contacts with Mesopotamia. However, round about 1750—and continuing down to 1400—there is evidence that groups of Aryans from the North descended into India, radically affecting the native civilization. They were not simply invaders, though archaeology has produced evidence of fighting at Mohenjo-daro—but settlers. The Aryan invasions were in fact migrations of peoples. Among other things they introduced the horse—hitherto unknown—to India, but much more significantly they brought a new language and a new religion whose effects are still profoundly important in India today.*

The Indian subcontinent, bounded on the north by the mountain ranges of the Himalayas and elsewhere by the ocean, has always been relatively immune from invasion. The would-be invader must show an extraordinary degree of resourcefulness and tenacity if such natural obstacles as these are to be overcome. On only two occasions in historical times has India been invaded: by the armies of Islam in the Middle Ages and by the British (a process of gradual infiltration rather than direct invasion) in the eighteenth and nineteenth centuries. Of the "prehistoric" invasions, that of the Aryans in the second half of the second millennium B.C. has left the profoundest marks on Indian culture, and may fairly be called a milestone in Indian history.

The precise dates and conditions of the Aryan invasion, for reasons we shall discuss later, may still elude scholarship, but this much is clear: between 1750 and 1400 B.C. India was forced to meet the onslaughts of waves of nomadic "barbarians" from the northwest. Materially, the nomads were far inferior to the peoples they were in the process of conquering; spiritually, they were perhaps not inferior, but they were certainly different.

The process of conquest, which appears to have been gradual rather than sudden, as successive tribes or groups of tribes crossed the mountains into the Indus Valley and the Punjab, was greatly facilitated by the Aryans' greater mobility, in which the domestication of the horse played a great part. But it cannot be stressed too strongly that this did not mean that the original inhabitants of the occupied area were simply exterminated. They were displaced or subdued; patterns of thought and conduct were imposed on them; and by the time of the Aryans' further migration into the Gangetic basin and western Central India, Aryan ideals were certainly dominant in those areas. But farther south and east, Aryanization was both gradual and incomplete: and it remains so to this day.

If history can be said to begin with the emergence of chronicles and other written sources, then the Aryan invasion belongs to prehistory. This is not to say that there is no accessible material from which knowledge of the invasion may be derived. Such material is of two kinds: oral-literary, the hymns of the *Rig Veda*, not reduced to writing until many centuries after the events they reflect but preserved with minute accuracy down through the ages; and archaeological, a constantly growing body of information that may yet require us seriously to modify many accepted opinions and many more tacit assumptions.

Neither source is absolutely precise or completely exhaustive. Literary material such as the *Rig Veda*, apart from not being susceptible to precise dating or location, is thoroughly partisan. Take, for instance, this quotation from a hymn dedicated to the warrior god Indra:

> With all-outstripping chariot-wheel, O Indra, thou
> Far-famed, hast overthrown
> the twice ten kings of men
> With sixty thousand nine and ninety followers . . .
> Thou goest on from fight to fight intrepidly
> Destroying castle after
> castle here with strength.      (*Rig Veda* 1:53)

The impression given by these and similar verses is of a campaign of conquest and destruction; not unnaturally, the hymns speak of the conquered peoples only in terms of contempt. In contrast to the light-skinned "nobles," they were dark, snub-nosed barbarians (in the sense of speaking an unintelligible language); contemptible phallus worshippers who were nevertheless wealthy, with

Priest-king, or deity, from Mohenjo-daro, in the Indus Valley (*opposite and above*). The people of this pre-Aryan city were not the primitive barbarians of Aryan legend.

Impressions of cattle and an elephant, from superbly carved steatite seals from Mohenjo-daro.

cattle and fields and fortified cities. If they were destroyed by the "nobles," it was no more than they deserved: such is the impression given by the Aryans' own literary sources.

Until fairly recently, although it might have been suspected that this was not the whole truth, historians took the evidence of the *Rig Veda* literally. Indian culture, it was assumed, was a product of the Aryan mind, modified in the direction of inactivity and contemplation (the two unjustly equated) by long residence on the Indian plains. The pre-Aryan strain in the Indian population could not, it was thought, have contributed anything of value. True, this left historians, and not least historians of religion, with many uncomfortable facts to explain away; but the validity of what the *Rig Veda* had to say about the people the Aryans found in India was not questioned. In his book *Indian Philosophy* (1923), Radhakrishnan was thus able to write: "When the Aryans came to India they found the natives of India whom they called Dasyus (a word of uncertain meaning) opposing their free advance. These Dasyus were of a dark complexion, eating beef and indulging in Goblin worship. When the Aryans met them

they desired to keep themselves aloof from them." When these words were written, it really seemed as though the natives of northwest India were no more than a rabble of aboriginal savages.

Over the last half century, thanks to archaeology, our picture of the Aryan invasions has to be completely revised. The reassessment ("revolution" might not be too strong a word) came early in the 1920s with the beginning of excavations at two sites: Harappa, in the Punjab, some 100 miles southwest of Lahore, and Mohenjo-daro ("the mound of the dead"), on the River Indus in Sind, two hundred miles north of Karachi. Since then further excavation over a very wide area has confirmed the fact that during the third and second millennia B.C. northwest India was the home not of barbarism but of a flourishing and in some ways extremely sophisticated urban culture, not unlike that of Mesopotamia. This is now known variously as the Indus Culture, the Harappa Culture and the Indus Valley Civilization. Some seventy sites are now known, covering an area of about half a million square miles. One of the most striking features of the Indus Culture is its elaborate and consistent practical development. This

Front and side views of a terracotta female figurine from Mohenjo-daro, probably a representation of the mother goddess still worshiped in various forms all over India.

extends to such details as weights and measures, town planning and architecture, drainage, pottery, trade and commerce, art and (apparently) religion. As far as we know, Harappa and Mohenjo-daro were the main centers, but we have no way of telling whether they were provincial or local capitals.

Despite such gaps in our knowledge, it is clear that the Indus Culture was far more advanced in practical ways than that of the invading nomadic Aryans. Spiritually, too, there is every reason to believe that the Indus Culture contributed much more to Hinduism than scholars were once prepared to allow.

One of the most celebrated finds from Mohenjo-daro is a seal bearing the image of a horned, three-faced male deity, seated in a yogic position and surrounded by animals—elephant, tiger, bull, rhinoceros and goat. This is evidently a prototype of the great god Shiva, lord of the beasts and prince of Yogins. Also connected with the worship of Shiva is the phallic symbol, or *lingam*, many representations of which have been found on Indus Culture sites. Many figures of nude or seminude females have also been found, explicable only as examples of the great mother-goddess still worshiped by various names all over India. The most spectacular building excavated at Mohenjo-daro—the "great bath"—probably points to the early practice of ritual washing, such as is still observed today in sacred rivers and temple baths in all parts of India. But the overriding impression of the spiritual basis of the Indus Culture provided by archeology is of a fertility religion: man's attempt to come to terms with the realities of his agrarian existence. Insofar as agriculture has remained the main basis of the Indian economy and way of life, Indian spiritual culture, still rooted to the soil, has taken over the heritage of the Indus Culture.

We must not, however, be too categorical when speaking of the intellectual aspects of the Indus Culture. There was a written language, but as yet no attempt to decipher the Indus script has met with undisputed success. It is thought that the language was probably Dravidian, perhaps therefore an ancestor of modern Tamil, but until a bilingual inscription is found—perhaps in Sumer?—the thought of pre-Aryan bronze age India must remain obstinately inaccessible.

Even the dates of the Indus Culture are a matter of dispute. It would probably not be too inaccurate to think in terms of an overall span of about a thousand years, from about 2500 to about 1500 B.C., since it is known that important trade contacts with Mesopotamia took place between 2300 and 2000 B.C., and radiocarbon dates have been obtained varying between 2300 and 1750 B.C. It seems relatively certain, however, that a decline began in about 1750 B.C., and that this decline and fall was in some way connected with the coming of the Aryans from the northwest.

But did the Aryans merely administer the final blows to a civilization already in decline? The

Formalized design showing three interlinked tigers, from a seal from Mohenjo-daro.

Three-headed animal seal from Mohenjo-daro, showing ibex, bull, and so-called "unicorn," which in fact is probably a bull in profile.

Horned deity with three faces, seated in a yogic posture and surrounded by animals; from Mohenjo-daro. This is evidently a prototype of the god Shiva, lord of the beasts and prince of Yogins.

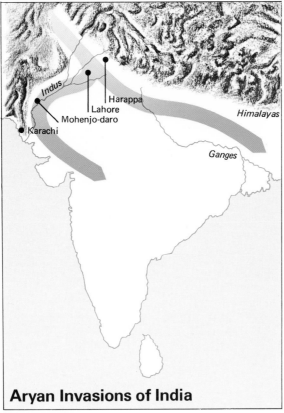

**Aryan Invasions of India**

The Aryan language belonged to the type classified later as Indo-European. The hieratic language of their religion was Sanskrit; the spoken language was probably one of the dialects related to Sanskrit, of the type since called Prakrits. The Indus language, on the other hand, was probably Dravidian, belonging to an entirely different linguistic family. Within a few centuries, Sanskrit was established as the sacred and official language of northern India: the language of hymns, prayers and commentaries, epics and lyrics, codes of religious and secular law. Belonging to the Prakrits group is Pali, the sacred language of Buddhism; among direct descendants of Sanskrit are modern Hindi, Bengali, Marathi and Gujerati. Hence, in a real sense, the linguistic consequences of the Aryan invasion are still with us. Attempts currently being made in north India to establish Hindi as the official language of the whole of India—attempts partly motivated by its direct descent from Sanskrit —have been objected to by Dravidian-speaking southern Indians in particular as "north Indian imperialism." It is an incontestable fact that classical Indian culture expressed itself very largely in the tongue of the Aryans.

The religion of the Aryans was essentially different from that of the Indus peoples. The latter followed a fertility religion, based largely on the earth as giver of life. Aryan religion was centered on the great deities of the sky and atmosphere, sun and moon, storm and fire. The earliest Indian religious writings, the hymns of the *Rig Veda*, were probably in part brought into India by later waves of Aryan invaders, and in part composed after the invasions. They reflect a priestly religion, concerned above all with the maintenance of the natural order, *rta*, by regular sacrifice. Many hymns are dedicated to the god of storm and war, Indra, to the god of the sacrificial fire, Agni, and to the deified sacrificial drink, Soma, as well as to the more remote celestial gods, Varuna and Vishnu. The *Brahmanas*, prolix commentaries on the hymns showing sacrificial theory and practice, probably date from the beginning of the iron age and the second stage of the invasions. The *Upanishads*,

*Below left* The Great Bath of Mohenjo-daro, probably the scene of ritual bathing.

*Below right* Drain at Mohenjo-daro, showing the high standard of building and engineering achieved by the pre-Aryan people of India.

evidence on this point is inconclusive. While in some areas the end of the Indus Culture seems to have been accompanied by extreme violence, elsewhere the transition may have been fairly peaceful. At Mohenjo-daro, the finding of unburied skeletons in the streets points unmistakably to unexpected attack from some quarter; at Harappa, on the other hand, the evidence seems to suggest that peaceful settlement took place. Much has been made of changing climatic conditions as a factor contributing to the weakened state of the Indus Culture at that time, but we do not know how far it had declined when the first Aryan incursions began. What we do know is that, in two closely related areas of its culture, India was decisively affected by the invaders. The first of these is language; the second, religion.

mystical treatises concerning man and the universe, reflect some of the earliest stirrings of the Indian speculative mind, possibly as a result of contact with Indus beliefs. On these foundations, though with many later elaborations, rests the complex edifice of Hinduism in its priestly aspect. To this day, one test of Hindu orthodoxy is the acceptance of the divine authority of these Vedic scriptures—largely, if not entirely, Aryan products.

But Hinduism is a social as well as a religious phenomenon. And there is probably no more tenacious social institution in the world than that of caste—still very much alive in India. It has been very extensively modified over the centuries, but that its roots date back to the Aryan invasion cannot be doubted. In the past, it has been too readily assumed that caste originated as a simple color bar between light-skinned Aryans and dark-skinned Dravidians. But this overlooks the fact that three of the four main caste groupings, those of priests, warriors and artisans, were classified as "twice-born," i.e. Aryan; only the fourth, the serfs, appear to have been non-Aryan. In fact, basic caste structure can be shown to correspond closely to the traditional structure of Aryan society: corroborative evidence can be found among other Indo-European peoples, such as the Celts and Romans. The conclusion must be that the invaders brought a rudimentary form of the caste system with them, and that after the invasions the conquered peoples were relegated in most cases to a subordinate role in society as serfs. In time, the emergent Indian society became more and more rigidly stratified under the growing influence of the Brahmanical priesthood—an influence that has persisted to modern times.

Down the centuries, the social and religious structure of Indian society became Aryanized in accordance with *varnàśrama dharma*, i.e. the caste law. To be a good Hindu, and by implication a good Indian, it was necessary to observe the laws of one's caste, as laid down in the priestly codes, such as the *Laws of Manu*. Language, trade and commerce, secular jurisprudence and education similarly followed Aryan patterns.

But this is not to say that India has ever become completely Aryanized. The contrast between the Aryan north and the Dravidian south is still marked, and India's conflicts are still to some extent unresolved. Hinduism, although its superstructure and many of its philosophies are derived directly from the Vedic Aryans, is noticeably non-Aryan at the popular, grass-roots level. For the culture of India is a complex and composite entity, reducible to no simple categories and intolerant of simple explanations. India proved hospitable to the Aryan invaders of three thousand years ago; their coming altered the entire pattern of her future history. But the fact that it is still impossible to read India's history solely in Aryan terms demonstrates clearly that she did not entirely submit to the invasion.

ERIC J. SHARPE

Terracotta female figurine with "pannier" headdress, from Mohenjo-daro.

*Below* Terracotta model of bullock cart from Mohenjo-daro. The people of the Indus Valley Civilization were still predominantly agricultural; the elaborate cities that have been excavated were probably centers of trade and government.

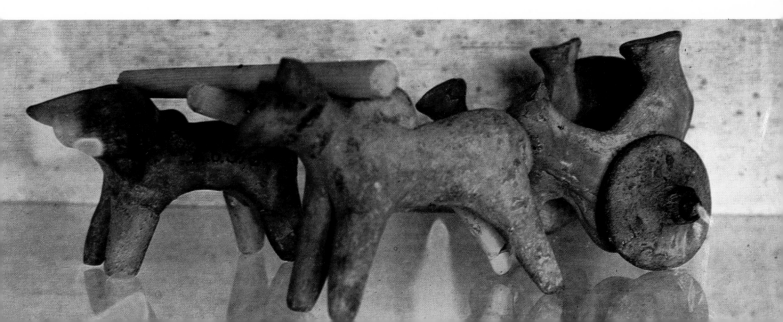

In the year 1887 an Egyptian peasant, digging in the ruins of an ancient city on the banks of the Nile, came across some baked clay tablets impressed with cuneiform writing. In due course these tablets came into the hands of dealers and eventually their importance realized. The city had once been the capital of Egypt,

Avenue of rams at temple of Karnak

pied with problems of their own and failed to set forth on those constant demonstrations of strength and tours of inspection that were necessary, if a ruler was to maintain a firm hold on his possessions. Moreover, the Hittites were again casting envious eyes on North Syria. Some of the Amarna letters, from the vassals of Egypt in this region, show clearly how they were being forced or cajoled by Hittite agents into deserting their

Cuneiform tablet from Tell el Amarna

for a brief time in the early fourteenth century B.C., and the tablets had come from the record office of the palace; they were letters, part of the files of the Foreign Office, the correspondence of the potentates and princes of the Near East with their ally, or in some cases their overlord, the Pharaoh of Egypt. They are written in Akkadian, the language of diplomacy in this age, as it had been in the time of the Mari letters, and we must imagine that in every prince's palace, even in countries remote from Babylonia, there were scribes who could read and write the language and would translate the

letters to their masters. The situation mirrored in these letters is a complex one.

The kings of Babylonia and Assyria, the kings of the Hurrian kingdom of Mitanni, and of the kingdom of Alashiya, which may be Cyprus, wrote to the Pharaohs as equals. They were bound to them by treaties of alliance cemented by marriage, and some of the letters discuss the amount of dowry which they propose to give to a daughter who is to be sent to Egypt to swell the Egyptian king's numerous harem. Rich presents were exchanged, and the vassal was to send a gift of gold equal value. This was, in fact, trade: an exchange of goods, value for value, on an official basis, and merchants were traveling as official agents of the kings and with their protection. Keftiu is not among those who sent these royal gifts: the Minoan envoys who once brought precious cargo from Crete to the court at Thebes came no longer. Knossos had been overwhelmed and was now in Mycenaean hands. But trade between Egypt and the Aegean continued, and Mycen-

aean pottery is found in some quantity at Tell el Amarna. It has recently been suggested that the memory of the Minoan civilization of Crete, after the disaster which overwhelmed Crete and the islands, was preserved in Egypt and was responsible for the legend of Atlantis, the fabulous island in the west where life was lived in fine palaces with elaborate drainage systems and which was overwhelmed by the sea. This story, according to Plato, was brought back from Egypt by his ancestor Solon. However this may be, it is true that in many details the description of Atlantis fits well

Daughters of Akhenaton and Nefertiti

with that which archeology tells us of Minoan Crete, and it is certainly tempting to see in the one a dim memory of the other.

Letters from the regents of vassal kingdoms, which form the bulk of the correspondence, protest their loyalty to the Pharaoh and frequently complain of the hostile activities of their neighbors and the treachery of fellow vassals. They paint a picture of turmoil and intrigue. It is clear that Egypt's control over her possessions in Syria and Palestine was far from complete, and that the Pharaohs Amenophis III and Amenophis IV (known by his own wish by the name of Akhenaton) were occu-

Deity from Assur

alliance with Egypt. Historical narrative texts from Hattusas (modern Boghazköi), the Hittite capital, carry on the story of the Hittite capture of the kingdoms of North Syria and of the eclipse of Mitanni, from the Hittite point of view.

Weather god from Ras Shamra

Tribute-bearers from Carchemish

# a national identity and settle in a new land

Tribute offered to El, god of Ugarit

## The Kingdom of Ugarit

One of the vassals of Egypt, whose king at this time was forced to change his allegiance and become a tributary of the Hittite king, was the ruler of the wealthy kingdom of Ugarit, on the Syrian coast north of the modern town of Lattakia. Excavations on the site of this city, the modern Ras Shamra, have revealed the size

Idrimi, King of Alalakli

and importance of the town and its palace and here, too, valuable hoards of tablets have been found. Some of them are letters, couched in the same language of international diplomacy as the Amarna letters; they include the actual terms under which King Niqmaddu of Ugarit was to surrender to the Hittite king and the amount of tribute he was to pay. Other

tablets refer to domestic matters and it is these, and in particular the large number which are written in a simplified, alphabetic script of only thirty cuneiform characters, which give us insight into the daily life and beliefs of the people of this region in the fourteenth and thirteenth centuries B.C. At Ugarit, which must be reckoned a Canaanite city, we find myths of the high god El, of the bloodthirsty virgin goddess Anath, of Baal the storm god, who

Goddess from Ras Shamra

was to be the adversary of Yahweh, the national god of Israel, and of Yam the god of the sea, with whom Baal did battle. Many of the rites of sacrifice, the festivals and even the poetic phraseology find close parallels in the Old Testament. And this reminds us that the Hebrews came as nomadic wanderers into a civilization already old, and absorbed and adopted from the Canaanites much that they found in the Promised Land.

## The mysterious Khapiru

Yahweh himself, as might be expected, has no part in the pantheon of Ugarit, but Ugaritic texts more than once mention a people called the Khapiru, a name which many historians equate with the Hebrews. The Khapiru are found over a wide area of the Near East. There is considerable doubt whether the word denotes some sort of ethnic group, a nation or a tribe, or whether it denotes a social class—a turbulent semi-nomadic element in the population of the kingdoms of Syria and Mesopotamia, who drove their flocks about the countryside and frequently succumbed to the temptation to plunder the fields and herds of their wealthier, settled

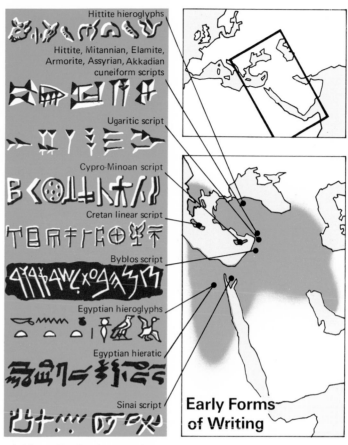

Hittite hieroglyphs

Hittite, Mitannian, Elamite, Armorite, Assyrian, Akkadian cuneiform scripts

Ugaritic script

Cypro-Minoan script

Cretan linear script

Byblos script

Egyptian hieroglyphs

Egyptian hieratic

Sinai script

**Early Forms of Writing**

neighbors. In the Amarna letters they are greatly feared marauders, a constant threat to the safety of the kingdoms of Syria and Palestine. They had evidently formed a not inconsiderable part of the population of "Retenu" (as the Pharaohs called Syria and Palestine together) in the time of Amenophis II, since he lists 3,600 of them among his prisoners. Later, about 1310 B.C., they were encountered by the army of Seti I during his campaign in the Galilee area of Palestine.

The Khapiru are first mentioned as an element of the population of Mesopotamia, much earlier. So too are other Semitic groups. One of these groups, which received scant mention in the early texts but later grew into a formidable nation, were the Aramaeans. Hebrew tradition later affirmed that Abraham, their ancestor, had Aramaean kindred; the story of his wanderings from Ur to Harran fits well into a context of the years after 2000 B.C., when the lower Euphrates valley and the northern steppe-country (called today the Jezireh) between the Tigris and Euphrates were alike the scene of bedouin movements and migrations. We will now see how they settled in Egypt and then at last went to a "Promised Land."

Syrian deity

49

# Let My People Go!

*The Hebrews were a nomadic people, some of whom settled in Egypt. They had their own God— Yahweh or Jehovah—and in this respect they differed little from the people around them. Yet the Israelites, led by Moses, were convinced that their God had promised them a land of their own, and that they must leave Egypt and go to Palestine. Their God was essentially a god of battle and, as such, invaluable as long as they were on the march. But what would happen once they settled down? Inevitably there were attempts to worship local gods also, but the basic conviction that there was only one god—and a moral god at that—the God of Israel, and that the Hebrews were his people, was never forgotten. For this reason the Hebrews are one of the most important peoples of antiquity. The Exodus or departure from Egypt was essential to the fulfillment of that role.*

The blazing heat of early summer beat down upon the rocks and sand of the vast and mountainous wilderness of Sinai. In a parched valley, far from any human habitation, a band of some hundreds— perhaps even some thousands—of fugitives from the Nile Delta waited for the orders of their leader, Moses.

These "children of Israel" formed part of a group of tribes who had migrated into the Land of Canaan from the north several hundred years earlier. All claimed a common ancestor in Abraham and all shared a common religious belief. Then famine had struck the land, probably in about 1650 B.C. Some of the tribes had found food nearby; others—the ancestors of Moses' group—had wandered as far as Egypt in the search for sustenance, and they had remained there as serfs of the pharaohs, engaged in building public works. Though the life had been hard, there was at least food and water.

The tribes had stayed some four hundred years in Egypt, then had left everything at the behest of Moses. There had been long and stormy arguments between Moses and Pharaoh (probably Merneptah of the next chapter), before the children of Israel had managed to leave; and the departure itself had been unforgettably dramatic and unexpected. It has come down to us in the legends of ten plagues, each one more destructive than the last. The plagues had driven Pharaoh and the Egyptians to surrender to Moses' demand that this group of despised serfs be allowed to go and celebrate some strange rite beyond the boundaries of Egypt. Pharaoh had then regretted giving his permission, and there had been a dramatic escape. The children of Israel had successfully crossed the "Sea of Reeds" or the Red Sea, and the Egyptian chariots and horsemen pursuing them had met disaster. What precise incidents lie behind these legends we do not know, but no scholar today would deny that the experience was real, taking place probably about 1280 B.C. Jewry has been celebrating that flight for more than 3,000 years in the festival of Passover, and we understand enough about primitive peoples to know that such a record arises only from experience.

The demand to "let my people go" had been made in the name of the God of Israel. For the tribe had retained belief in a single God who had called their ancestors to his especial service. It was to renew this service that, in spite of many misgivings and frequent complaints, they had followed Moses into the vast and deserted region of Sinai. And the culmination of their pilgrimage was the day of meeting with their God.

Moses was a man who had the irresistible power to gain complete acceptance and obedience from a whole people. While his life has attracted so many strange trappings that it is difficult to disentangle truth from legend, we could deny his existence only by creating someone with similar powers living at the same time and performing the same dynamic role in the spiritual evolution of a little band of former serfs. For the sojourn in Egypt of some of the people of Israel is history, and the survival of the Jewish people today as a result of the Exodus from Egypt and the events in the Sinai Desert is also history.

Though an Israelite, Moses had not been brought up to the drudgery of making and laying bricks. The Old Testament says that he grew up in the household of Pharaoh himself. If so, it had not made him forget the traditions of his ancestors, the worship of a God of whom there was no image, and the discipline of an ethical and moral, as well as a ritual, service to the Deity. Legend speaks of long years in the dry, steppe country east of Sinai, where he married and tended the sheep of his father-in-law, until a vision called him to his law-giving mission to his people.

If legend has surrounded the flight from Egypt and the life of Moses, still more has it surrounded

A view of Mount Sinai, at the summit of which Moses received from God the tables of the Law. Scholars do not doubt that the ethical discipline taught by Moses is the basis of the Biblical Ten Commandments.

*Opposite* The parched desert lands of the Middle East recall the grim terrain crossed by the Israelites under Moses in the Exodus from Egypt. (The picture shows the cracked soil and sparse vegetation of the Negev, near the Dead Sea.)

An Egyptian war-chariot of the type used in the pursuit of the Israelites. According to Hebrew tradition, the Egyptian army was drowned in the Red Sea, through which the Israelites had miraculously passed dry-shod. The feast of the Passover annually commemorates the Israelite Exodus from Egypt. The picture shows the Pharaoh Seti I; it is carved on the wall of the Temple of Amun at Karnak (ancient Thebes).

the "giving of the Law" at the foot of the mountain to which the Bible gives the names of Sinai and Horeb. The Bible recounts how Moses climbed to its summit and there spoke face to face with Yahweh, God and Redeemer of the children of Israel. The people waited below, awed by the lightning and thunderclouds hiding the summit of the mountain. We have no reason to doubt that the Ten Commandments—which prohibit murder, adultery, theft, lying and envy and which establish the Sabbath as a holy day—embody the core of the ethical discipline taught by Moses and accepted by the people as a whole. Nor would most scholars today hesitate to ascribe to the same period much of the communal law embodied in the Old Testament. Of particular interest are those laws embodied in the "Code of Holiness", in which the sanction is not a penalty, but a reminder of the covenant between God and Israel and the obligations that result therefrom. Typical of the laws are these two, concerning the poor and the weak:

When you reap the harvest of your land, you shall not reap your field to its very border, neither shall you gather the gleanings after your harvest . . . you shall leave them for the poor and the sojourner: I am the Lord your God. (*Leviticus* 19: 9–10)

You shall not curse the deaf or put a stumbling block before the blind, but you shall fear your God: I am the Lord. (*Leviticus* 14)

The central discipline is not any particular set of regulations, but the conviction of the whole people

that they had accepted an obligation to live according to the Law, not as an act of obedience to an earthly ruler, but as a covenant between themselves and their God.

These words ascribed to Moses may have been written centuries later, but they contain the essence of the covenant:

See, I have set before you this day life and good, death and evil. If you obey the commandments of the Lord your God, by loving the Lord your God, by walking in his ways, and by keeping his commandments . . . then you shall live and multiply, and the Lord your God will bless you . . . But if your heart turns away and you will not hear . . . I declare to you this day that you shall perish. (*Deuteronomy* 30: 15–20)

The subsequent history of the children of Israel is the record of continual recall to the true meaning of the covenant, of continual struggle both with idolatry and with social injustice which defiled that covenant.

Some forty years after the giving of the Law, the children of Israel abandoned their nomadic life in and around the deserts of Sinai for a settled habitation in Palestine. According to their tradition, this had been promised them by their God. Palestine at that time contained an agglomeration of city-states, small kingdoms and semi-nomadic tribes of mixed ethnic origin. Still scattered among these people of Palestine were relatives of the children of Israel, who like them claimed descent from Abraham and to some extent retained the worship of his God. But they had not completely resisted

52

the local gods and goddesses and the fertility rites by which they were worshiped.

There was little to distinguish the newcomers from the rest of their neighbors. They interpreted the divine will in terms of very human ambitions. They were prepared to massacre and enslave other tribes, and they regarded the covenant with their God as an exclusive privilege. But the experience of the desert had given them particular status. One of the most remarkable developments during the next few centuries is that their settled relatives, who in fact had not undergone the long humiliation of Egyptian servitude, came to adopt the Egyptian experience as that of their own ancestors. The nature festivals that they shared with the peoples around were transformed into historical commemorations and remodeled as anniversaries of the Exodus from Egypt, the experience of Sinai and the acceptance of their God, Yahweh. Even that name was brought to them by those who had experienced the hardships of Egypt and the rigors of the desert.

In the earliest days of the settlement in Palestine the religion of Yahweh was preserved by groups of ecstatic devotees. Gradually they became dominated by the prophets, who proclaimed righteousness, denounced social injustice as fervently as religious idolatry and spoke with deepening insight about the nature and demands of a righteous God. It needed all their eloquence to instill into the people the true meaning of the covenant, and the fact that it involved responsibilities rather than privileges. "You only have I known of all the peoples of the earth," cries Amos in the name of Yahweh. "Therefore I will punish you for all your iniquities." (*Amos* 3:2) But the prophets also had to teach their people that the statement "you only have I known of all the peoples" did not mean that God had no concern for the rest of his creation. It is again Amos who says:

"Are you not like the Ethiopians unto me, O people of Israel?" says the Lord. "Did I not bring up Israel from the land of Egypt, and the Philistines from Caphtor and the Syrians from Kir?"    (*Amos* 9:7)

The children of Israel were soon to meet disaster. They had established two small kingdoms which were constantly engaged in foolish quarrels with each other. The northern kingdom, with its capital at Samaria, was swallowed up by the Assyrian empire in about 721 B.C., and the ruling classes were deported to northern Mesopotamia. As an identifiable and creative society it disappeared from history. Less than two hundred years later, in 587 B.C., the southern kingdom, with its capital at Jerusalem, was likewise overthrown and its ruling classes deported by the Babylonians, who had succeeded the Assyrians. When Babylon was in turn destroyed by the Persians, Cyrus, the Persian king, issued an edict in 538 B.C. allowing the descendants of these exiles from the southern kingdom to return, and many did so. At the center of the southern kingdom had been the tribe of Judah, hence its inhabitants were known as "Judahites"—Hebrew, *Yehudim*; Latin, *Judaei*; English, *Jews*.

Though the story deals henceforth with "Jews," it is probable that descendants of the northern kingdom who wished to remain loyal to Yahweh migrated from northern Mesopotamia to the great centers of Jewish cultural life established by the Babylonians in the southern part of the land between the Tigris and the Euphrates. This was to be a center of the Jewish world for many centuries, indeed surviving until modern times.

During the century before Cyrus allowed them to return, the exiles had made two vital contributions to the future of their people. First, deprived of their Temple in Jerusalem, they had evolved a nonsacrificial form of worship, Sabbath by Sabbath, wherever Jews lived. This was the worship of the synagogue, and its present form is familiar to millions today wherever there are Christian churches or Muslim mosques. For it was without priestly sacrifices or rituals and consisted of prayer, praise and instruction, centered on Holy Scripture. The second achievement of the exiles lay in the collecting and editing of national records, history, prophetic utterances, psalms and sacred songs, from which the Scriptures were compiled. What is most striking about this compilation is that the whole of Jewish history is written in terms of obedience to the covenant. Kings whose victories added wide dominions and the revenue of subject peoples are dismissed in a few verses, with the words that they "did evil in the sight of the Lord." Kings like David, who were the object of deep affection and veneration, were represented without any attempt at whitewash. And the words of the

*Above* An Asiatic prisoner, a tile in the palace of the Pharaoh Ramses II at Tell el Yahudijah, in the Nile delta.

*Below* Three Canaanite idols: the weather god (*left*), holding a thunderbolt; deity holding a spear and a sword (*center*)—possibly Resheph, god of thunder and lightning: female figure from Beirut (*right*), possibly the goddess Astarte.

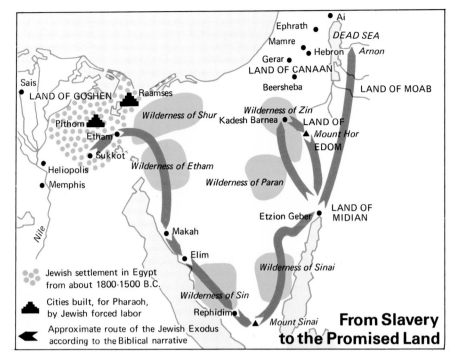

Map legend:

- Jewish settlement in Egypt from about 1800-1500 B.C.
- Cities built, for Pharaoh, by Jewish forced labor
- Approximate route of the Jewish Exodus according to the Biblical narrative

**From Slavery to the Promised Land**

Map labels: Ai, Ephrath, DEAD SEA, Mamre, Hebron, Arnon, Gerar, LAND OF CANAAN, Sais, LAND OF GOSHEN, Raamses, Beersheba, LAND OF MOAB, Wilderness of Zin, Wilderness of Shur, Kadesh Barnea, LAND OF, Pithom, Mount Hor, Etham, EDOM, Sukkot, Heliopolis, Wilderness of Etham, Memphis, Wilderness of Paran, Nile, LAND OF MIDIAN, Etzion Geber, Makah, Elim, Wilderness of Sinai, Wilderness of Sin, Rephidim, Mount Sinai

in their hearts not to eat unclean food. They chose to die, rather than to be defiled by food or to profane the holy covenant; and they did die" (*Maccabees*: 62–63). In consequence ordinary men and women became the first recorded martyrs in the long history of religious persecution.

The return to Judaea was a remarkable event, for in Babylon Jews had been prosperous and self-governing. They had a rich territory, which, compared with the infertile hills and ruined towns and villages around Jerusalem, should have argued in favor of staying in exile. But Jerusalem (often called Zion) and "the land of Israel" arouses an affection in the Jewish mind that may be illogical, may be irritating to others, but is a quite certain fact of history. The land of Babylon, for all its wealth, was *exile*, as the psalmist so well expressed:

> By the waters of Babylon we sat down and wept,
> when we remembered thee, O Zion.
> As for our harps we hanged them up upon the trees
> that are therein.
> For they that led us away captive required of us
> then a song and melody in our heaviness: "Sing us
> one of the songs of Zion."
> How shall we sing the Lord's song in a strange land?
> If I forget thee, O Jerusalem, let my right hand
> forget her cunning.
> (*Psalms* 137: 1–5)

The return did not take place all at once, but in a series of caravans, and the future leader of the Jews came in one of the later groups. His name was Ezra, and he, together with his companions and disciples, ensured by their wise leadership the future of Judaism and the Jewish people. They brought with them from Babylon the institution of the synagogue and the main elements of a sacred Scripture. Ezra, however, added provision for a system of adult education by which the Law was regularly taught to the whole people.

When Jerusalem had been rebuilt from its ruins,

Ivory plaque from Megiddo, showing prisoners being led before a Canaanite ruler. The artist has imitated an Egyptian style.

prophets, who spared no one in their denunciations, are preserved with the utmost care.

The books of the Old Testament cover the traditions and chronicles of more than a thousand years. We can trace through them the slow growth of a national conviction that obedience to the covenant was the true goal of national life. But it was not until after these books were completed that those who had for many generations been pioneers and fighters for righteousness had their reward. In the supplementary books, called *The Apocrypha*, it is recorded how in 166 B.C. Antiochus, King of Syria, tried to make Israel desert its God. They were commanded to eat forbidden meats, "but many in Israel stood firm and were resolved

*Left* An Egyptian fresco showing a carpenter at work. *Below* Wooden model of Egyptian brickmakers. The Israelites were doubtless engaged in such activities when building "treasure cities" for Pharaoh in Egypt.

and the Temple was once more the center of national worship, Ezra arranged a solemn reading of the whole Law "before the Water Gate." The reading covered several days and was followed by a renewal, by the whole people, of the covenant with Yahweh. But Ezra did not merely read. He "gave the sense and caused the people to understand the meaning" (*Nehemiah* 8:8). Systematic teaching of the Law continued not merely on special occasions, but in every town, week by week, and by a trained body of teachers, recruited at first from local priestly families. They came to be known as scribes, because it was their duty not only to teach the Law, but to write copies of it, so that gradually every synagogue came to possess its own copy as well as its own teacher of the Law.

The inevitable consequence of this permeation of the whole life of the people by the revelation of Sinai soon followed. The local teachers became the local magistrates, for much of the Law dealt with matters, criminal and civil, that required adjudication; and the local magistrates in turn found themselves involved in the responsibility of reinterpretation necessary when a written code must be constantly adjusted to changes and developments in society. Judaism and Jewry were thus equipped to survive when Temple and State were destroyed in the disastrous wars with Rome.

JAMES PARKES

Although the Exodus of the "children of Israel" from Egypt is rightly to be regarded as one of the greatest milestones in human history, in the context of the age in which they lived it must have seemed a very small, even trivial event. The Egyptians themselves would have regarded it as just one more tiresome episode in a constantly recurring situation. For centuries the bedouin tribesmen of Sinai and south Palestine had been permitted from time to time to bring their flocks to the fringes of the fertile Delta in search of pasture; whenever there was famine on the steppelands, the cry would go around, "There is corn in Egypt!" And from time to time, when the nomads, grown numerous, sought to move farther in and settle, the army of Pharaoh would be sent to expel them from the borders once more. They had outstayed their welcome.

Archaeology has not yet provided any material remains that

Egyptians harvesting corn

Statues at Abu Simbel

could throw light on the story of the sojourn in Egypt and of the Exodus. Circumstantial details contained in the narrative, however, and our knowledge of the wider history of the age, suggest that Joseph and Moses fit best into the context of the Nineteenth Dynasty, when the residence city of the Pharaohs was not Thebes or Memphis, but Pi-Ramesses in the eastern Delta, probably that same city called "Raamses" which the Hebrews are said to have helped to build. The Pharaoh of the Exodus in that case is likely to have been Ramses II, who founded this new city and embellished it with fine buildings and gardens.

## The reign of Ramses II

Ramses II is one of the most impressive figures in the whole history of the ancient Near East. His long reign of sixty-seven years (he lived to the age of ninety) was a time of great prosperity for Egypt. The resources of the country were developed, trade and industry flourished and a vast program of temple building was carried through. In every city in Egypt and Nubia his monuments proliferated. Quarries and mines were opened and wells dug in desert places to ease the lot of the miners. In front of the astonishing temple of Abu Simbel, carved in the living rock, there are four colossal figures representing, not the great gods of Egypt, but the king himself seated in fourfold

Hittite king and queen

Ramses II

majesty, his face towards the rising sun. In the lofty hall of this temple and on the walls of others throughout the land, Ramses caused to be depicted, in flamboyant detail and in huge size, scenes from the great battle which he fought against the combined forces of the Hittites and their allies in the year 1300 B.C., the fourth year of his reign. The battle took place near the city of Kadesh in Syria. Almost singlehanded, if we are to believe his account, he

had charged the enemy in his chariot and driven them sprawling backwards into the river Orontes. It was a theme of which the court poets and sculptors did not tire. In spite of his claim to have won a great victory, however, this trial of strength seems to have ended in stalemate. His greater achievement was the treaty of "brotherhood" which, after years of negotiation, he subsequently made with the Hittite king, Hattushil III, and which proved to be lasting. By a fortunate chance of survival, the text of this treaty survives in both the Hittite and the Egyptian versions, the one carved in hieroglyphics on a stone stele in the temple of Karnak, the other in

cuneiform on tablets found in the Hittite capital, Hattusas, the modern Boghazköi.

The treaty was cemented by the marriage of Ramses to the daughter of the Hittite king. She was sent to Egypt with an escort befitting so important a traveler and

Hittite war chariot

her way was made easy, we are told, by the storm god who caused the winter snows of Lebanon to melt and the sun to shine as she passed by. The *entente cordiale* was not thereafter broken by either side. The Hittites became increasingly preoccupied with struggles to maintain their empire in Anatolia and were content to maintain their position in North Syria, while Egypt was left in possession of the Phoenician coast and all of Palestine, and probably also of the land beyond the Jordan. If the armies of Joshua and Gideon were at this time moving into "the land of milk and honey," they must have found themselves in territory still at least nominally Egyptian, and in part garrisoned by Egyptian troops.

## Canaanite strongholds

Unfortunately, archaeological evidence for the destruction of the Bronze Age cities of Palestine mentioned in the Biblical narrative is curiously inconclusive. The

Hittite warriors

# topples the Hittite Empire and threatens Egypt

The Hittite storm god

dramatic story of the fall of Jericho cannot nowadays be substantiated by the remains of fallen walls. On the sites of Lachish and Hazor—both mighty Canaanite strongholds—the evidence of pottery suggests a date late in the thirteenth century for the conquest, and Tell Beit Mersim, which is thought to have been the ancient city of Kiriath-Sepher, fell at about the same time. But in each case, no break in civilization is apparent between the levels below the layer of rubble and ash that marks destruction, and the levels of rebuilding above. It may rather be that one of the campaigns of Merneptah, the son and successor of Ramses II, was responsible for the calamity; in one of his inscriptions he claims to have crushed rebellion: "Canaan is plundered, Askalon is taken and Gezer seized; the people of Israel are desolate and have no seed. Palestine is widowed for Egypt."

This mention of Israel is unique in Egyptian writings and suggests that by 1230 B.C., the approximate date of the events described in the long text of the stele, some Israelites were already established in the Promised Land.

## Threats to the Hittites

The Hittite kingdom, meanwhile, was already running into difficulties. Assyrian armies were marching west and threatening Syria from across the Euphrates, and the turbulent Gasgas, barbarians from the northeastern mountains, constantly menaced the homeland. Hattushil had kept both at bay by military action and adroit diplomacy, but after his death in about 1250 B.C. his son, Tudkhaliya IV, met with opposition from a different quarter: from a hitherto friendly neighbor on the Aegean coast. This was the king of Ahhiyawa, who now began unwelcome interference in the affairs of the western dependencies of the Hittite empire.

The land of Ahhiyawa is still not certainly located. Many scholars, however, believe that the Ahhiyawans were the people who play the chief role in the Homeric epics—the Achaiwoi or Achaeans, warlike Greeks from the mainland and the islands who mustered their ships and under their leader, Agamemnon, sailed to attack

The Fall of Troy; Hellenistic bas-relief

Troy. The story of the ten years' siege of Troy by the Achaeans is the story of the *Iliad*. Now, judging by the geographical distribution of the confederate cities, and the description of the warriors' dress and accouterments as transmitted in

Achaean warriors

the tradition that survived till Homer's day, it is clear that these Achaeans were the same people whom archaeologists have named the Mycenaeans, the Greek-speaking warrior race who occupied Crete and the islands of the Dodecanese after the fall of Knossos (see third chapter). Their seafaring merchants established colonies or trading posts over the whole of the eastern Mediterranean and even penetrated west of Sicily to the coasts of Italy, France and Spain. Mycenaean pottery is found in Cyprus, in the cities of the Levant and in Egypt, and some has been found, too, on the west coast of Turkey.

The kings of Ahhiyawa who sheltered fugitives from the Hittite court may well have been Achaean Greeks whose kingdom—somewhere on the fringe of the Hittite empire, perhaps in Caria or on the island of Rhodes—now constituted a threat to peace. In a treaty between Tudkhaliya IV and one of his vassals, the king of Amurru, the Hittite king refers to "the kings who are of equal rank with me: the king of Egypt, the king of Babylon, the king of Assyria and the king of Ahhiyawa." But the words "and the king of Ahhiyawa" were subsequently deliberately erased from the tablet. Fortunately the signs are still legible, and we are left wondering what crisis in Hittite affairs had led to the hasty removal of the offending phrase, perhaps by some scribe who had been lacking in discretion.

## End of the Hittite Empire

In the reign of Tudkhaliya's successor, Arnuwanda III, the situation became more critical: a rebel made common cause with Ahhiyawa and occupied wide territories in the southwest of Asia Minor. In the east, a hostile attack by one Mita, or Midas, suggests that the Phrygians, who were destined later to occupy the Hittite

homeland, were already in league with other mountain peoples against their former overlords. In these texts we can dimly perceive the first stirrings of great movements of populations, the origin and direction of which we do not yet understand, but which were to topple the great empire of the Hittites and change the map of the Near East.

The end came in the reign of Arnuwanda's brother, Shuppiluliuma II, ill-fated bearer of a great name. At his accession, a little

Warrior from Boghazköi

before 1200 B.C., he must already have found himself at the head of an army fighting for its life. The records from Boghazköi tell of naval battles. Tablets from Ugarit, still a Hittite dependency, reflect a state of emergency in North Syria at the approach of an enemy who is not named. These tablets, some of them letters, were found in the oven in which they had been packed for baking; there had been no time to take them from the kiln when the city met its final destruction. Ugarit was sacked and burned, never to be rebuilt. Other cities of Anatolia and Syria met the same fate. Hattusas itself suffered a great conflagration, and wherever excavation has been undertaken on Hittite sites, the destruction is only too apparent. So complete was the disaster that no written record of it has survived, save in the annals of the one kingdom that was able to withstand the invaders. That kingdom was Egypt.

# Ramses III Defeats the Sea Peoples

*For several years the Sea Peoples from the north had been drawing closer and closer to Egypt. Syria and Libya fell to them, and under the leadership of Merai of Libya they began to prepare for an assault on Egypt itself. Merneptah, son of Ramses II, decided to take the initiative and attack first. His strategy was justified by his resounding victory, but the Sea Peoples learned a lesson and devised a new tactic. They began to infiltrate the country in families and groups. Unknown to the Egyptian administration, a new onslaught of Sea Peoples was about to occur. Happily for Egypt there was a man equal to the situation in the person of Ramses III.*

Captive Sea People held by the hair; from Cairo Museum.

*Opposite* Battle between the Egyptians and the Libyans; detail from the relief in the temple of Medinet-Habou commemorating Ramses III's second Libyan campaign.

In the eighth year of his reign, in 1191 B.C., Ramses III mobilized the Egyptian armies, together with their mercenaries, auxiliaries and allies, to halt an invasion of the Sea Peoples. Egypt was facing some of the toughest enemies in its history. Who were these mysterious Sea Peoples, as they are referred to in the official documents that chronicled the numerous campaigns fought against them during the reigns of Ramses II and Merneptah?

The Sea Peoples were nations of very diverse origins, engaged in joint expeditions of conquest and plunder. They included the Aqaivasha, who were probably Achaeans; the Tursha or Tyrrhenians; the Shakalsha or Zekel, who came from Sicily; the Shirdana or Sherden, who originated in Sardis or possibly Sardinia; the Denyen or Danaeans, originating from Greece; the Peleset, referred to in the Bible as Philistines; and the Louka or Lycians. These men, although from different stock, had one thing in common: Indo-European racial characteristics, with features astonishing to the Egyptians. They were "all northern peoples," declare the victory inscriptions of Merneptah in his temple at Karnak, "coming from all sorts of countries and remarkable for their blond hair and blue eyes."

These people were nomads, or perhaps they had been forced into a nomadic way of life by the great migrations of about 2000 B.C., which had completely changed the Near East and the Middle East. The descent of the Indo-Europeans into Greece, Asia and to some extent India had been irresistible and devastating. The Peleset, for example, who originated in Crete, established themselves first in the region of Syria and then in Palestine, warring against the Hebrews; while other tribes invaded the banks of the Orontes and the kingdom of the Amorites.

The conquest of Kheta, which had tried to oppose the insidious infiltration and brutal aggression of the Sea Peoples, and the defeat of the Hittites put Egypt in great danger; for the great Delta, networked by numerous tributaries from the Nile, offered easy entry to the warships of the Indo-Europeans who aimed to command the seas. Some of these people already had entered the service of the pharaohs, who admired their military valor and gladly employed them as mercenaries. Among these were the Shakalsha, the Shirdana and the Louka. Others, like the Aqaivasha (the Achaeans who are found in Greece at virtually the same period) were newcomers.

Seti I had already been alarmed by the establishment of these Sea Peoples in Syria, and their obvious appetite for attacking neighboring countries and their large-scale irruption into Libya, where the native tribes had been overwhelmed. One of the principal aims of Seti's campaigns in Libya had been to neutralize their power. In this he succeeded, and he gave Egypt a long period of peace from these particular enemies. It was not until the end of the reign of Ramses II, Seti I's successor, that the threat from the Sea Peoples caused the pharaohs any great concern. Then came a considerable upheaval in Eastern Europe, principally in the Balkans and around the shores of the Black Sea, and nomads moved in the direction of Asia Minor, Greece and the Aegean islands, and finally Libya—that is to say, they moved in closer to Egypt. Once again it became necessary to take the offensive and fortify the frontiers, or better still, to attack the nomads before they became invincible.

Ramses II was eighty, too old, too tired and too disheartened to take the initiative. He handed the responsibility and the honor to his son Merneptah, who, in the fifth year of his reign (*c.* 1227 B.C.) attacked Libya. Merneptah justified this action in view of the preparations made by the Libyan king Merai, who was gathering the Sea Peoples together under his command. Tempted by the fertility of the Nile Valley, they were preparing to

*Right* Detail showing three of the prisoners. From Medinet-Habou.
*Below* Captive Philistines, in feathered headdresses, being led away by the Egyptians.

invade either by chariot along the land routes, or by sea.

The inscription called the "Stele of Israel," discovered in Merneptah's temple tomb in Thebes, records the events of the war and Merneptah's success; the inscriptions on the walls of the temple tell us more. The engagement took place at Per-Ir in the Delta, to the north of Memphis. After a battle lasting six hours, the Sea Peoples retreated; 9,000 prisoners were taken. In order to make his victory yet more effective, the Egyptian ruler pursued Merai's troops as far as Palestine and ravaged their settlements in the lands of Canaan and Ashkelon. This punitive expedition did not spare the Hebrews: "Israel is laid waste and its people no longer exist," the inscriptions record.

After this triumph, Merneptah had no more trouble with the Sea Peoples, nor did the five pharaohs who succeeded him. But Egypt was possibly enjoying a false sense of security. The Sea Peoples had learned prudence from their failure and never again risked a full-scale attack on their neighbor. But neither did they abandon the idea of infiltrating the Delta and taking possession of it.

It has been rightly said of Ramses III that he was "the last great king of the ancient empire." From the moment he succeeded to power in 1198 B.C., he was conscious of the vital need for reforms in his kingdom, above all in the administration and the army. Under his predecessors, foreign policy in regard to Asia had been feeble and neglected. Libya had re-established its power, and the Sea Peoples, in spite of their defeat at Per-Ir, were once again planning an attack on Egypt.

Their tactics, however, had changed. Unobserved by the frontier garrisons, they infiltrated the Delta in small groups of a few families each, then gradually moved south. Without the knowledge of the administration, they set up small collectives, apparently peaceful settlements but capable of becoming formidable instruments of war if their inhabitants banded together. The Egyptians over a long period had employed aliens, sometimes as soldiers and sometimes as workmen, and this facilitated the integration of these foreign races, who little by little mixed with the native population despite racial differences.

In the melting pot of this Afro-Asian immigration were Bedouins, Syrians, Cretans, Lydians and Canaanites. They were a motley crowd, lacking in discipline and hostile to the edicts of the administration and to the laws of a country to which they owed neither physical nor moral allegiance. Such internal disorder and lack of civic sense among people who lived in Egypt as though they had conquered it, yet who refused all the obligations that conquest entails, endangered the security and prosperity of Egypt. And this was at a time when Palestine, Syria, Naharin, Cilicia, Cyprus and the lands of the Amorites were in the hands of the Sea Peoples, before whose onslaughts even the powerful Hittite bastion had collapsed.

It was providential that at this time of great danger, a king who was wise, intelligent, energetic and bold succeeded to the throne. The bas-reliefs of the temple that Ramses built at Medinet-Habou record, in epic style and imposing pictures, the triumphs of the sovereign, the wheels of his war chariot grinding his enemies into dust. Along the north wall of the temple, a gateway almost 230 feet wide, scenes of the tremendous battles that brought about the undoing of the Sea Peoples unfold. But how could enemies so strongly entrenched around Egypt and so well established even in the Nile Valley itself have been defeated so completely? For after the victories of Ramses III they never again represented a serious danger to Egypt.

To understand the brilliance of Ramses III's tactics, one must recognize the patience, care and

Ramses spearing one of the enemy. In Egyptian battle scenes it was customary to show Pharaoh in the thick of the fight, personally responsible for the Egyptian triumph through his semi-divine power.

61

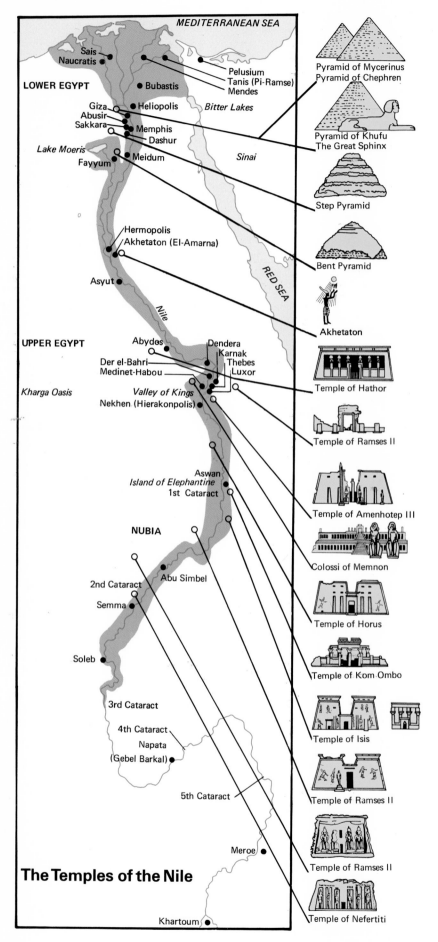

**The Temples of the Nile**

tenacity with which he pursued his policy of reconquering Asia. The triumphant bas-reliefs of Medinet-Habou indicate a first expedition dating from the third or fourth year of his reign, or perhaps even earlier. This was against the Amorites, and the inscription reads: "The capital is reduced to ashes, the people taken into captivity, their race obliterated." Ramses III may well have used this opportunity to march against the Libyans and the Asians who, he said, had been the ruin of Egypt on former occasions. Perhaps he also stopped the Delta invasion of two new Indo-European bands of troops, who had come from Libya in swift warships and were disembarking along the coast.

This counter-blow, however effective temporarily, could not deter the aggressors, who were themselves being pressed by their own enemies. In the fifth year of Ramses' reign Libya was the scene of a concentration of hostile tribes, among whom were the Mashouash—who were beginning to acquire an alarming hegemony—and the less numerous Seped and Rebou. The Libyans had been restive ever since Ramses II, in order to assert his authority over this area, had installed as king a Libyan prince brought up in Egypt and loyal to the Pharaoh. The adherents of the legitimate Libyan dynasty overthrew this foreign intruder. Then, after summoning to their assistance all the scattered tribes of the Sea Peoples, they attacked the Egyptian garrisons at a place believed to be Canopus, where the Nile debouches. Their intention was to push on from there as far as Memphis.

Ramses III quickly surrounded the invaders, trapped them in swampy ground and slaughtered them so effectively that it would seem the whole race of the Sea Peoples must have been destroyed. However, the satisfaction gained from this victory was short-lived. Scarcely three years later, in 1191 B.C., the Denyen, the Tjeker, the Peleset, the Shakalsha and the Washash, more insolent and bolder than ever, and supported as always by the native population of Libya, the Tehenou, again attacked Egypt.

This war of 1191 B.C. finally broke the spirit of the Sea Peoples and disorganized their coalition. The tribes from Asia arriving by sea found the Delta protected by an Egyptian squadron much larger than any gathered there before. If one is to believe the accounts of the battle, each mouth of the Nile was blocked by ships close enough together to touch sides. Along the land frontier toward Palestine the Egyptians had built forts and had assembled a number of infantry regiments as well as squadrons of chariots. All the doors into Egypt had been securely locked.

Ramses' strategy was skillful: the enemy's assault would be broken by these impenetrable walls, and Ramses then would have only to drive back the discouraged and weakened aggressors to their point of departure. The bas-reliefs of Medinet-Habou show the fury of the naval battle. The Egyptian galleys rammed and sank the ships of the

Sea Peoples, whose prows, like the Viking long-ships, terminated in birds' heads; Egyptian sailors pierced with their lances the invaders, some of whom wore the horned helmets so characteristic of the Germanic nations during the later great migrations.

The invaders, annihilated at sea by a better-armed fleet and blocked by land, retreated. They left more than 12,500 dead and about a thousand prisoners. The enemy dead were counted by a curious system: each soldier cut off one hand (or the genitals, if uncircumcized) of his victim and took it to the scribes responsible for the census and rewards.

Ramses III wished his glory to be recorded for all time on the walls of his funerary temple, and it is to this that we owe the magnificent and realistic battle scenes. The Pharaoh—larger than life,

*Above* The gateway of the temple of Medinet-Habou built in the style of an Asiatic fortress.

*Left* Nubians bringing tribute to the Pharaoh; wall painting from the tomb of Sebekhotep at Thebes.

*Below* The Pharaoh Ramses III, depicted on each of this row of colossal statues at Karnak.

according to the convention for a figure already semi-divine in his own lifetime and after his death destined to be revered as a god—is piercing his enemies with his lance and crushing them with his mace. The sculptors have carved with great precision the racial peculiarities of the different peoples who allied together against Egypt: the projecting jaws of African Negroes, the Semitic noses, the feathered headdresses of the Philistines, the beards (presumably blond) and horned helmets of the northern tribes, huddled together in a single group, pitiful and suppliant. Elsewhere Ramses III, standing upright in front of a sort of rostrum, receives homage and reports from his generals, while lower down his secretaries count the corpses.

The victorious king was not exaggerating the glory of his successes. It is clear from the records of the Harris Papyrus and the inscriptions at Medinet-Habou that Egypt had escaped a catastrophe comparable to that which had wiped out the Hittites. Yet decisive as this victory was, it did not assure the impregnability of Egypt. Three years later, in the eleventh year of his reign, Ramses III had to take to the field yet again.

The Mashouash, who had occupied Libya and imposed their rule on the native Tehenou, had chosen as king a fearless and cunning tribal chief called Kaper. He first united all the small Indo-European tribes established in Libya and coerced the more or less reluctant Tehenou to join his federation. He then marched against the Egyptian frontier fortresses, and pushed forward to within fifty miles of the Nile before being halted by the royal chariots. Once again Ramses III was able to put on his victory memorials the triumphant inscription: "The race of men who menaced my country no longer exist, they have been ground into the dust, their hearts and souls have disappeared for all time."

We know from the inscriptions at Medinet-Habou that more than 2,000 Mashouash were killed, and that survivors were pursued for more than twelve miles. Prince Meshsher, who commanded the invading army, was taken prisoner, along with a considerable number of his men; when Kaper, the vanquished king, came to entreat Ramses to spare his son's life, they executed the prince in front of his eyes. Kaper himself was put in chains and condemned to slavery. The prisoners taken in the three campaigns (in the fifth, eighth and eleventh years of Ramses' reign) provided the king with 62,226 slaves, whom he employed to build and maintain his funerary temple.

The unruly neighbors of the Two Kingdoms were henceforth politically impotent. Dispersed, denied the cohesion that had made them so dangerous, driven out of all Egyptian territories, the Sea Peoples were once again reduced to piracy by sea and a nomadic life on land. The prestige of Ramses III was immense and his authority

A section of the Harris Papyrus, which records the exploits of Ramses III. It is the longest papyrus in the world. In this section the scribes have recorded instances of the justice meted out to his subjects by the Pharaoh. The papyrus is written in the hieratic script, which was developed by the scribes from the earlier hieroglyphic writing.

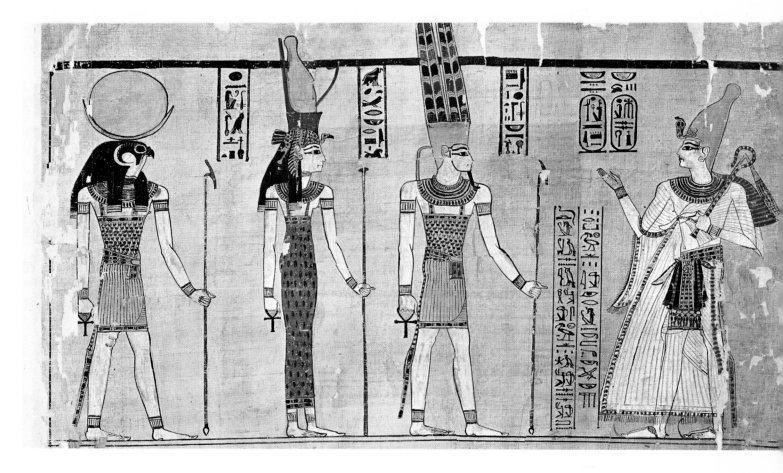

indisputable. The subject nations once again began to pay him tribute, and the sea routes once more were open to commerce. Ramses consolidated his empire by taking five cities of the Amorites and reducing the remnant of the Hittites in Syria to complete subordination. As for the Bedouins in Nubia, a few policing operations proved sufficient to reduce them to servility. Until Ramses III's death in 1166 B.C. nothing disturbed the prosperity and power of Egypt.

Ramses' personal life, however, was not so tranquil. In spite of the debt that his people owed him, showered as they were with glory and blessings, his life was endangered by several plots, one of which was engineered by his own vizier. At last, one of his wives, Queen Tiye, to further the covetousness and ambition of her son, resorted to a sorcerer who used magic charms and probably concocted poisonous drugs.

The plot was denounced and about sixty people, including six women, were condemned to death. Some of these were granted the favor of committing suicide; others were strangled or buried alive. The status and offices of the conspirators are known: a general by the name of Peyes, the commander of the Nubian archers, five senior officials, three royal scribes, five sculptors, the sorcerer Panhouibaounou, and certain concubines. Ramses never knew the outcome of the trial: he died some days before the verdict, after a reign of thirty-one years and forty days.

MARCEL BRION

*Above* Ramses III depicted with the "Theban Triad," the three principal deities of Thebes—Amon, Mut and Khons. From the Harris Papyrus.

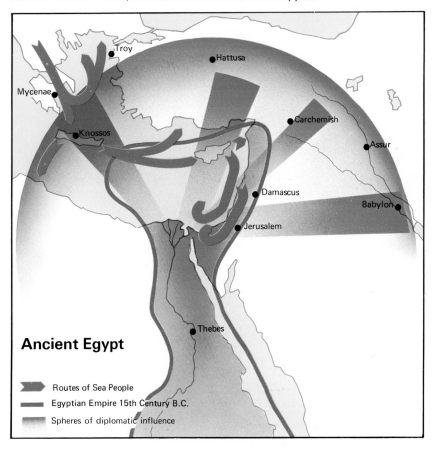

**Ancient Egypt**

Routes of Sea People

Egyptian Empire 15th Century B.C.

Spheres of diplomatic influence

65

Hittite inscription

Ashurbanipal hunting

The vacuum left in Western Asia by the passage of the Sea Peoples was soon filled. New peoples infiltrated into the devastated areas and settled there. Some cities like Alalakh and Ugarit were never rebuilt; others rose again from their ashes. Tribes of Phrygians from Europe and their kin, the Mushki or Moschoi, divided the Anatolian plateau between them, but remnants of the Hittite peoples still continued to survive under their rule. Others, remaining outside the Phrygian orbit, retained their old traditions in the cities of southeastern Anatolia, the Taurus mountains and the plains of North Syria. Here they built temples to the old gods of the Hittite empire, and the inscriptions in their palaces are written in hieroglyphic script, the ancient writing that had coexisted with cuneiform since its beginning in Anatolia. In many of these "Neo-Hittite" states, however, the ruling element was soon Semitic, for camel-riding tribes-

men from the North Arabian desert moved into settled areas and took control of cities, setting up a series of political states. Once established, they flourished on commerce, acting as middlemen between the Mediterranean coast and the cities of Babylonia and Assyria. Competition, however, was to be their downfall: they proved incapable of combining. Their historical inscriptions celebrate victories over rivals, whereas a much greater danger threatened them from across the Euphrates.

## Assyrian expansion

The Assyrians, now welded into a mighty military machine of formidable efficiency, were bent on expansion. One after another, as the Assyrian armies swept westwards, the Aramaean states crumpled and were swallowed up; one after another the cities of North Syria, Carchemish and

Arpad, Hamath and Damascus fell, and Israel and Judah paid tribute. The wealthy coastal cities of Phoenicia bought their freedom for a time, but they too were occupied, and by the seventh century Egypt herself was prostrate under the heel of Assyria. It was an empire such as the world had not seen before. The only kingdom to resist occupation, in spite of repeated campaigns, was the mountainous realm of Urartu, to the north of Assyria. Urartu's capital on the shores of Lake Van was impregnable to the attacks of the Assyrian siege engines. The Urartians, distant relatives of the Hurrians, had developed in their hilly fastness a remarkable civilization of their own, about which more is now beginning to be known, as excavation on sites in south Russia and northeastern Turkey uncovers their temples and palaces. Long at loggerheads with the Assyrians, who coveted their mineral resources, they eventually made a treaty with them. To the Assyrians, friendship with the Urartians had become desirable, for they were the last bulwark against a threat that now once more loomed terrifyingly large.

We have shown earlier how certain groups of nomads, some of them Indo-European in speech and custom, had poured over the mountains from the north and established themselves in Anatolia, Mesopotamia, Iran and northern India. But the steppelands of Central Asia continued to be a reservoir of nomadic peoples who periodically, in response to various pressures—famine maybe, or the impact of other, more distant migrations—invaded the civilized lands on their borders, from China in the east to Europe on the west. In about 1000 B.C. Indo-European groups began once more to overrun Persia from the direction of the Caucasus. Their bronze horse trappings and weapons are found in stone-built graves in the Luristan hills. Some were Iranian tribes,

forerunners of the Medes and Persians whose fortunes we shall briefly relate. Other invaders from the Russian steppes traveled more slowly and later, from about 800 B.C., nomadic groups known to classical writers as the Cimmerians, Thracians and Illyrians invaded the plains north of the Black Sea and the Danubian basin. Not long afterwards, a white-skinned horde of horse-riders known as the Yueh-Chi were troubling China.

Babylonian demon

## The Scythian onslaught

The Cimmerians who invaded Asia Minor in the eighth century B.C. were escaping, so Herodotus tells us, from the Scythians who were hard on their heels. About the Scythians we are well informed, for a number of Greek writers describe their appearance and their customs and way of life. They were a short, bearded people who wore tunics and baggy thick trousers. Their covered wagons were drawn by oxen, and these were their only habitations. They were brilliant horsemen, skillful archers, scalp-hunters, and they practiced witchcraft and shaman-

Capture of Lachish

# ew peoples emerge and new empires rise

Coin of King Kanishka

ism, and drank from cups made from the skulls of their enemies. They succeeded, as the Cimmerians had not, in bringing to an end the Phrygian kingdom in Asia Minor. For fifty or perhaps a hundred years, their advance was stemmed on the west by the armies of Lydia, and to the south by those of Urartu and Assyria. Waves of Scythian onslaught beat in vain against the rocky strongholds of the armies of Van. But at last the kingdom of Urartu fell. At Karmir Blur, a rocky stronghold near the Russian border with Turkey, signs of a desperate last stand have been found: meals abandoned half-eaten, wine jars overturned, arrowheads of Scythian type embedded in the skeletons of those who had fallen in the streets or on the battlements.

## Medes and Persians

The Assyrians, too, were to succumb. In 612 B.C. the Scythians joined an alliance with two other of Assyria's enemies, the Medes and the Babylonians; Nineveh fell and the empire was partitioned between the victors. It was, however, the more highly developed military power, the Medes, rather than the wild Scythians, into whose hands the northern part of the empire fell, while Babylonia took over Arabia, Phoenicia and Palestine.

We first hear of the Medes and Persians in the eighth century B.C., when both "Madai" and "Parsua" paid tribute to the Assyrian king Shalmaneser III. At this time the Medes were concentrated around the south of Lake Urmiah, in the north of Iran; later they moved south and made Ecbatana, the modern city now called Hamadan, their capital. Farther south, in Fars, the modern Shiraz district, a king of Parsua named Cyrus, a descendant of one Hakhamanish, or Achae-

menes, became a client of the last great king of Assyria, Ashurbanipal. After the fall of Nineveh, the Persians became vassals of the Median empire, but it was they, and not the Medes, who were destined to create the first Iranian empire, far wider than that of Assyria. It is often called the Achaemenid empire, after the founder of the line. In 539 B.C. a second and greater Cyrus, who had already captured Ecbatana and united Medes and Persians under his rule, conquered Babylon.

North Assyrian tribesman on camel

This date was truly a milestone in history, for it marked the end of the long political dominance of the Mesopotamian powers and the shift of leadership to Iran. Under its successive Achaemenid kings, Persian domination spread over the known world and into regions hitherto outside the ken of civilized peoples; not only the Fertile Crescent and Egypt, but the whole of the peninsula of Asia Minor as far as the Ionian coast was made subject, and to the east huge territories including Bactria and the region of the Hindu Kush, and even the Indus Valley, were made tributary. This empire, the greatest the world had yet known, continued until its overthrow, two centuries later, by the young and remarkable Macedonian adventurer, Alexander.

## The rise of Persia

The success of the Achaemenids was perhaps due in part to their freshness of outlook, their youthful energy and their freedom from the shackles of tradition. In part it may

be ascribed to the bankruptcy and exhaustion of the ancient civilizations of the Near East, torn by internal discord and harassed by enemies from without. But largely it was due to the wise and liberal policy of the Achaemenid kings, a policy of adaptation and reconciliation whereby the old could be welded together with the new. The Persians respected local traditions, honored the gods of their subject peoples and interfered as little as possible in the affairs of their subjects. Their liberal attitude is in keeping with the tone of moral enlightenment and ethical balance which characterizes their religious outlook.

For great though their political achievement was, it is in the realm of religion that the Achaemenids left their mark indelibly on the world. For this, one man is responsible, Zarathustra—or Zoroaster as the Greeks called him. To him also is owed the earliest compositions of Persian literature, the *Gathas*, religious poems that were later incorporated into the sacred book known as the Avesta. We know very little of Zoroaster's life. The Gathas, which record his utterances, are difficult to interpret. Even the very date of his birth is widely disputed. Many authorities consider that the prince at whose court he found protection and encouragement was the father of Darius the Great; others consider that he lived some centuries earlier, or else that, although he may have lived in the sixth century, the effect of his teachings was not felt until much later. The question of whether or not the Achaemenid kings of Persia were themselves followers of Zoroaster is a matter of debate, though it is certain that they upheld one of the essential tenets of Zoroaster's faith: the belief in Ahura Mazda, the embodiment of goodness and wisdom and

Bronze buckle from the Caucasus

Axehead from Luristan

truth. Zoroastrian influence extended far beyond the frontiers of Iran; it had a profound effect on Judaism, especially in the realm of eschatology—the concepts of the afterlife, of purgatory, judgment and resurrection—and these ideas passed over into Christianity and became an integral part of orthodox Christian belief. In India today, Zoroastrianism continues as the faith of the relatively small but influential community of Parsees, and in Iran there are still areas where the ancient faith is still followed and the ancient rites performed.

Symbol of Ahura Mazda

It has been said that most scholars believe the most likely date for Zoroaster's birth is the early sixth century B.C., perhaps around 570, in the lifetime of the father of Darius. By a strange coincidence, within a few years, another great teacher was born whose religious doctrines, different though they were in many respects, were to have an equally profound effect on the lives of many millions. This was Gautama, the Buddha.

*As a young man, Gautama, or the Buddha as he came to be known, followed the usual pursuits of someone of his class. He hunted, played games, feasted and had many friends. He also inspired great personal devotion, which was to stand him in good stead later. Growing discontented with his life and determined to find enlightenment, he renounced his wealth and left Kapilavastu in order to lead an ascetic life. But Gautama found that this kind of existence, practiced in isolation, did not satisfy him. He believed that compassion for his fellow men should find practical expression. He returned to Gaya where he became the "fully-awakened", or Buddha, and began to teach. Although Buddhism—the faith he founded—did not become supreme in India, it won many followers in Ceylon, Burma, Thailand and Tibet and played a crucial role in the development of China and Japan.*

In the forested foothills of the Himalayas, in the region that is now central Nepal, there was born around the year 563 B.C. a man whose life and teachings were to have a profound influence throughout Asia and beyond. His personal name was Siddhartha, but he was known also as Gautama, the name of the family group to which he belonged. The Gautama family were Sakyas, one of a number of clans who inhabited the area between the river Ganges and the Himalayas, roughly to the northeast and northwest of the modern city of Patna.

The young Gautama, who was later also to be called Sakyamuni, or "Sage of the Sakyas," grew up in the hill town of Kapilavastu. As the son of the leading clansman, Suddhodana, his lot must have been fairly pleasant, and Buddhist tradition tells us that he was protected from contact with the harsher of life's problems. Tradition also ascribes to his father the deliberate policy of shielding his son from knowledge of the evils of life, because at birth it had been predicted that the child was destined to become either a great ruler or a great ascetic, and his father was determined that it should be the former.

The nature of the human condition could not be hidden indefinitely, however, and Gautama's disillusionment with the artificially soft life he was enjoying came about in early manhood. Tradition represents this as happening through four chance encounters. First he met a very old man, "bent, decrepit, leaning on a staff, tottering as he walked, afflicted . . . ," a sight that caused the young Gautama to reflect that the same fate awaits all humanity. Next he encountered a sick man, suffering great disease, unable to raise himself, in acute pain, needing to be tended and washed by others; again the young man became aware that debilitating illness was a possibility that lay in store for all. Then he saw a corpse being carried out to the funeral pyre, attended by sorrowing

parents, relatives and friends. The same fate, he realized, awaits us all. Finally he encountered a *samana*, an ascetic holy man, with yellow robe and shaven head. Questioning him about his way of life, Gautama, concerned with the uncertainty and suffering that attends mortal existence, became attracted to the idea of the holy life.

As Gautama thought about these four encounters, he became convinced of the need to find a solution to the intolerable problem of suffering that he saw life entailed. He then resolved to leave the temporary and illusory pleasures of his privileged life in Kapilavastu and set out in pursuit of salvation.

Up to this point there is nothing to distinguish the young Gautama from other samanas who were seeking some kind of salvation from mortal ills. In his case, however, the ascetic life did not prove the answer. He engaged in the most rigorous of ascetic practices, in the course of which his body was reduced almost to a skeleton, yet he found no satisfying answer to his quest. Turning aside from the extreme rigors of asceticism, he took some food and came to a place on the bank of the river Neranjara, a tributary of the Ganges. There he saw a large tree, known subsequently to Buddhists as the bodhi or "enlightenment" tree. Here he sat down and remained for a long time, at length passing through certain well-defined, progressive stages of meditation. In the course of his meditation he was assailed by Mara the Evil One (literally, "the destroyer," or "lord of death"). Mara tried by various stratagems to deflect the Buddha-to-be from his progress toward enlightenment. Having failed to intimidate him, Mara then tried to divert Gautama by sending his three daughters to seduce him. But all Mara's efforts were futile. The earlier, Pali Buddhist scriptures present the temptation by Mara as a mental and spiritual attack by the elemental forces of mortal existence, the forces of *Kamadhatu*, the sensual

*Above* Shakravartin—"he who turns the wheel"—the ruler of the world, is shown in this marble relief of the school of Amaravati, dating from the first century B.C. or A.D.

*Opposite* The attack of Mara, a marble relief of the second century from Amaravati. In this relief the Buddha himself is not shown but is represented by the royal throne below the tree of enlightenment.

sphere, which ultimately lead to death rather than life. In later versions the story of the temptation is embellished with highly sensational descriptions of Mara and his army in grand array, and of the seductive wiles of Mara's daughters. The temptations later became a favorite subject for pictorial decorations in Buddhist temples and monasteries in India and southeast Asia. The form of the *Buddha-rupa* or "Buddha image," in which the Buddha is shown seated in meditation with one hand pointing toward the ground, is sometimes known as the "Mara-renouncing" position.

At length, after being immersed in profound meditation throughout the night, there came to Gautama the clear insight by which he saw the true nature of all things; as day dawned he became "fully-awakened," or "Buddha." Buddha is in no sense a personal name, since in the view of Buddhists there had been other Buddhas before Gautama, and there will be others after him. The title Buddha, namely the "Awakened One" or "Enlightened One," indicates a spiritual or ontological status, a certain order of being. When he reached this state, the Buddha understood the transience that characterizes all mortal life and saw the ultimate transcendental end of existence, in Sanskrit called *nirvana*.

After this momentous insight, the Buddha remained for a week under the bodhi tree in continual meditation. Then, for a few weeks, he walked in the neighborhood of the tree. Once again Mara is said to have approached him and to have urged him to abandon mortal existence and enter fully and finally into nirvana. The Buddha rejected this subtle attempt of Mara's to get him out of the way, as he did all subsequent attempts. He replied that he must first instruct others in the truth he had experienced, set up an order of monks and see the order well established before he left this life. Mara, it is said, once again retired in defeat. It was to the

mission he had described to Mara, and which Mara henceforth did everything he could to hinder, that the Buddha devoted the remaining forty years of his life.

To understand the significance of the Buddha's doctrine and the new religious community that he gathered round him, it is helpful to look first at what we know of the India he was born in. Our evidence comes mainly from the ancient Pali literature of the Buddhists, which shows a generally keener historical sense than either the Hindu Vedic texts or the Prakrit texts of the Jains, another contemporary religious group. Various critical studies have revealed that the republican groups of northeast India, such as the Sakyas, were suffering attacks from newly arisen neighboring monarchies, particularly those of Magadha and Kosala. These monarchies were absorbing the territories and people of the repub-

## The Spread of Buddhism

CHINA

TIBET

*Himalayas*

INDIA

Scenes from the early life of the Buddha, depicted in carvings of the school of Amaravati.
*Left* The mother of the Buddha has a dream (*top right*), which is interpreted by a sage (*top left*). The birth of the Buddha ensues (*bottom right*), and he is presented to the tutelary spirits of the sakyas (*bottom left*).
*Right* The Buddha with his father, surrounded by women of the harem. Shielded by his father in a life of luxury, the Buddha grew to early manhood before realizing the sorrow of life.

lics, although the Sakyas themselves were probably not invaded during the Buddha's lifetime.

It was thus a time of social disturbance and political change and, consequently, a time also of psychological malaise. Men were asking with a new urgency questions about the meaning of existence and ultimate human destiny. The destruction of the old republican clans meant that people were being swept into the larger, more impersonal autocratic organization of the monarchy. They could no longer rely on the close-knit structure of the clan to give their lives ready-made significance. The individual became more acutely aware of his isolation and faced problems of personal conduct in which the old rules no longer applied. What, men were asking, are the causes of the indignities and injustices suffered by the individual? How should a man conduct himself? What other possible goal was there but to make the most of such opportunities as life provided to eat, drink and be merry? Such questions were not new in India, nor was the Buddha the first to suggest an answer. The need for answers was, however, being felt more acutely, and the Buddha offered a doctrine significantly different from others already available.

The religious philosophies and systems that existed in India at that time were broadly of two kinds; the distinction is epitomized by two characteristic classes of religious functionary, brahmans and samanas. The brahmans were priests brought by the Aryan invaders a thousand or so years earlier. They regarded themselves as a sacred elite, in whose keeping was the hereditary practice of the sacrificial system by which they believed the cosmos was maintained. It was a stupendous claim. To the ordinary householder, farmer or merchant, however, it was a claim that had little relevance to personal problems.

It was to the needs of such men that the samanas addressed themselves. The metaphysical views and ascetic disciplines that they recommended were various and often conflicting, but common to most of them was a belief in the liberation of the soul, or ego, by personal discipline, asceticism or esoteric meditational practices. These often involved renouncing the life of the householder and undertaking a rigorous training in self-mortification to enhance the soul's psychic powers, so that it might break out of the mortal realm into the sphere of supernatural bliss. The term "samana" indicates "one who labors," in this case spiritually.

Such was the background against which the Buddha set forth his doctrine, or *dharma*—according to tradition, in a deer park near the city of Benares. Unlike the teachings of most of the other great religions of the world, the Buddha-Dharma did not require belief in a supreme and omnipotent deity or creator, or make any reference to such a being. It consisted of an analysis of the human condition, as something given, rather than as a situation to be explained by speculation about cosmic origins. The latter kind of speculation was the basis of the brahmans' position; their theory of the importance of sacrifice the Buddha rejected. He also rejected their élitism: the doctrine he taught was true of all and true for all.

There are various ways of summarizing the Buddha-Dharma. One is in terms of the "four holy truths." The first truth to be apprehended is that all living beings have to suffer the disorder and imperfection of ordinary earthly existence; this may be variously described as "illness," "unsatisfactoriness," "imperfection," or "suffering." At times one may be temporarily unaware of this imperfection, but eventually it will always assert itself.

The second truth is that this suffering is caused by an attitude of craving, an insatiable thirst for that which one has not.

The third truth is that the experience of suffering

Buddhist pillar, decorated with scenes symbolizing the four main events of the Buddha's life—his birth, enlightenment, first sermon, death. The pillar with the Wheel of the Law, shown in the photograph, symbolizes the first sermon, given in the deer park at Benares.

The great departure. The Buddha leaves home, escorted as a prince for the last time, to abandon his luxurious life and become an ascetic.

*Above* Buddhists worshipping the Bodhi tree, beneath which the Buddha received enlightenment.

*Below* The miracle of Saraswati.

"soul," to which such importance had been attached and which was the cause of division between men through ideas of "I" and "mine," that real awakening was to be found. Destroy this egocentric view of the world, said the Buddha, and enter a freer, wider realm of being, which is nirvana. Moreover, it was a process that needed the experience of living in a community dedicated to the negation of the egoistic principle. Such a community was the Buddha-Sangha or Buddhist religious order.

The sangha, or order of *bhikkhus* (almsmen), provided the optimum conditions for living the Buddhist life. This community, which came into being when the first disciples attached themselves to the Buddha, was unique. Other groups of samanas sometimes formed groups for the period of the monsoon rains, when traveling was impossible and it became necessary to take shelter in one place. But these groups had only a temporary existence. Out of this practice, however, the Buddha and his disciples established a permanent community that existed to facilitate the practice of the Buddhist way. A recognized rule of life and conduct and a high standard of moral discipline were outstanding features of the order from the beginning.

In the course of the Buddha's lifetime, as the number of disciples grew, the code of conduct for members of the order was worked out and formally established. This code subsequently became embodied in the basic tradition as the *Vinaya*, that is, the Discipline. The other main feature of the tradition was the dharma, which had come to mean, besides the doctrine, the actual collection of discourses uttered by the Buddha. This took the form of parables, allegories, discussions, stories and verses, in order to render the doctrine as clear as possible to as many as possible, since the Buddha's teaching was intended for all men, whatever their station. Within the sangha there was no hierarchy apart from seniority in spiritual attainment; all social distinctions were (and still are) abandoned by those who entered.

The sangha thus offered some replacement for the communal life that India had lost with the destruction of the old republican societies. Later it was to acquire far wider significance, over a far greater area. For more reasons than one, a man went for refuge to the sangha. The common formula used by Buddhists from the earliest times as a simple affirmation of faith, and still universally adopted, runs as follows: "To the Buddha I go for refuge; to the dharma I go for refuge; to the sangha I go for refuge."

Among the early members of the sangha who accompanied the Buddha on his many journeys throughout northeast India and Nepal, and who devoted themselves to his mission and his needs (as Buddhist monks still minister to one another), are certain well remembered names, especially those of Ananda, often referred to as the "beloved disciple," Sariputta and Maha Kassapa. It was

ceases with the end of desire in all its aspects—greed, anger and false views of life. The cessation of craving is nirvana, the Buddhist goal.

The fourth truth is that there is a way by which such cessation can be achieved here and now, namely the way of the Buddha, the way opened up by him, to be followed by all men who have faith in the Buddha's knowledge. Such faith, however, is not blind faith, but "faith-with-a-view-to-verification." According to the Buddha, the following of the way itself provides the verification. The invitation that the Buddha offered was summed up in the phrase *"ehi passako"*—"Come and see," that is, verify the transcendent truth for yourself.

In addition to characterizing all human existence as suffering imperfection, the Buddha also emphasized its transitoriness. In ordinary earthly existence no state of being persists; all is continually in flux, and nothing endures. The third characteristic of existence, according to the Buddha, is the absence of any permanent individual ego. It was this that most clearly distinguished the Buddha's teaching from that of all the other samanas of India, and also from that of the brahmans. These others asserted the existence of a real permanent self or *atman* in each individual, and bade each man find within the depths of his *atman* the ultimate reality. The Buddha's doctrine was stigmatized by these "orthodox" teachers, as being *nairatmya*, that is, a "nonsoul" doctrine. But the Buddha asserted that it was in relinquishing this notion of a permanent

Ananda who approached the Buddha with a request from some of the women disciples that a parallel order for women should be established. After some hesitation the Buddha is said to have consented to this. From the earliest days an order of nuns, with its own parallel code of discipline and regulations, has been a feature of Buddhism.

At the age of eighty, his mortal body having come to the end of its span of existence, Gautama passed from the intermediate stage of the Buddha who still retains a mortal body to that of final and complete nirvana, or parinirvana. His bodily remains were cremated with great reverence, and his ashes were distributed among various groups who claimed a share in these sacred relics. The ceremony is described in one of the longest of the Pali texts, the *Parinirvana Sutta*. Over each share of the ashes, it is said, a memorial mound, or stupa, was raised. The stupa was a hemispherical structure of stone or brick with the sacred relic enshrined at its center. For Buddhists such structures became symbols and reminders of the Awakened One who had first taught them the dharma. In their later, developed form, known in Ceylon as *dagobas*, or pagodas, these stupas became a familiar feature of the Asian countries to which the Buddha-Dharma was carried by its missionary-monks.

In India the Buddhist sangha gradually grew in size and spread from the Ganges Valley around Patna northwestward toward the Punjab and Kashmir, where its monks came into contact with elements of Greco-Roman culture in the kingdom of Bactria (on the northwest borders of modern West Pakistan). There, some five centuries after the Buddha's death, a new form of Buddhism, known as the Mahayana, developed. It perhaps owed something to Greco-Roman influences, and something to the increasing numbers of brahmans who had by then, especially since the reign of the Buddhist emperor Asoka (third century B.C.), begun increasingly to enter the order.

These brahmans did not easily discard their old attitudes and ideas when they donned the yellow robe of the Buddhist monk. The result was the development within the Buddhist community of a high degree of speculative philosophizing, and an increasing use of non-Buddhist cults and practices among its lay supporters. By about A.D. 1200, partly for this reason, the practice of the way of the Buddha had disappeared almost entirely from India. From then on, however, Buddhism was expanding in influence in the neighboring lands of Tibet, Burma, Thailand, Laos, Cambodia and Vietnam, as well as in China and Japan, where it was already well established. Even in India the effects of the Buddha and his community influenced the philosophy, ethics and religious institutions of what had by then become Hinduism. In modern times India has begun to rediscover the way that was taught and practiced by one of her greatest sons, and the Buddhist community has once again begun a remarkable revival.  TREVOR LING

One of the gates of the stupa at Sanchi. A stupa is a Buddhist temple designed to house sacred relics or to commemorate the sacred character of a place or of an important event. In shape it is based on the funerary mound of the Vedas, and symbolizes the cosmic mountain, the pivot of the world.

The dagoba, or stupa of Thuparama, in Ceylon. The oldest parts of this stupa date from the third century A.D.

73

The destruction of Knossos in 1450 B.C. precipitated the end of a brilliant period in Cretan civilization. The focus of power subsequently lay on the Greek mainland, in the great fortress-cities of Mycenae and Tiryns. These cities were remembered in Homeric legend, in the poems of the *Iliad* and the *Odyssey*. Confirmation as fact of what scholars had credited merely as legend was provided by the excavation of the site of Homer's "Mycenae rich in gold" by the German merchant-turned-archaeologist, Heinrich Schliemann, in 1876. His discoveries there brought to light the "Mycenaean" civilization, which we now know to have been widespread in Greece from *c.* 1400–1200 B.C. It was the product of Indo-European settlers, and these Mycenaean Greeks took control of Crete, from where much of their culture originated, as the presence of Linear B tablets on both Crete and the mainland indicates.

The society which Homeric legend describes is not a society at its peak, as many scholars have noted, and the epics of "Homer" (whoever or whatever Homer might represent) foreshadow the downfall of the Mycenaean civilization. The decline of the Achaean Greeks was speeded by an abrupt end to their political supremacy, when the Dorian tribes swept southwards in about 1100 B.C. This may well have been part of a larger pattern of migrations that affected the western Mediterranean at about this time. The empire of the Hittites was overthrown, and Egypt was attacked by the "Peoples of the Sea." The Dorian invasion precipitated emigration of earlier Greek inhabitants from the mainland—Ionians from Attica fled to the coastal lands of Asia Minor, as did Aeolians from Thessaly; Achaeans moved into Arcadia and Cyprus.

The Trojan Horse of Homeric legend; from an early Greek vase

The Dorian invaders themselves settled in the Peloponnese and Crete, and in part of Asia Minor. The regional differences established during this period of movement and settlement were remembered by the Greeks—Sparta was always thought of as Dorian. After the Dorian invasion, Greece gradually assumed the political configuration that was to last until Alexander of Macedon reorganised the civilized world.

## The city-state

The key to Greek political development, and indeed to Greek civilization, is the Greek city, or more accurately, city-state, the *polis*. The physical geography of Greece—small plains separated from each other by steep hills and mountain chains—must have influenced the development of small, closely-knit communities, though the choice of organization was the Greeks'. They saw the *polis* as the only and the ultimate form of political and social life. Unlike elsewhere in the eastern Mediterranean, the Greek city was not part of a larger unit, such as a kingdom, but was an independent state in itself.

The cities of Greece must have provided their inhabitants with a stable and secure existence, for population in the cities had increased until it became a problem by the eighth century B.C. The geographic confinement which had partly determined the development of the cities also determined the limits of their growth—land was scarce. So still another migratory movement got under way. Yet this time it was not the helter-skelter movement of whole tribes, but the planned sending-out of real colonists. The knowledge that the Greeks possessed of the Mediterranean was somewhat hazy, but enough for many thousands to set out optimistically to find a new

life. They headed in the direction of southern Italy and Sicily, Asia Minor and the Black Sea, each pioneering group with its *oikistes*, the official "founder" of the new city. This colonization was not like the colonization of, for example, the British Empire, where the parent-country retained political control over its colonies. Once the settlers had made a landfall and established themselves in their new environment, they were on their own, virtually independent of their mother-city. Regular trading contacts were in many cases set up, the parent-cities tending to trade with their individual offspring. The wealth of a city like Corinth was undoubtedly augmented by trade with her many colonies, but the offspring prospered too—the Corinthian colony of Syracuse became one of the greatest of the Greek cities. The colonizing movement lasted for about two hundred years, from the eighth to the sixth century, and towards its end trade and commercial motivations had taken supremacy over the original "land-hunger" motive.

The political and economic

Mycenaean warrior; ivory

consequence of colonization for the Mediterranean world was that Greek influence and interests had spread far afield, ranging into the territories of diverse peoples. Southern Italy became predominately Greek (with Sicily, it was known as *Megale Hellas*, *Magna Graecia*), all along the coasts of Asia Minor there were Greek settlements, and Greeks even penetrated Egypt, establishing trading stations at Naucratis and Syria, and a colony at Al Mina.

The Phaistos Disk

Part of Linear B tablet from Knossos

Aramaean script

# Mediterranean focus moves to Greece

"Mistress of the Beasts"; Etruscan

## Cultural interchange

Colonization was not the sole prerogative of the Greeks. Greek expansion in Sicily was limited by the colonizing efforts of the Phoenicians, the skillful sea-farers who inhabited the area of present-day Lebanon. They founded several important cities on the Mediterranean coast of Spain also, though perhaps their most important foundation was the city of Carthage in North Africa, whose famous son Hannibal will be the subject of a subsequent article.

Greek settlement in southern Italy was also limited by the expansion of the Etruscans in central Italy in the seventh and sixth centuries B.C. Etruscan kings ruled the small city of Rome during the sixth century, and the fate of the Greeks, the Carthaginians, the Etruscans and the Romans are all interlinked, as future articles will show. Political confrontation was to occur between various groupings of these powers, but an example of the importance of cultural interchange during this formative period is provided by the spread of the alphabet. The Linear B script was difficult and clumsy to write—only the Greeks

of Cyprus retained it for long—and in the eighth century the Greeks took over the Phoenician alphabet, and developed it in various forms. From the Greeks of Chalcis, the Etruscans adopted a version; from them the Romans borrowed and modified it. You are reading it now.

Cultural interchange on a large scale followed the Greek colonization of the East. The Greeks were eager to assimilate and learn from the eastern cultures. The "orientalizing" trend is evident in Greek pottery from the eighth century, with the use of motifs from Syria and Phoenicia (and the Phoenicians borrowed from the Egyptians). From the Greeks in Italy the Etruscans learned the arts of civilization; they were eager for all the trappings of Hellenization, as the material remains of their culture indicate. From them Rome absorbed Greek culture.

Our next article takes us to the point in Mediterranean history at which the expansion of the colonizing period has become with only minor exceptions a thing of the past, and expansion now means large-scale political confrontation. The cities of Greece were forced to unite to save themselves from domination by the mighty empire of Persia.

## Political organization

However, the Greece that confronted Xerxes had evolved politically. Within the city-states of Greece, internal government went through a variety of forms. Sparta had two kings, whose power could vary according to the strength of their individual personalities *vis à vis* the council of elders—the ephors—who also made up the governing body of the state. Below the kings and ephors was an elite of citizens; and below them, various grades of semi-slaves and slaves. But, during the Achaean period, most Greek cities were

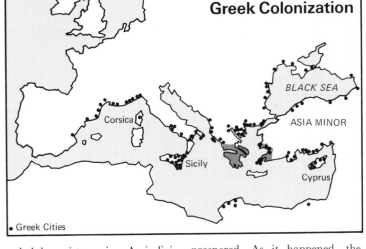

**Greek Colonization**

BLACK SEA

ASIA MINOR

Corsica

Sicily

Cyprus

• Greek Cities

ruled by aristocracies. As individual cities grew, and new economic interests and commercial expansion emerged, the hold of the landed aristocrats was challenged and gradually superceded by people of new wealth. The form of government thus tended to shift from aristocracy (rule or power of the best) to oligarchy (rule of the few). This shift in political power was often accompanied by improvements in justice—subjecting the administration of city life to the relative impartiality of written laws rather than the arbitrary and biased decisions of powerful land-owners, the "princes who devour bribes and give crooked decisions" mentioned by Hesiod. The process of changing political organization to represent new interests was often hastened, from the seventh century on, by the appearance of "tyrants," individual leaders, frequently of noble ancestry, who were hostile to the aristocracy as a whole. Tyrants (only later did the word become symbolic of oppression) arose mainly in the coastal cities of Greece that had trading interests: the first tyrants were at Sicyon and Corinth. Athens, too, had her tyrant, a noble called Cylon, in 630 B.C., but her internal problems remained, and a reformer was given power to clear up some of the inconsistencies in Athens' political and social organization. The work of this senior citizen and law-giver, Solon, gave political recognition to new forces within Athenian society, but still many problems were unresolved, and thirty years later another tyrant emerged. He established himself firmly enough to found a dynasty. Although short-lived, the dynasty of the Peisistratids gave Athens a period of stability during which she

prospered. As it happened, the fall of the Peisistratids paved the way for democracy in Athens. In Greek politics, the tendency was for tyrants (individual rulers) to be succeeded by a coalition of important men, oligarchs. Two factions of nobles competed for control when the last tyrant had been deposed, and one faction, headed by a noble called Cleisthenes, had enlisted popular support. When Cleisthenes gained control, he carried out a thorough reform of the Athenian constitution, and considerably reduced the remaining power of the nobles that was vested in the council of the Areopagus. The assembly of the people of Athens became paramount: democracy (the power of the people) was achieved, and given perhaps its fullest expression ever.

At Salamis, the democratically elected leaders of the Athenian people confronted the power of an oriental autocrat, the fleet of Xerxes, Great King of the Persians. The empire that he ruled had emerged from the ruins of Assyrian and Median power. The Persians were given a new-found unity by Cyrus (559–529), and under his rule the Achaemenid empire expanded at a phenomenal rate. Lydia was conquered, then the Persians advanced to the edge of the Mediterranean, conquering the Greek cities there. Caria, Lycia and Cilicia came under Persian domination, Babylon fell, and Syria and Palestine were subdued. Egypt was conquered after Cyrus' death by his son Cambyses (525 B.C.). Thus the whole of the eastern Mediterranean was in Persian hands. The next chapter shows how the European expansion of Persian power was stemmed by a great naval battle in the Aegean.

Italian terracotta head; ivory head from Nimrod; head from Carthage

# Victorious Athens

*Greece was threatened by the advance of the Persians. But even in the face of such a threat, the Greeks were unable to unite as a nation. The basis of Greek life was the "polis" or city-state, and the concept of nationhood was completely foreign to this system. Eventually, however, a Hellenic league of Greek cities was formed, led by Athens and Sparta, and in 480 the Persians were defeated at sea at Salamis and in 479 on land at Plataea. Had the Persians been the victors, it is hard to tell how our civilization would have developed. Possibly democracy, as we know it, would never have survived. Paradoxically it was precisely because of Greece's weakness—the independence of the city-state—that democracy, particularly in Athens, reached its highest peak of development. Thanks to Salamis it was handed on to future generations, enshrined in the legacy of Greece.*

Themistocles, whose far-sighted proposal that the Athenians should fight the Persians at sea rather than on land paved the way for the defeat of King Xerxes.

*Opposite top* The Pnyx at Athens, where Themistocles addressed the assembled citizens. In the distance on the Acropolis is the temple of Athena Parthenos, the most sacred spot in Athens.

*Opposite bottom* Greek warriors bid farewell to their womenfolk before setting out to battle; from a vase.

The Assembly on the Pnyx, Athens' "parliament hill," was packed; this would be a crucial debate. The mighty Xerxes of Persia, with the greatest invasion force that Greece had ever seen, had crossed the Dardanelles and was now advancing inexorably across Thrace towards Macedonia. His engineers had even cut a canal through the peninsula of Mt. Athos for the safe passage of the force's navy. The ruling dynasty of Thessaly had decided to collaborate with the invader, and the Macedonians had given him earth and water in token of submission. The district of Boeotia was rife with Persian sympathizers. The Spartans were ready to make a stand against Xerxes; the crucial question was, where would they make it? Their traditional line of defense was the Isthmus of Corinth. If they chose to hold that line now, Athens—to the north—would be left in isolation, exposed to the advance of the Persian war machine.

In two months or less, if nothing was done to halt him, Xerxes' fleet and army would reach Attica. The chance of the northern Greek states holding out—or indeed not actively collaborating with Xerxes—was plainly slim. Worse still, Xerxes had publicly declared that the prime purpose of his expedition was to punish Athens for the part that she had played, nearly twenty years earlier, in the revolt of Greek cities in Ionia against Persia. Any other state, then, might expect reasonable treatment from the Persian king; the Athenians could expect no mercy. Their alternatives were flight or resistance. The Delphic Oracle—while merely counseling other states to remain neutral—had already advised flight for the Athenians.

The big, thick-set man who stood on the speaker's platform of the Pnyx on that fine day in 480 B.C. was already a familiar figure. The crier's voice called out: "Pray silence for Themistocles, son of Neocles, of the Phrearri parish." Themistocles must have stood for some time, perhaps waiting till the buzz of voices died away, trying to

sense the Assembly's mood as he gazed out towards the plain of Marathon. There, he would have recalled, once before, only ten years earlier, Athenians had beaten off a Persian invasion. Themistocles had fought—and fought well—in that battle; so had many of those waiting this day for him to speak. But this crisis was different. At Marathon a citizen-army—men of property and breeding, who could afford their own armor—had marched out to defend their city and their country estates. Some of the men in his audience today, Themistocles knew, were anxious to do so again. Yet no infantry force Greece could put in the field would hold up this new invasion for long. To fight the Persians at sea was the only chance.

Three years before, against strong conservative opposition, Themistocles had put through a motion for Athens to build two hundred new warships, financed by the proceeds of a rich new lode in the Laurium silvermines. By June, 480, that fleet was ready, and Themistocles was determined to use it. We have no record of his actual speech to the Assembly on that historic occasion, but the arguments he employed are not in dispute.

Ever since the accession of King Darius, forty-two years earlier, in 522, Persian expansion had threatened Europe. Meanwhile, Egypt and Libya had fallen; so had several key islands in the eastern Aegean Sea. Darius had then boldly crossed the Bosporus, annexed Thrace and secured Macedonia's submission. The collapse of the Ionian Revolt (499–94) had made an invasion of the Greek mainland inevitable. In 490 the invasion came, to be repulsed by the Athenians at Marathon. Rebellion in the Persian empire, and the death of Darius in 486, had merely postponed the next, inevitable attack. Now Darius' son Xerxes was on the march.

Hysterical rumors estimated Xerxes' fleet at over 1,200 ships, and his army at well over a million (the actual figures are probably 650 and

*Above* King Xerxes of Persia; from the palace at Persepolis.

180,000 respectively). Themistocles' attempt to sell a naval-defense policy to the Greeks had already once fallen on deaf ears. The Hellenic League—a group of those Greek states determined to resist—had voted instead to send a land force of 10,000 men to hold the pass of Tempe in northern Greece, and Themistocles had agreed to serve as its commander. The expedition ended in a complete fiasco. The Greeks found that Xerxes could easily outflank them through central Greece; and the Thessalians, on whose help they had relied, went over *en bloc* to the enemy. It was immediately after this setback that Themistocles made his great speech to the Athenian assembly.

In a few days, there was to be an emergency meeting of the Hellenic League at the Isthmus of Corinth; but how the states would vote no one, at the moment, could foresee. Themistocles hoped for the acceptance of his own plan—a land-and-sea holding action at the pass of Thermopylae and in the waters off Artemisium. Yet he was a realist. No one had forgotten that the Spartans had arrived too late for Marathon. Worse still, they might vote to hold the Isthmus line and let everything to the north go. Cynics at Sparta might sacrifice their rival Athens to Xerxes and allow Persia to run northern Greece in the same *laissez-faire* way that she did Ionia. Sparta, south of the Isthmus, would retreat still further into isolation. In either case, Themistocles realized, adequate plans must now be made for the protection of Attica.

Thanks to archeology, we now know what those provisions were. In 1959 Professor Jameson of the University of Pennsylvania discovered a third-century B.C. inscription which preserves, in edited form, the motion passed by Themistocles in June, 480 B.C. Here are the key clauses from it, in Jameson's translation:

King Darius of Persia, whose attack on Greece had been repulsed ten years before Salamis, hunting lions; from an engraved cylinder seal.

Gods. Resolved by the Council and People. Themistocles, son of Neocles, of Phrearri, made the motion. To entrust the city to Athena, the Mistress of Athens, and to all the other gods to guard and defend from the Barbarian for the sake of the land. The Athenians

themselves and the foreigners who live in Athens are to send their children and women to safety in Troezen, their protector being Pittheus, the founding hero of the land. They are to send the old men and their movable possessions to safety on Salamis. The treasures and priestesses are to remain on the Acropolis, guarding the property of the gods.

All the other Athenians and foreigners of military age are to embark on the two hundred ships that are ready and defend against the Barbarian for the sake of their own freedom and that of the rest of the Greeks along with the Lacedaemonians, the Corinthians, the Aeginetans, and all others who wish to share the danger . . . When the ships have been manned, with a hundred of them they are to meet the enemy at Artemisium in Euboea, and with the other hundred they are to lie off Salamis and the coast of Attica and keep guard over the land. In order that all Athenians may be united in their defense against the Barbarian, those who have been sent into exile for ten years are to go to Salamis and stay there until the people come to some decision about them . . .

To get this motion passed was a real triumph for Themistocles: its measures were bound to be unpopular with those who had an old-fashioned attitude towards defending hearth, home and the shrines of one's ancestors. What landed gentleman would support a motion proposed by a man whose backing came from the "sailor rabble" of Piraeus—not least when its direct consequence might be the destruction of all farms and estates in Attica? When he called on Athens to evacuate Attica and trust to the fleet, Themistocles had the whole weight of prejudice and tradition against him.

Yet, somehow, he won. He argued that the "wooden wall" which—according to the Delphic prophecy—would not fail Athens in her hour of need, must refer to the fleet. He spoke of freedom and the glories of sacrifice. He changed his mood, becoming brisk and practical as he outlined the evacuation plan in detail. And he ended with a call to unite against the Barbarian. When he stopped speaking, the Assembly rose and cheered.

The Hellenic League, too, was swayed by Themistocles' arguments. Naval and land forces moved north to hold the Thermopylae-Artemisium line. The army, commanded by Sparta's King Leonidas, included some 4,000 Lacedaemonians, of whom only 300 were full Spartan citizens. Athens provided by far the largest contingent in the fleet: 147 triremes out of an initial 271. The priests at Delphi advised the Greeks to "pray to the winds." Meanwhile the Great King's host trudged southwards.

By the end of July the Greek fleet and army were in position. On August 12 the Persian fleet was anchored in minor harbors and anchorages around Cape Sepias and along the Pallene peninsula. Fire-signals from Skiathos brought the news to Artemisium. To prevent dissension, Themistocles had surrendered his command to the Spartan Eurybiades, but one can see his hand in what followed. The Greek fleet retreated to Chalcis, in the Straits of Euboea: Themistocles hoped to

tempt the Persians into fighting in a confined space. Xerxes had dried out his fleet at Doriscus; the Greeks had not dared risk a similar operation. Thus the Persian vessels were now faster and more maneuverable than those of their opponents. Somehow this disadvantage had to be neutralized.

At dawn on August 13 the *meltemi*, the seasonal northeast winds, began to blow and for the next three days the Persian fleet was storm-bound, with heavy damage. As early as the fourteenth, the Greek naval commanders learned of this disaster—and heard also that the Persian land forces were approaching Thermopylae. The fleet now returned to Artemisium: it was strategically vital that King Leonidas should not have his right flank exposed. It was essential to maintain close liaison between land and sea forces.

For a day or two, nothing happened. The storm blew out by August 16, and the battered Persian fleet limped into Pagasae harbor. But on the following day Xerxes prepared for action. A squadron of two hundred ships was sent round Euboea to take the Greek fleet in the rear; perhaps news of this action drove the Greeks to fight their first naval engagement, on August 18. This clash coincided with the first land assault on Thermopylae, and it was equally inconclusive.

Praying to the winds seemed highly efficacious. Xerxes' outflanking squadron was now caught in a driving rain off the Hollows of Euboea and largely destroyed. Since the danger of an outflanking movement was now largely removed, the Greeks reinforced their Artemisium fleet with fifty-three ships relieved from the duty of guarding Attica. They hoped to snatch a decisive naval victory from the Persians. They were disappointed. On August 20 a bitter battle was fought with Xerxes' remaining squadrons, but its outcome was indecisive. Yet the Greeks still held the straits.

"They learned from their own behavior in the face of danger," Plutarch wrote, "that men who know how to come to close quarters and are

determined to give battle have nothing to fear from mere numbers of ships . . . they have simply to . . . engage the enemy hand-to-hand and fight it out to the bitter end." The engagement at Artemisium paved the way for Salamis. But while this encounter was taking place, another more famous and more desperate battle had been fought in the pass of Thermopylae.

For two days King Leonidas and his inadequate force held the pass against endless assaults by Xerxes' infantry. Then a traitor showed the Persians a concealed path over the mountains, a natural "corridor" by which Leonidas could be taken in the rear. The Phocians guarding it fled, possibly by design; the sources are not clear. At

Two Persians, from a frieze at Persepolis showing subjects paying homage to the Great King.

The Persian court, as seen by the Greek artist of the "Persian Vase," which was found in a burial chamber at Canossa.

this news the bulk of the Peloponnesian units withdrew south. Once Xerxes' cavalry was through the pass, those retreating Greek troops would be cut to ribbons. So Leonidas, without fuss or bother, made his last stand. The Spartans fought to the last man; when their spears were broken, they fought with their swords; and after that, with their hands and teeth. But they went down at last, and the pass to the south lay open.

Thermopylae and Artemisium were far from useless sacrifices. Their effect on Greek morale was incalculable, and they delayed the Persian advance just long enough. More important, and in conjunction with those two lucky storms, they had destroyed so many Persian ships and men that Xerxes hesitated to make the one move almost guaranteed to win him the campaign: a division of his forces. Demaratus, the renegade Spartan king

who was acting as the Great King's adviser, urged Xerxes to detach a task force of three hundred ships to the Peloponnese, while at the same time pressing home his attack on Athens. But Xerxes' brother Achaemenes vetoed such a project—too many ships had been lost already.

Battered and bloody, the Greek fleet withdrew south from Artemisium under the cover of darkness. The Athenians alone had had about half their vessels put out of commission. The allies made directly for Salamis, where the reserve fleet was to join them. The Athenians meanwhile sailed to Phaleron, to complete the evacuation of Attica before Xerxes' advance land forces crossed the frontier. The news that Themistocles and his exhausted crews received at Athens was not encouraging. The Peloponnesians—predictably—were reported to be "fortifying the Isthmus and

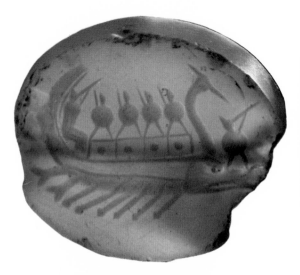

*Right* A Greek warship, from a seal. Such ships as this defeated the Persian navy at Salamis.

Aerial view of Salamis. Part of the island can be seen to the left (beyond the island of Psyttaleia), opposite Piraeus, the port of Athens.

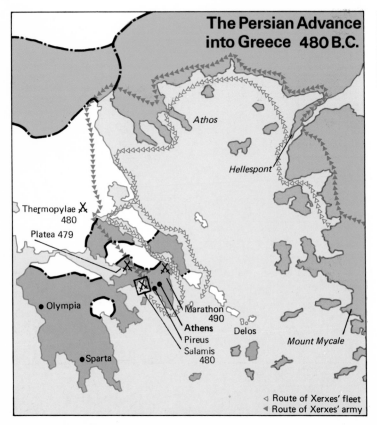

**The Persian Advance into Greece 480 B.C.**

*Athos*

*Hellespont*

Thermopylae ✗✗
480

Platea 479

✗✗

✗✗

⊠✗

● Olympia

● Sparta

Marathon
490

**Athens**

Pireus

Salamis
480

Delos

*Mount Mycale*

◁ Route of Xerxes' fleet
◀ Route of Xerxes' army

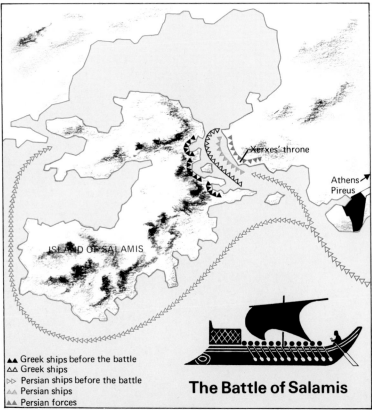

Xerxes' throne

Athens
Pireus

ISLAND OF SALAMIS

▲▲ Greek ships before the battle
△△ Greek ships
▷▷ Persian ships before the battle
▲△ Persian ships
▲▲ Persian forces

**The Battle of Salamis**

Greek hoplites (infantrymen) fighting in formation, protected by their round shields. Such soldiers defeated the army of Xerxes at Plataea, in the year following the battle of Salamis; relief from the Siphnian Treasury, at Delphi.

letting all else go." Some men still hoped to hold the Cithaeron-Parnes line with Spartan support. Again Themistocles acted swiftly and decisively. A token garrison was left on the Acropolis; within forty-eight hours the evacuation of Attica was complete, and the allies were firmly established on Salamis. Even then, Peloponnesian representatives at the council of war that followed were still in favor of pulling out and holding the Isthmus line.

Meanwhile the Persian army, virtually unopposed, was pressing on southwards. Delphi, mysteriously, was spared—perhaps as a reward for so many pro-Persian oracles. Boeotia surrendered, and collaborated. News came that the Persians were already in Attica, burning the countryside as they came. About August 27, Xerxes' advance column clattered through Athens' deserted streets to the foot of the Acropolis; his fleet reached Phaleron two days later, leaving behind a trail of smoke-blackened coastal villages. Soon after the beginning of September, the Persian army arrived in force, and on the fourth or fifth, watchers from Salamis saw a pall of smoke rise over the burning Acropolis.

Defeatism was in the air: several commanders were so alarmed that they walked out of a council meeting and "hoisted sail for immediate flight." Again there was talk of a retreat to the Isthmus. Themistocles told Eurybiades, in private, that once this happened, the whole allied fleet would break up. The Greeks, notorious individualists, possessed singularly little team spirit. In public, however, Themistocles argued that sea and land strategy were indissoluble. To fight in the Salamis channel would give the Greeks every advantage. In a confined space, tactics were more important than numbers or speed. Finally, Themistocles resorted to threats: if they refused to fight at Salamis, he said, he would pull out the entire Athenian contingent. At this, Eurybiades gave in, and the other commanders followed suit.

Xerxes had problems of his own. He could not attack the Peloponnese by sea until he had dealt with the fleet at Salamis. Whatever he did, he must act fast: it was already mid-September. Themistocles, who was a first-class judge of human nature, guessed that the Great King would grasp at anything that seemed to offer a quick solution. The Athenian therefore summoned his children's tutor, an Asiatic Greek named Sicinnus, and secretly sent him to Xerxes with a letter. In this letter Themistocles made three claims: that the allies were quarreling among themselves, that many would desert or change sides in a showdown battle, and that some already planned to slip away to the Isthmus during the night. If Xerxes blocked both exits from the straits, Themistocles advised, and struck at once, the Great King would capture or destroy the entire Greek fleet.

What Themistocles wrote was not only plausible, but in many respects was all too true. It was also just what Xerxes wanted to hear and he was therefore completely taken in by the deception. The duped Great King acted at once. The Egyptian squadron was sent to block the channel between Salamis and Megara. A large body of Persian infantry landed on the island of Psyttaleia at the entrance to the narrows. Other Persian and Phoenician squadrons moved up along the Attic coastline. Thus Xerxes' crews were up and active most of the night—and exhausted by morning. Xerxes had taken the bait, the blockade was complete. It only remained to be seen whether he would press home his attack into the sound. On that everything hung. As was said afterwards, all Greece that day stood on the razor's edge.

At first light of day on September 29, the Greek crews assembled by their ships, ready for action. Themistocles was chosen to address them and his speech, on the theme "All is at stake" became legendary. It fired his men's hearts, and, fiercely elated, the crews rowed out into the channel. But something more than mere patriotic fervor was needed to win the day and accounts of the battle suggest that meticulous planning had been under-

Two Greek soldiers, from a marble tombstone found at Salamis.

81

The theater of Dionysus, at Athens, where Aeschylus' play *The Persians* was produced in 472 B.C. Aeschylus wrote the play for performance here, after having taken part in the Salamis campaign.

Horsemen in procession, taking part in a festival in honor of Athena; a frieze from the Parthenon.

taken well before the battle actually took place.

The allied contingents were distributed among three harbors—Salamis itself, and the two shelving inlets north of the town, where the main force was concentrated. In Salamis harbor, detached from the fleet's battle formation were stationed the crack squadrons of Aegina and Megara. The northernmost position of the main force was held by the Corinthians, who had orders to guard the Bay of Eleusis against a surprise attack by the Egyptians in the Megara channel. The central allied line—Spartans on the right wing, Athenians on the left—moved out from shore to form beyond St. George's Island. At first the ships peeled off northwards—a critical moment, for this move was a carefully calculated feint to lure on the enemy.

Seeing the main part of the fleet heading north, the Persians must have believed that it was what they had been told to expect—a demoralized Greek retreat. A decision was taken at once. The Persian rowers bent to their oars, and the line moved forward through the narrows into the sound. From his golden throne, set on an eminence above the Attic shore, Xerxes watched their advance—at first with pride, then with mounting anxiety, and finally in anguish and despair. As more and more of his warships crowded into the narrows, they began to foul each other. Some had to be pulled out of line, causing considerable disorder. Xerxes was not the only commander to discover that it is much easier to start an advance than it is to stop it.

The leading Persian squadrons naturally slackened their speed when the Greeks—in battle formation now, and far from demoralized—came sweeping towards them in a wide crescent. To create yet greater chaos, the Persian admiral was killed almost at once, and his subordinate officers began shouting contradictory orders from every side. With such a press behind them, they could hardly have backed water now even if they had so wished. In a few minutes the whole channel was a logjam. The only alternative left to the Persians was to attack. But the Greeks, with more room to maneuver, encircled them in a tightening noose, pressing them still closer, brazen rams smashing through their timbers or shearing off their oar-banks. As the jammed Persian vessels struggled to withdraw, the Aeginetan squadron moved out from its reserve position and took them in the flank.

As the battle turned into a rout, Xerxes sprang up from his throne in agonized and impotent fury. Aeschylus, who fought at Salamis, afterwards

memorialized the scene in his play *The Persians*:

Crushed hulls lay upturned on the sea, so thick
You could not see the water, choked with wrecks
And slaughtered men: while all the shores and reefs
Were strewn with corpses. Soon in wild disorder
All that was left of our fleet turned tail and fled.
But the Greeks pursued us, and with oars or broken
Fragments of wreckage split the survivors' heads
As if they were tunneys or a haul of fish:
And shrieks and wailing rang across the water
Till nightfall hid us from them.

Against all odds—and at the eleventh hour—Greece had been saved; and not even his many bitter enemies could deny that Themistocles had saved her. Persian strategy had depended on close cooperation between fleet and army; the fleet was now virtually out of action, and the vast land force had no option but to retreat. Xerxes' son-in-law Mardonius remained in Greece, with perhaps 60,000 men; but a year later, in 479, an allied army led by the Spartan Regent Pausanias destroyed him also. Hostilities with Persia continued, sporadically, for years, but the specter of invasion and occupation vanished after Salamis, never to return.

Writing of Leonidas at Thermopylae—but it might equally well have been of Themistocles at Salamis—William Golding says, in a memorable and moving essay: "If you were a Persian . . . neither you nor Leonidas nor anyone else could foresee that here thirty years' time was won for shining Athens and all Greece and all humanity . . . A little of Leonidas lies in the fact that I can go where I like and write what I like. He contributed

to set us free." Salamis was the triumph of free men over autocrats, of men who won, against odds, precisely because they were fighting for an ideal. Only free men, proud of their freedom, could have produced the imperishable achievements in architecture, sculpture, and drama that have made Athens immortal: the vision of a Phidias, the thundering choruses of Aeschylus, the proud, gay, confident humor of Aristophanes. Under Persian overlordship, Athens might have achieved much; but not this, and not in the same spirit.

This story does not have a happy ending; not, at least, in the short run. Less than ten years after his great victory, Themistocles was hounded into exile. He eventually died by his own hand, a reluctant hanger-on at the court of the country he had defeated, Persia. Pausanias was executed by his own countrymen, probably on a trumped-up charge. Under her new leaders, Athens, having fought in the name of freedom, proceeded to build an imperial system of her own, of "subject-allies" who were not barbarians, but Greeks.

The fifth century, which had dawned so brightly, ended in defeat and despair, with the long, drawn-out struggle between Athens and Sparta. Yet there is a moral here. Freedom means, in the last resort, the freedom to go to hell in your own way; better Athenian irresponsibility on an Assembly vote than benevolent autocratic paternalism. That is the lesson which Salamis bequeathed to Greece, to Europe, and, ultimately to the whole Western world. We forget it at our peril.

PETER GREEN

Pericles, the Athenian statesman who was chiefly responsible for the disastrous war with Sparta. The drain on the resources of Athens caused by this lengthy and bitter struggle led to her defeat and to the temporary collapse of the democracy that had defeated the Persians.

83

The "classical" period of Greece, during which the finest products of Greek civilization were achieved, has been defined as beginning after the victory over the Persians. Its end is marked by the appearance of Macedonian soldiers in Greece, and the capitulation of the Greek cities to their semi-Greek conquerors from the north. This was the first stage in the vast program of military expansion under the Macedonian king, Alexander, which ended with his death, the subject of the next chapter. Macedonian expansion changed the whole face of the East: in the West events were less momentous, though in the same year as the battle of Salamis the Greeks of Syracuse held back a major attack on Sicily by the Carthaginians.

Achilles and Patroclus

The sea victory at Salamis had been engineered by the brilliant Athenian commander, Themistocles. The land victory at Plataea, which so decisively put an end to the Persian campaign in Greece, was the work of the Peloponnesians, especially of the Spartan commander, Pausanias, and his men. Pausanias was then given the task of liberating the Ionian coastal cities from Persia, but they seem to have feared his potential as a new tyrant, as did the Spartan *ephors* or elders, and he was relieved of his mission. Athens then took up the coastal war for which she was obviously so much better suited than Sparta, organizing the islands and cities into a confederacy under Athenian leadership, the Delian League. This league was put on a formal basis, with the allies contributing ships and money for defense. But, dominated as it was by Athens, it was only a question of time before it became a *de facto* Athenian empire. The Ionian kinship shared by its members might have been expected to form some basis for a closer tie, but the tradition and outlook of the

*polis* or city-state was not compatible with the idea of "nation" as we understand it today. The formation of a league was the nearest the Greeks came to national unity until the conquests of Alexander imposed a temporary unity on the Greek world. This meant that mainland Greece achieved an identity, if only through its geographical insignificance within a wider community, that of the *oikoumene* (the whole inhabited world).

But meanwhile, the formation of the Delian League consolidated the division of Greece into two main power blocs: the Peloponnesian League with Sparta at its head, and Athens and her "empire." These groups developed mutually hostile ideologies, based on the very different political system of Sparta and Athens.

## Athens

Athens at this period had achieved the ultimate in Greek democracy. It was not total democracy, as we would understand it, for a large percentage of her population were

Relief of Demeter and Persephone

slaves, with very limited political rights. But Athens had developed a greater measure of popular representation than perhaps any other city or state has ever done.

## Sparta

In contrast, Sparta was still theoretically ruled by her two kings and council of elders or ephors, below which were the citizen-élite, the *perioeci* and *helots*. Thus, oligarchy (rule of the few) was the basis of Spartan government, and democracy (the power of the *demos* or people) in Athens.

Athena

While the Delian League was successful in holding the allies together under Athens' leadership, and while Persia remained an obvious threat and a symbolic enemy to hold the Greeks together, no confrontation with the Peloponnesian bloc occurred. Persia was decisively beaten off Salamis (Cyprus) in 451, and obliged to conclude a peace with the Greeks. The Delian League clearly had less raison d'être now that the Persian menace had been contained, but Athens did not want to relinquish her position of dominance. The chains of empire were tightened by the establishment of colonies of Athenian citizens (*cleruchies*) at vital points in allied territory, guarding all-important supply routes to Athens. The champion of democracy might after all be a tyrant in disguise.

Leonidas, King of Sparta

## Pericles

This extension of temporary military leadership into control of an empire took place under the rule of the great Pericles (470–429). The stability that lasted while Athens and her navy remained unchallenged in the Aegean enabled the arts of civilization to flourish in an unprecedented way. Athens itself was the glittering hub of intellectual and artistic activity. In the fifth century it became the center for philosophy, drawing together philosophers from all over the Greek world who previously had had no one meeting place. While the Greeks took much of their knowledge from the East—mathematics and astronomy in particular—they developed their own methods of scientific inquiry and philosophy. The power of pure reason led to the questioning of treasured concepts about life and society; and the Sophists, who advocated such a critical use of knowledge and education, provoked a strong reaction from the more conservative elements in Athens.

## Socrates

The great teacher and philosopher became notorious for his ability to criticize anything and everything, though he was in fact challenging the extreme and wayward scepticism of the Sophists. He nevertheless became a scapegoat for the excesses of the Sophists' philosophical contortions, and preferred to die rather than recant. Such was the seriousness with which philosophy was treated by both its practitioners and the people of Athens.

## Religion and temples

Philosophy did not entirely dispense with the gods, who were still an integral part of Greek culture everywhere. Since religion centered on the performance of the cult of a particular god or goddess, ceremonies mattered much more than doctrine, so philosophy was not a radical alternative. Religion was essentially bound up with the life of the *polis*, and large sums were spent on erecting temples to tutelary deities. These magnificent temples offered perfect opportunities for the expression of the

Socrates, Plato and Herodotus

Greek artistic genius, and the architecture and sculpture of this period has haunted European civilization from that time to the present day.

## Greek drama

The Greeks of this period also produced remarkable new developments in literary form. The creation of the theatre, or more specifically, the creation of a permanent repertory of written plays, dates from the birth of Attic tragedy in the incomparable works of Aeschylus (525–456), written at the time of the struggle with Persia. Sophocles (497–406) and Euripides (480–406) continued the tradition of Attic drama,

Comic actors

and Aristophanes' (444–380) delightful plays, full of wit and sharp digs at the politicians, developed the new art of comedy.

## Plato

Socrates' unwritten teachings were put into elegant and powerful words by the philosopher and writer Plato. His works, models of lucidity and style, include two stimulating and fundamental treatments of political theory, *The Republic* and *The Laws*.

The Athenian search for truth was passionate and pragmatic. Plato's works examined the real world of the Greek *polis*, and formulated more or less ideal solutions to the problems of city life, but he even tried out his theories in a practical experiment. The tyrant Dionysus II of Syracuse was at his own request carefully educated by Plato to be the "ideal ruler," the embodiment of Plato's wise philosopher-king. The experiment failed, as Dionysus proved too easily distracted by human pleasures, but it shows the extraordinary status of philosophy in Greek society.

## Herodotus and Thucydides

The politics of the Periclean age profoundly influenced historical as well as other literary forms. Herodotus of Halicarnassus, proverbially "the father of history," produced a study of the Persian Wars that initiated true historical analysis where before only the uncritical tabulation of chronicles had existed. Athens' tight hold on the Aegean and the exacerbation of her relations with Sparta came to a head in 431, and war broke out. The ensuing conflict brought down the Athenian empire. Such a momentous event caused the historian Thucydides to ponder on the reasons for such a calamity. His work on the Peloponnesian War and the destruction of Athens' greatness, analyzing one of the most exciting and disturbing periods of history, is one of the most penetrating and skillful pieces of historical writing ever produced.

## Victorious Sparta

The Peloponnesian War left Sparta victorious, and the Athenian navy and defenses were destroyed. Sparta was to enjoy only a brief period of hegemony in Greece. The war was concluded in 404: by 401 Sparta was embroiled with the Persians and, in Greece, was faced with an attack from her allies who were dissatisfied with her treatment of them. War followed.

## Thebes

The city of Thebes, which had developed a highly efficient army under the brilliant general Epaminondas, emerged as victor from the struggle, destroying the Spartan army at Leuctra in 371. Victory brought with it leadership of the other Greek cities, but Thebes' domination was resented just as Sparta's (and Athens') had been. The pattern of intermittent wars, the shattering of one city's armed power to permit the emergence of another to dominate a federation of cities, was ominous in its repeti-

Head of charioteer

tion. Clearly the economic and political decline of Greece was a reality. The situation of the Greek cities could conceivably be exploited by a number of external powers—the Carthaginians' sphere of influence dangerously overlapped the Greek settlements in the western Mediterranean, and Persian ambitions might flourish again in the East. As it happened, the resolution of Greece's discord and decline came firmly from a direction that few people could have expected at the time.

## Philip of Macedonia

To the north of Greece proper lay the kingdom of Macedonia, peopled by "barbarians" in Greek terms, though the ruling family was recognized as Greek. Feudal wars and local quarrels with the Illyrians were the Macedonians' traditional occupations, but a strong state emerged under King Philip II. He had spent some time as a hostage in Thebes and had absorbed knowledge of the Greek way of life, and, more important, knowledge of military procedure from the famous Theban troops. Under his rule the military potential of Macedonia was developed and organized.

The new power of Macedonia grew visibly as Philip intervened in Thessaly and had himself elected as military commander. The presence of a strong state to the north produced various reactions among the Greeks. One line of thought, voiced by the orator Demosthenes, warned against Philip as a threat to the "liberty of Greece." The orator Isocrates championed the idea of Philip as the strong leader who was needed to unite the Greeks and lead them out of the morass of their political and military conflicts. The choice of the Greeks hardly mattered anyway. Philip was obviously aiming at the leadership of Greece, and there was no effective way to limit his designs. Military conflict with the Macedonians followed, and the last remaining Greek army of consequence, that of Thebes, was defeated together with Athenian soldiers at Chaeronea in 338. Philip became *hegemon*, or ruler, of

Philip II of Macedonia

yet another Greek league, comprising all the major Greek cities except Sparta, whose absence hardly mattered since she was no longer powerful.

## Alexander

At the battle of Chaeronea, Philip's son Alexander played a decisive role in the victory, and proved himself a great military commander. His father dreamed of taking final revenge against the Persians on their own ground. Alexander inherited this ambition, and how he achieved this and much more is the subject of our next chapter.

# The Death of Alexander the Great

*In 336 Philip of Macedonia, in northern Greece, was assassinated. His successor, both as king and as leader of the League of Corinth, was his twenty-year-old son Alexander. In addition to the throne the young Alexander inherited his father's mission—to take revenge on the Persians on their own ground. The fulfilling of that mission and its consequences constitute one of the most glittering pages in the history of the ancient world. Alexander may not have wanted to fuse the traditions of East and West in the empire he created, but he gave Hellenism to posterity, thus bequeathing a truly international culture for the civilized world.*

Twelve years had passed since Alexander, the young king of Macedonia and captain-general of the League of Corinth, had stood at the helm of his ship, guiding it over the Hellespont to the shores of Asia—twelve years and twenty thousand miles of Asian roads. Now, in 323 B.C., in a world that he himself had shaken and transformed, he lay dying in his Babylonian palace, and at the doors the soldiers clamored to see their leader. The rumor had spread that Alexander was dead already, and that his death had been concealed by the guards. At last the doors were thrown open to the rough horsemen and pikemen of Macedonia; with bewilderment on their faces, they crowded silently past the king's bed. Alexander was in his last fever, beyond speech and almost beyond life, but he made the effort to raise his yellowed face and nod some kind of greeting.

That night his generals—Seleucus and Peucestas, Peithon and Cleomenes—went to the temple of Serapis and asked if they should bring their leader to the god, but the oracle answered that it would be better for him to remain in his palace. There, soon afterwards, Alexander died. His illness had been malaria, the last of many bouts he had suffered on his campaigns; but it was malaria assisted by hard drinking and by the fury of a man fighting against unaccustomed ill-fortune.

Alexander died only seven years after the king he had displaced on the throne of Persia—Darius III, last of the Achaemenid line founded by the great Cyrus in the sixth century B.C. For almost two hundred years, since the fall of the Ionian cities to Cyrus in 545, Persia and Greece had been intimately linked. Darius I had been defeated at Marathon in 490, Xerxes at Salamis in 480 and Plataea in 479. But Persians still ruled over Greeks in Ionia, and by playing upon the rivalry between Sparta and Athens, they contrived to interfere in the affairs of the Greek states in Europe. Greeks sold their services to Persia, as mercenaries and craftsmen; they helped to build the great palaces at Susa and Persepolis; and as the Persians themselves grew soft from easy living, the paid Hellenes gradually became the most reliable corps in the vast and unwieldy army of the Persian King of Kings.

Accepting Persian pay, the Greeks observed Persian weaknesses. The epic story of the Ten Thousand—the Greek mercenaries who alone in the army of Cyrus the Younger stood firm at the battle of Cunaxa in 401, then fought their way to the Black Sea—became not only a literary classic in the hands of Xenophon, but also an inspiration to more ambitious men. King Agesilaus of Sparta was certainly not without hopes of considerably reducing the Persian domain in Asia Minor, and periodically the Athenians thought of revenge when they remembered how Xerxes had desecrated and destroyed their temples.

The great Attic orator Isocrates preached not only the union of the Hellenic world, but also a crusade against Persia, the natural enemy of the Hellenes. When he saw no one among the Greeks likely to fulfill his wishes, he looked to Philip II of Macedonia, a Hellenized barbarian who claimed descent from Achilles, Hercules and, for good measure, Perseus. Philip aspired to become the protector of neighboring Greece, and in 338 the League of Corinth entered into an arrangement for mutual defense with him and appointed him captain-general of the joint Greek and Macedonian armies. Philip persuaded the League to approve a war against Persia; before he could lead it, however, he was killed by an assassin. In 336 his son Alexander, twenty years old, succeeded to the throne of Macedonia and the captaincy of the League.

Never has any man been more fitted for his hour—an hour that offered a whole world to conquer and remake. Alexander's phenomenal beauty may be a legend fostered by flattering

Bust of Alexander as a young man; probably an idealized representation.

*Opposite* Alexander, on horseback, at the battle of Issus. This mosaic, found at Pompeii, is thought to be a copy of an original painting of *c.* 330 B.C.

Greek soldiers fighting Asiatics; a relief panel from the "Alexander Sarcophagus," which was found in the royal cemetery at Sidon, Phoenicia, and dates from the late fourth century B.C.

artists and chroniclers; but of his genius there can be no doubt. His strategic vision, his tactical originality and his grasp of military engineering are too well known to need discussion here. From the beginning the savage courage of Alexander the warrior was balanced by other, more humane forms of audacity. The influence of Aristotle, his childhood tutor, had not been in vain. Alexander's ruthlessness was Macedonian, but his intellectual curiosity and tolerance were Hellenic. More than any other great man of action, with the exception of Pericles, he represented the questing Greek mind. He became a great explorer and the inspirer of generations of geographers. In planning his expeditions he included philosophers, naturalists and topographers as well as military engineers. "If I were not Alexander, I would like to be Diogenes," he is supposed to have said. It is this combination of conqueror and philosopher that makes Alexander so fascinating and so historically significant.

The story of his conquests is familiar. He set out in 334 from his Macedonian capital of Pella, which he was never to see again. Crossing to Asia Minor, he defeated the Persians at the Battle of Granicus and liberated the Ionian cities. Late the next year, campaigning down the coast of Phoenicia, he defeated the main Persian army at Issus, and put Darius to ignominious flight. Taking his time to besiege and destroy Tyre and Gaza, he proceeded to Egypt, acquired a legendary parent in the god Amon, and showed a new, constructive side to his leadership by founding the first and greatest of all the Alexandrias, the queen city of the Hellenistic world.

Having consumed in such methodical fashion the western perimeter of the Persian empire, Alexander next aimed a blow at the heart. In the autumn of 331 he marched into Mesopotamia and met Darius on the field of Gaugamela. The elephants and the scythe-armed chariots of the Persian king, the multitudes of warriors he had drawn from every distant corner of the Achaemenid dominions, were of no avail against Alexander's cavalry and the Macedonian phalanx.

Totally defeated, Darius fled into the depths of Bactria; Alexander proceeded as conqueror to Babylon and Susa, then eventually to Persia proper, the center and birthplace of Darius' power. At last Alexander sat on the throne in the palace of Persepolis, built by Ionian craftsmen. The champion of Greece was transformed into the Great King of Asia, yet without entirely ceasing to be the champion of Greece. From then on the effort to reconcile his Hellenism with his Oriental power became the overriding element in Alexander's life.

The campaigns continued. Darius, pursued into Central Asia in a series of extraordinary marches, was killed by his own general, Bessus. Bessus and other Persian captains were slaughtered or incorporated into the Alexandrian pattern of government. Then, in 327, Alexander launched an expedition to India.

It was at this point that Alexander's incredible run of luck was reversed. Ironically, the first defeat of his life came at the hands of his own men. In 326, on the bank of the Jhelum River in India, his troops refused to pass beyond the Punjab into the lands of the great kings who ruled in middle India. "A commander like you, with an army like ours," his general Coenus said to him then, "has nothing to fear from any human enemy; but remember, fortune cannot be foretold, and no man may protect himself from what it will bring." Fortune had taken Alexander to the throne of the Achaemenid King of Kings in Persepolis, to the heartlands of Central Asia where Samarkand and Bukhara would later rise, and over the Hindu Kush in search of the great River of Ocean which he imagined washed the foothills of the Himalayas. But after the events on the Jhelum, he turned reluctantly back from the Punjab to fight his way down the Indus Valley, nearly dying from an arrow that pierced his lung when he assaulted the fortress of a fierce tribe in Sind.

There followed a terrible march over the deserts of Gedrosia, with men and beasts dying of thirst and Alexander sharing the privations his infantry endured. On his return to Babylon he found that many of the men he had left in charge had taken advantage of his absence in India to plunder the people and desecrate monuments. It was bad enough that Persians, who were indebted to him for his clemency, should do this; it was more bitter news to hear that Harpalus, his companion since childhood, had plundered the Persian treasure and then had fled to evade Alexander's wrath, dying at the hands of a fellow robber on the way back to Greece. Then, at Opis, there had been a mutiny by the Macedonian veterans, whom Alexander proposed to send home and replace by Persian levies; thirteen of his men were executed for that revolt. Finally his beloved friend Hephaestion had died in Ecbatana—perhaps also of malaria—and Alexander had abandoned himself to a prolonged and immoderate grief.

From all these misfortunes, Alexander emerged in the spring of 323 to plan an expedition that would revive his military glory and satisfy his perennial longing to know the unknown. To explore and subdue Arabia, a region little known even to the Persians, would make up for his failure to conquer India. A great harbor to hold a thousand ships had been dredged beside the Euphrates, and fleets had been assembled and manned by Phoenician and Ionian sailors. Troops had been recruited in Persia and Lydia and Caria; it would no longer be a Macedonian army that Alexander led, but an army of all the peoples under his rule. June 7, 323, was fixed for the start of the expedition. Five days before the scheduled departure, Alexander performed sacrifices to assure his success, gave wine to his men and drank heavily with his friends. Medius, his favorite since the death of

*Above* The pass of Issus, site of the battle in which Alexander defeated the main Persian army and put King Darius to flight.

*Below* Asiatics in Persian dress fighting a lioness; a relief panel from the "Alexander Sarcophagus."

*Above* Temple relief from Persepolis, showing a lion attacking a bull. The vigorous carving is typical of the art of the Persian empire at the time of Darius.

*Below* The ruins of the palace of Persepolis, the heart of Darius' great empire. It was built largely by Ionian Greeks, and was destroyed by Alexander.

Hephaestion, induced him to continue drinking late into the night, and, before he went to sleep, the fever had already seized him. During the next few days Alexander insisted on continuing his sacrifices and giving orders to his army officers and to Nearchus, his admiral. But his condition became grave, and he was carried to a summer house beside the river, and finally to his palace. By this time he had lost the power of speech. Eleven days after the outset of his fever he died, at the age of thirty-three. The expedition to Arabia was never undertaken.

During his lifetime Alexander and his empire remained a disturbing enigma to his Greek and Macedonian followers. Remembering the leader who stood at Issus and exhorted his men with the cry, "We are free men, they are slaves," the Greeks were puzzled when Alexander tried to introduce into his court the Persian custom of prostration before the throne. When the sophist Callisthenes openly voiced his disapproval, he died—no one knows how—as a martyr to his own philosophic candor. Alexander's companions murmured angrily when the conquered Persians were welcomed as equals at the court. Finally, one night, after drinking heavily, the king quarreled with Cleitus, who had saved his life at the battle of Granicus, and killed him. The division between the ambitions of Alexander and the reservations of his followers put an end to the Indian expedition and sparked off the mutiny of Opis. After Alexander's death, there would be many Hellenes to claim that he turned away from Greece and became an Oriental ruler.

In a way, this was true. One can even mark a turning point at Ecbatana, in the spring of 330, when Alexander dismissed as allies the Greek soldiers of the League and rehired as mercenaries

The excavated remains of the Persian palace at Susa, in eastern Mesopotamia.

those who chose to stay. His role as captain-general of Greece was discarded; now he claimed the Persian empire as his by right of conquest. Already, that winter, he had begun to fill his army with Persian recruits, trained in the Macedonian manner. In 325 he arranged an interracial mass marriage festival at Susa. Alexander had already in 327 married a Persian princess, Roxana, daughter of the Bactrian chieftain Oxyartes. Now he chose as a second wife the daughter of Darius, persuading eighty of his closest companions to pick Asiatic wives and ordering ten thousand soldiers to do likewise. Later, after the mutiny of Opis, there was a festival of reconciliation attended by nine thousand people; led by Greek priests and Persian Magi, the assembled guests prayed that the Macedonians and Persians might rule the empire together in true harmony.

For the claims that have been made that Alexander was the first ruler with a truly international vision, there is little further evidence. Diodorus Siculus, writing as a contemporary of Julius Caesar, certainly saw Alexander as believing in a real union of the people of Asia and Europe, but his view of history was necessarily influenced by the Stoic and Epicurean egalitarian ideas. It is difficult to argue against historians who claim that Alexander conceived not a true internationalism, but merely a renovated Persian empire, streamlined by Greek logic and efficiency and ruled by a dual master race.

What did Alexander plan for the physical extension of his empire? He had already won the greater part of the antique world. After Arabia he hoped to conquer the lands around the Caspian Sea. He had left garrisons in the Punjab and at the mouth of the Indus, and there is little doubt that one day he meant to complete the conquest of India. We can only speculate about his plans for the Mediterranean, but the fact that the Carthaginians, the Etruscans and even the far Iberians sent ambassadors to congratulate him on his conquests suggests an unseemly rush to make terms before his deep-eyed look turned westward. Writing his history of Alexander's expeditions, in the second century A.D., Arrian speaks of his

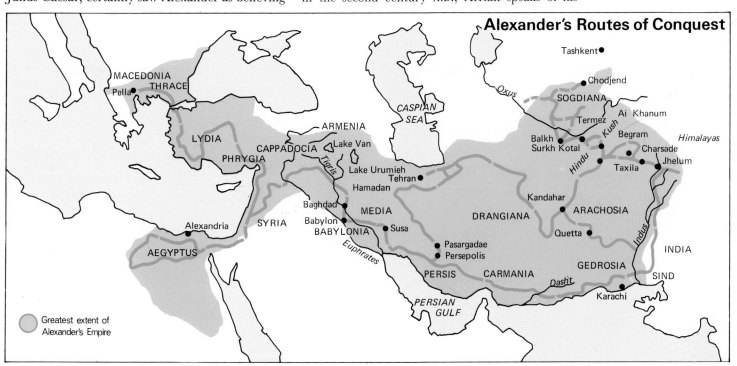

**Alexander's Routes of Conquest**

Greatest extent of Alexander's Empire

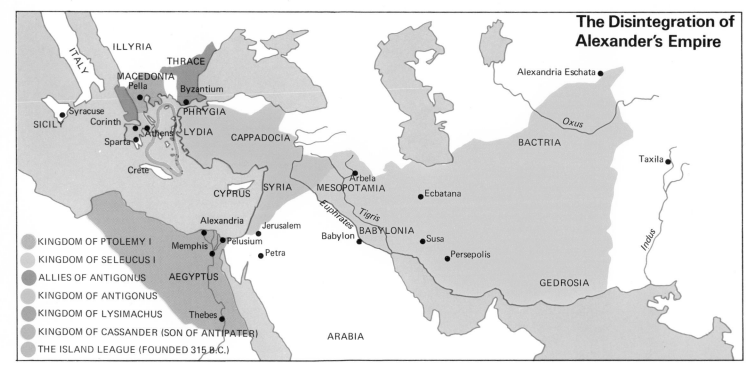

ILLYRIA
ITALY
THRACE
MACEDONIA
Pella
Byzantium
PHRYGIA
SICILY
Syracuse
Corinth
LYDIA
Athens
Sparta
CAPPADOCIA
Crete
CYPRUS
SYRIA
Arbela
MESOPOTAMIA
Ecbatana
Alexandria
Jerusalem
Euphrates
Tigris
BABYLONIA
Memphis
Pelusium
Babylon
Susa
Petra
Persepolis
AEGYPTUS
GEDROSIA
Thebes
ARABIA
Alexandria Eschata
Oxus
BACTRIA
Taxila
Indus

KINGDOM OF PTOLEMY I
KINGDOM OF SELEUCUS I
ALLIES OF ANTIGONUS
KINGDOM OF ANTIGONUS
KINGDOM OF LYSIMACHUS
KINGDOM OF CASSANDER (SON OF ANTIPATER)
THE ISLAND LEAGUE (FOUNDED 315 B.C.)

"insatiable desire to extend his possessions," and it is unlikely that, if he had lived, he would have left unattempted the conquest of Italy, France and Spain, where the Greeks had already long-established colonies. His eventual aim was almost certainly to unite under his own rule the whole of the known world.

Alexander profoundly affected the world through which he passed. At his death his empire was frozen within the boundaries he had created, and the only later extension of Hellenistic rule was in the eastern marches where he had merely con-

Gold armlet from the Oxus Treasure.

quered and passed on. Two centuries after his death the Greek kings of Bactria sent their cavalry probing toward the boundaries of the Chinese empire, and in the middle of the second century B.C. Menander, the Greek king of the Punjab and a philosophic warrior of the same temper as Alexander himself, fulfilled his predecessor's ambition by leading an army of Greeks and Persians down the valley of the Ganges to capture Pataliputra, the capital of Hindustan.

After Alexander's death, his empire fell immediately into disunity. His heir was Roxana's yet unborn child, the unfortunate Alexander IV, who was eventually murdered in 311 by Cassander, the son of Alexander's general Antipater. Antipater was nominal regent; in fact Alexander's generals, known as the Successors—Seleucus, Ptolemy, Antigonus, Lysimachus, Eumenes—divided the empire. Ptolemy departed first to his satrapy of Egypt, taking with him the body of Alexander to bury it in Alexandria. In 306, when all the heirs had been eliminated, the Successors, or *Diadochi*, named themselves kings. Only one of them, Ptolemy, died peacefully in his bed; the rest were killed in the bitter struggles dividing them. For a while it seemed as though Antigonus might reunite the empire, but Ptolemy and Seleucus were too strong for him, and the Hellenistic world remained divided between three great kingdoms—Macedonia, under the descendants of Antigonus, Egypt under the Ptolemies, and Syria, embracing also Persia and Mesopotamia, under the Seleucids. Smaller realms like Pergamum arose under the shadow of these great kingdoms, and new city-states like Rhodes and Byzantium became commercial powers in their own rights.

Despite all this fragmentation, the Hellenistic age was a time of vigorous civilization. It has been

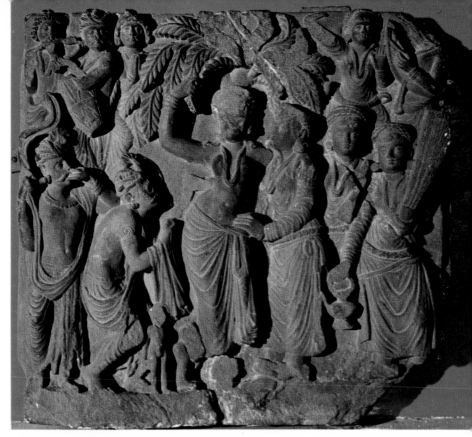

given too little credit for its achievements because historians have concentrated on its divisions and on the dramatic decline of its kingdoms in the face of the threat of Rome. The Successors, in spite of their conflicts, ruled over a surprisingly homogeneous world. Asian kingdoms in Pontus and Bithynia and Cappadocia adopted the Hellenistic culture and political systems, and even the Parthian and Scythian rulers, finding their way into Greek Bactria, became Hellenized.

It was not entirely the kind of empire Alexander may have envisaged. The Successors had no use for his visions of copartnership between Greeks and Asians. Only Seleucus retained the Persian wife he had been given at the great marriage feast of Susa, and the ruling castes of all the Hellenistic kingdoms consisted either of Greeks—with a dwindling proportion of Macedonians—or of Hellenized members of the native aristocracy. This elite inhabited its own enclaves, typically Greek cities with democratic constitutions, and its settlements included people of all classes who migrated from the overpopulated Greece of the third and second centuries. The native people remained in the villages and retained their own cultures, so a marked horizontal rift, which Alexander had probably not foreseen, developed between Greeks and Asians. Yet, unlike the Romans, the Greeks of the diaspora never conceived a universal citizenship. They were citizens of their individual communities, subjects of the Greek kings, but the bonds that united a man in Alexandria of Egypt with a man in Alexandria Bucephala of the Punjab were cultural and not political.

The most durable of the Hellenistic states were those that eventually made some compromise with the native cultures. By the beginning of the second century the main states were decaying fast; by the middle of the century Macedonia and the Seleucid kingdom had been overwhelmed by the Romans, and the Greek kingdom of Bactria by the Sakas. But the Ptolemaic kings, who had accepted a place in the Egyptian religious hierarchy and had turned Alexandria into a great intellectual meeting place of East and West, survived; so did the Greek kings in India with their Buddhist affiliations. In fact, Cleopatra, last of the Ptolemies, and Hermaeus, last of the Indo-Greek monarchs, died at about the same time; the battle of Actium in 31 B.C. finally ended the political legacy of Alexander's conquests.

Yet even at Actium only one aspect of Alexander's heritage was destroyed. As Rostovtseff has pointed out, "the 'romanization' of the Hellenistic world was slight, the 'Hellenization' of the steadily expanding Latin world much more conspicuous." Later, from the eastern Rome of Constantinople, the Hellenistic world helped to give Eastern Christianity its special forms. To India, Alexander and his successors gave much of its art—the techniques of building and carving in stone and the Gandhara style—and the concept of a united rule that Chandragupta adopted when he founded the Mauryan empire. Even the Arabs, who finally

Greek influence on the art of western Asia was considerable. *Above* Sculptured scene in the Gandhara style of northwest India, an area once ruled by Hellenistic kings. *Left* Funerary busts from Palmyra, probably early-third century A.D. They illustrate the surviving influence of Hellenistic art.

destroyed the Greek cities of the East, retained Hellenistic science. Through Rome, Constantinople and the Arab world, Alexander contributed something to the new West of the Renaissance, even to lands he never conquered. If he failed to unify the world politically, he helped to turn it into an intellectual community, particularly when one remembers how much the great religions of Christianity, Mahayanist Buddhism and Islam owed to the exchange of ideas between Europe and Asia that he so materially assisted.

GEORGE WOODCOCK

93

The empire of Cyrus and Xerxes was vast. The empire left by Alexander on his death was even larger, and it did not outlast its founder. The most obvious reasons for its immediate breakup were the lack of overall homogeneity, the variety of individual characteristics and political traditions in the area it covered, and the virtual impossibility of establishing a strong central authority to hold it together. The theme of empire is a recurrent one throughout this volume: Xerxes, Alexander, Hannibal, Shih-huang-ti and lastly Augustus—all these men commanded empires. If we seek a key to the relative endurance of such empires, we should look for a durable and comprehensive administration. The great emperor Shih-huang-ti thoroughly organized the administration of his empire, and even though his dynasty was overthrown, the essential framework of the Chinese state remained. And we shall see that after the milestone of the battle of Actium, Augustus was to devote the greater part of his energy and ability to developing and improving an administration that would provide a lasting basis for the Roman Empire. Alexander's successors were more concerned with dividing the Near East among themselves than with pushing the territorial limits of their empire, as he had done, farther toward the mysterious East, as yet largely unknown to them. Contacts did

Skull of Peking Man

undoubtedly exist between the ancient Near East and China. Some scholars have sought to trace Mesopotamian influences in early Chinese culture, but they were extremely tenuous. However, a great civilization had been developing there from the second millennium B.C., and our next chapter will deal with a significant epoch in it. In preparation for it, we must now consider some of the fundamental aspects of Chinese civilization.

The Chinese thunder god

## Prehistoric China

China has provided evidence of one of the earliest precursors of the human race (*homo sapiens*). In 1929 at the village of Chou K'ou Tien, about 26 miles southwest of Peking, skeletal remains were found of the so-called "Peking Man" (*Pithecanthropus pekinensis*). With a cranial capacity of about two-thirds of *homo sapiens*, this hominid, who lived about 300,000 B.C., made crude tools of stone and used fire. However, despite this early start, the subsequent development of culture in China during the Palaeolithic and Neolithic period remains obscure, chiefly because there has been relatively little archaeological excavation.

The history of civilization in China is only adequately documented by archaeological data from the Shang Dynasty (*c.* 1500–1027 B.C.). Later Chinese literature includes a rich mythology which tells of many emperors, beginning from 2356 B.C. As in similar records of other early peoples (e.g. the Sumerian King List and the genealogies in the *Book of Genesis*), incredibly long reigns are attributed to these emperors, who generally appear to have been of the culture-hero type. There are also a number of flood-myths, probably because the earliest centers of civilized life were in the area of the lower course of the Yellow River.

## "Great Shang"

The most illuminating information about the culture of the Shang Dynasty has come from the excavation of its capital city, known as "Great Shang," near Anyang in north Honan, which dates from the twelfth and eleventh

centuries B.C. The most spectacular finds have been the "royal graves," which parallel, in the richness of the deposits and the number of skeletons, the "royal graves" found at the Sumerian city of Ur, in Mesopotamia. The remains of chariots, horses and their drivers show how important it was considered for the dead lord to take his transport with him into the tomb. The fine ritual bronzes which were found, some decorated with the celebrated *t'ao t'ieh* pattern, show the high quality of contemporary craftsmanship and the existence already of the distinctive characteristics of Chinese art.

## "Oracle Bones"

Another kind of evidence, less impressive in appearance but of great historical significance, has been the so-called "Oracle Bones." It was apparently the practice at Anyang for augurs to apply a heated bronze implement to selected animal bones, and the resultant cracks were interpreted as answers to questions previously put. These questions and answers were often inscribed on the bones, and constitute the earliest extant evidence of Chinese writing.

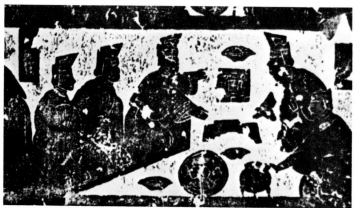

A Confucian fable

## Ancestor Worship

In primitive Chinese thought ancestor worship also involved a deep attachment to the soil, particularly to that bit of it where each family lived. It was the ancient custom to place both the newborn and the dying on the earth, thus symbolizing the need for contact with it at these two crises of man's life. In the primitive rural communities of China it was the custom also for marital intercourse to take place in the southwestern corner of the house, near to where the seed-corn was stored, and the dead, too, were buried close to this spot. Such customs sprang from the belief that the "family stock" lasted as long as the earth upon which the family lived. Thus, at any given moment, the greater part of the "family stock" lay buried in the family soil, with the living members, as it were, forming the individualized portion active above ground.

Within the ordinary family this sense of integration was expressed in a devoutly practiced cult of its ancestors. Their memories were preserved on tablets in the ancestral shrine, poor and meager though it may have been. On the son devolved the duties of being the chief mourner of his deceased father and minister of his mortuary ritual, while the grandson represented his deceased grandfather at the family cult. With the development of the ancestor cult in the feudal states of ancient China (*c.* 722–481 B.C.), the family of the ruler came to epitomize the various families of the state. The primitive connection between mankind and the soil was carefully preserved by siting the ancestral temple of the ruler in the seignorial town, close to the altar of the gods of soil and harvest.

## Yin and Yang

It was probably during the feudal period of the later Chou Dynasty that another idea, which reflects a basic intuition of the Chinese mind, developed and found expression—the idea of *yin* and *yang*. This concept saw all cosmic existence as the product of an alternating rhythm of two complementary creative forces. The *yin* force or principle was regarded as feminine; it was associated with darkness, softness and inactivity. *Yang* was the male principle, characterized by light, hardness and activity; it was also associated with heaven, whereas *yin* was of the earth.

## Human Nature

The *yin-yang* dualism was also used to explain human nature. Man was conceived with two souls which together with the body constituted him a living person. The *yin*-soul was identified with the primitive *kuei*, because it was of earthly origin and associated with the body from the moment of conception. During the individual's lifetime this *yin*-soul was called the *p'o*, and after death the *kuei*; it lingered on near the tomb but gradually faded to nothing. The *yang*-soul was regarded as the animating principle, which came from heaven as air or breath. It announced its presence in the first cry of the new-born infant, and it left the body as the last breath at death—there was a special ritual used by relatives for recalling this soul before it departed too far from the body. The *yang*-soul was known as the *hun* during life, and *shen* after death.

Ritual bronze vessel; Shang dynasty

## Confucius

The greatest figure in Chinese culture has been K'ung Fu-tsu or Confucius, as he is known in the West. He is reputed to have lived from 551 to 479 B.C., mainly in the small but cultured state of Lu (now in modern Shantung). Although his name has become associated with Confucianism, which is often regarded as the traditional religion of pre-Communist China, Confucius was not a religious prophet or teacher as, for example, were Moses, Zarathustra or the Buddha. Indeed, according to tradition, he definitely refused to discuss religious or

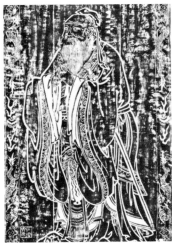

Confucius

metaphysical questions concerning divinity or human destiny. Confucius was essentially an ethical teacher. He taught that there was a *Tao*, or Way of Life, prescribed for men to follow, in order to maintain the proper balance or harmony that is fundamental to social happiness and the well-being of mankind.

## Love of ancient rites

Confucius lived at a time when the old feudal society was breaking up, with resultant confusion of ideas and standards, strife and injustice. He seems to have belonged to, or became identified with, the *Ju*. These formed a scholar-class who were experts in the performance and interpretation of religious rites and exponents of a traditional learning. Looking back to what seemed the Golden Age of the Chou Dynasty, Confucius concluded that the proper observance of the ancient rites was necessary to integrate and preserve an ordered society. This Confucian view of the past profoundly affected the earliest extant records of Chinese history, particularly of the early Chou Dynasty. For these are largely idealized accounts of the establishment of the institutions and customs which Confucius and his followers approved.

## Ti'en

Confucius certainly believed that the *Tao* or Way, which he presented, had divine authority. But his view of deity seems to have been essentially impersonal. Instead of using the ancient term *Shang Ti*, the Supreme Ancestor-Spirit or High God of the Shang Dynasty, he preferred *T'ien* (Heaven). He did, however, associate *T'ien* with a number of moral qualities, so that it does not appear only as a cold cosmic entity. Ritual in its various social forms, from the official sacrifices offered by the ruler to the mortuary service, owed by the individual to his ancestors, was essential to virtue.

## Confucianism

Confucius achieved meager success during his lifetime, but his Way of Life appealed to the Chinese temperament, for his reputation steadily grew until he was recognized as China's greatest sage. He was honored by other high-sounding titles, and temples were dedicated to him; by some he was virtually regarded as a deity. There has been much discussion as to whether Confucianism, as the movement that stemmed from his teaching, should be described as a religion, for it lacks many distinctive religious attributes. Some scholars have preferred to call it an ethico-political philosophy.

## Taoism

The idea of the *Tao* or Way, which Confucius invoked, was ancient and fundamental in Chinese culture. Confucius was primarily concerned with its social significance, although he was careful to emphasize its divine derivation. His idea, interpreted rather as an all-embracing cosmic process, was developed by other sages as a rival faith and practice; it appealed to

Han tomb interior

many who sought a more metaphysical creed than offered by Confucius and his disciples. Known as Taoism, with Lao-tzu as its legendary founder, this movement was based on the Chinese belief that man is a part of nature.

In time this Taoist belief produced a kind of nature-mysticism, and these ideas also inspired some beautiful painting, in which the Taoist sage merges into a landscape of mystical loveliness. Taoism, at its best, demanded of its devotees a high standard of intellectual ability as well as a capacity for mysticism; but because these qualities were not always to be found, the movement easily declined into forms of popular superstition. In this way, Taoism helped prepare the gradual establishment of Buddhism in China.

## Sixth-century climacteric

Our milestones of history show the development of civilization throughout the world, and it is therefore worth noting here a curious but inexplicable phenomenon. The sixth century B.C. witnessed the beginnings of some of the great religions of mankind: Gautama, the Buddha, lived *c.* 563–483; Zarathustra was born about 570; Confucius about 551, and the foundations of Judaism were laid after the return of the exiled Jews from Babylonia. In the sixth century also came the dawn of a different movement which in the distant future was destined both to undermine and aid religion—in the cities of Ionia, Greek philosophy was born.

# Building the Great Wall of China

*Finding his country a patchwork of disparate states, Shih-huang-ti, the first Emperor of China, imposed upon it unity and coherence. Centralized administration demanded swift communications, so a vast network of roads and canals was thrown across the country. Weights and measures were standardized and the same writing script introduced throughout the land. But unity was of little avail without security, and to protect his new empire from the repeated invasions of Turco-Mongolian hordes, Shih-huang-ti built an immense wall that survives to this day. Across hill and valley, mile after mile, the mighty bastion is a vivid testimony to the willpower of an absolute monarch and the imagination of a creative genius.*

The Great Wall (*opposite*) extends across some 1,400 miles of northern China. The section illustrated remains as it was when rebuilt by the Ming emperors (A.D. 1368–1644). The Wall had some 25,000 watchtowers, and models of it were a popular subject of Chinese art. The one above is of pottery, 33 inches high, and dates from the Han dynasty.

The Great Wall of China is probably the world's most stupendous monument to human ingenuity and industry, and purportedly is the only one of man's works that could be seen from the moon. The *Wan-li ch'ang ch'eng* or Wall of Ten Thousand *Li* (a *li* is approximately one-third of a mile) forms the country's northern boundary, extending some 1,400 miles from the Gulf of Chihli in the east to the sources of the Wei River in the far west of Kansu province.

Even today, centuries after its construction, the Wall remains an awe-inspiring sight. It climbs the sides of ravines and crests the watersheds of mountain ranges, doubling back on itself so frequently that its actual length is more than double 1,400 miles. In some stretches, particularly in the desolate desert regions of the far west, the Wall has been reduced to mere mounds of earth a few feet in height; other portions hundreds of miles in length are still in excellent repair—their stone, brick and mortar facings intact. The average height of these sections is twenty feet, and at top they are wide enough to permit six horsemen to pass abreast.

Although the Great Wall has been repaired and enlarged many times, the existing structure is mainly the result of restoration work undertaken during the Ming dynasty (A.D. 1368–1644). All reliable Chinese sources attribute the original building to the Ch'in dynasty ruler Shih-huang-ti, the self-styled First Emperor of all China. His imperial reign lasted only eleven years (221–210 B.C.), but for the preceding twenty-one years Shih-huang-ti had ruled the semi-barbaric border state of Ch'in in northwest China. With the assistance of able ministers, he had turned the full energies and resources of the Ch'in state to production and defense, and his kingdom rapidly became an irresistible military power.

In the year 211 B.C. the Ch'in ruler defeated the last of the feudal states into which China had been divided for centuries and proclaimed himself the First Emperor of China. Shih-huang-ti set himself the task of unifying his vast territories under the control of a strong centralized government and thus ending centuries of all but incessant internecine strife. Shih-huang-ti soon realized that the unification and pacification of his empire would be thwarted unless he could ensure the defense of his northern frontier, vulnerable to the constant incursions of China's traditional enemies, the warlike, nomadic Turco-Mongolian tribes who inhabited the northwestern steppes. Those barbarians, who "moved from place to place according to the water and grass, and had no walled cities or towns, settled habitation or agricultural occupation," had united under the Hsiung-nu, or Hun tribesman, by the time of the First Emperor.

From the beginning of his reign, the Emperor had been forced to send one expedition after another to drive back the swiftly moving Huns, who retreated over the wide Mongolian plains after each successful raid. Conquering the Mongols proved impossible; containing them within their own territories was all Shih-huang-ti could hope to achieve. To do so he embarked upon a construction project unparalleled in world history: the building of the Great Wall.

Shih-huang-ti was determined to construct a chain of strong fortifications and watchtowers along the entire length of his northern frontier and then to join them together by a massive wall. In 215 B.C. he dispatched General Meng-T'ien to the northern frontier with an army of 300,000 laborers and an uncounted number of political prisoners, convicted felons and other elements of the population that were considered dangerous or unproductive. There were already hundreds of miles of fortifications in existence along China's northern borders, built in earlier times by the states of Ch'in, Chao, Wei, and Yen to protect themselves from the Huns and the eastern Hu tribes. Those barriers were well

*Above* Head of a singer, from the period of the Warring States (fifth to third centuries B.C.), which ended with the establishment of the Ch'in dynasty under Shih-huang-ti, who proclaimed himself the first Emperor of China.

*Below* Bronze buckle with motif of struggling beasts, typifying the nomadic themes and vigorous execution of much early Chinese art.

maintained, and wherever possible Meng-T'ien's engineers simply rebuilt and strengthened earlier fortifications.

Though there is little reliable information, numerous legends testify to the immensity of the builder's task, its appalling toll in human life and suffering and the remorseless speed of the Wall's construction. It has been estimated, for example, that if the materials used in building the Wall were to be transported to the equator, they would provide a wall eight feet high and three feet thick, encircling the entire globe. The Wall reportedly had 25,000 watchtowers within signaling distance of one another, each capable of accommodating one hundred men. Between the watchtowers, two parallel furrows, about twenty-five feet apart, were chiselled out of the solid rock. On this foundation, solid, squared granite blocks were then laid, and these were topped by two parallel courses of large bricks. The inner core was then filled with tamped earth. According to legend, the unwieldy granite blocks were often tied to teams of goats, who dragged them up the almost inaccessible ridges. It has been estimated that at one time roughly one-third of the able-bodied men of the empire were engaged either in building or defending the Wall, or in conveying the necessary supplies to the inhospitable regions that the Wall traversed.

So long as it could be effectively garrisoned, the Wall undoubtedly provided the rich agricultural plains of north China with some protection from Hun incursions, but it served another purpose as well. The Wall proved an effective barrier to those dissident indigenous groups within the empire who had been dispossessed of their lands and desired to defect to the enemy. Chinese scholars and peasants alike had much to offer the less sophisticated northern barbarians in the way of political, agricultural and economic expertise, and Shih-huang-ti was resolved that all defection attempts by sizeable groups should be frustrated.

The Wall solved another of Shih-huang-ti's domestic problems as well. Decades of almost ceaseless warfare had led to the creation of a huge standing army. Those soldiers, spread over the empire and inured to fighting, might easily prove a threat to the centralized government. Thus, the garrisoning of the Great Wall served a dual purpose, for besides protecting the frontier, it also kept a large part of the army permanently occupied some distance from the capital. In addition, it solved the problem of providing useful employment for China's vast numbers of landless vagabonds, prisoners and disillusioned scholars.

The sheer logistical problem of supplying those garrisons with food and equipment was an enormous drain on the economic resources of the empire, however. Apart from the Yellow River, few of north China's rivers were navigable for any appreciable distance, and the loaded supply barges

had to be manhandled upstream against swiftly flowing currents. Carts traveling the barren regions often used up many of their supplies before reaching their intended destinations. Shih-huang-ti's attempts to supply provisions to the troops stationed along the Great Wall were a contributory cause in the speedy collapse of his empire.

Nevertheless, the Great Wall was a mighty material symbol of empire, an indication that for the first time in East Asian history a great power structure had arisen under the unified control of an absolute monarch. By almost every act, Shih-huang-ti repudiated China's centuries-old feudal-istic system. He saw himself as the inaugurator of a new era, and he ruthlessly destroyed the feudal states and their territorial magnates. The Emperor divided his lands into thirty-six (later forty-one) military districts, in which both military and civil authorities were responsible to the Emperor himself. In those districts, the influence of the Confucian scholars was severely curtailed, and in 213 B.C. the Emperor moved to diminish further the power of the Confucians by ordering the destruction of those Confucian classics that the scholars invoked as "mirrors of the ancient golden age of universal peace and prosperity, under Sage-kings who ruled, not by force, but by virtue." State histories, except for those of Ch'in, and the writings of ancient philosophical schools were also destroyed.

The Confucian ideal of rule by etiquette and propriety and appeal to ancient precedents was replaced by standardized laws, which, though extremely harsh, were applicable to all. Peasants were given the right to own, buy and sell land. Agriculture was encouraged; commerce, which Shih-huang-ti regarded as non-productive, was repressed. Currency, weights and measures were all standardized—and by fixing the length of cart axles, communications along the roads through the loess-land of north China were measurably improved. Equally important was the unification of the written language through the introduction of a simplified script—a measure that, perhaps more than any other, advanced the cultural continuity of Chinese civilization.

To make organized revolt difficult, the weapons that had belonged to the feudal lords were melted down and their local fortifications were destroyed. Barbarian tribes that had inhabited north China for generations were expelled, while the southern barbarian tribes, who lived in what are now Kuangsi and Kuangtung provinces, were brought under Chinese jurisdiction by a brilliant campaign that included the digging of a twenty-mile-long canal to connect the great river systems of central and southern China.

The building of the Great Wall was not the First Emperor's only grandiose scheme. He put 700,000 convicts to work building a capital city, Hsien-yang in Shensi province, of a size and magnificence never before attempted. According to Chinese historians, 120,000 of the richest and most powerful families in the empire were transported

to the new capital. The Emperor sought to win them over by building exact replicas of the palaces those families had left behind and by loading them with titles and empty honors. For himself, Shih-huang-ti built an enormous palace near the capital, and a sepulcher under the shadow of Mount Li. Tree-lined radial roads fifty paces broad spread from Hsien-yang to all parts of the empire.

The First Emperor made frequent tours to different parts of his empire, and he often ascended the sacred mountains in outlying areas to make sacrifices. Extremely superstitious and morbidly fearful of death, Shih-huang-ti became the dupe of Taoist magicians, as he eagerly sought after the elixir of immortality. Impetuous, violent, cruel and despotic, Shih-huang-ti came to believe that

Kneeling girl, and convict without hands; two clay tomb figures from the early Han period. The amputation of the hands of convicts was a common punishment in China, but whether this is depicted here is uncertain, because of the state of preservation of the figure.

99

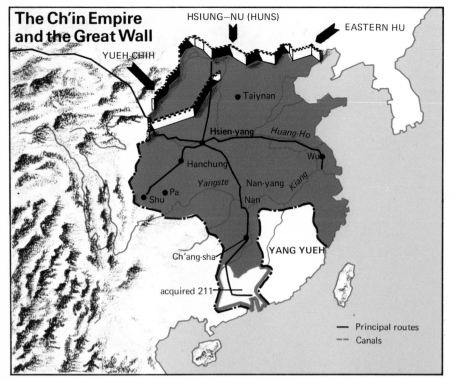

## The Ch'in Empire and the Great Wall

HSIUNG–NU (HUNS)

EASTERN HU

YUEH-CHIH

Taiynan

Hsien-yang    Huang-Ho

Wu

Hanchung

Yangste    Nan-yang

Kiang

Shu    Pa

Nan

Ch'ang-sha

YANG YUEH

acquired 211

— Principal routes
--- Canals

Bronze dagger and scabbard (Chou dynasty, seventh to sixth centuries B.C.), which owes much to nomadic influence both in its shape and in its decoration. The interlacing motif is probably derived from plaited ropes and leather thongs used by the nomads for their harness gear.

he was semidivine, and erected self-laudatory tablets throughout the empire. Gradually he became so mistrustful of even his closest associates that he segregated himself from his ministers and each night changed his sleeping quarters. Thus, towards the end of his life, the ruler of all China often could not be found when important matters needed decision.

Soon after the death of the First Emperor rebellion broke out, and within four years, in 206 B.C., the Ch'in dynasty came to an ignominious end. The concept of empire and the idea of the unity of all who lived south of the Great Wall were not lost, however, and even in times of imperial breakdown the vision of a united China remained. A centralized government had been established to promote large public works, exercise a monopoly over certain basic products, promote a common coinage and a common written language and maintain a large standing army.

The first ruler of the succeeding Han dynasty was astute enough to enforce most of the First Emperor's measures. There was a partial return to the old feudal system, however, as the new monarch granted fiefs to relatives and favorites. Furthermore, in his search for capable men to staff his huge administration he found it necessary to employ those who had been trained in Confucian ideas—and during the Han dynasty Confucianism came into its own.

The Huns, powerless against the First Emperor, once more renewed their pressure. Breaking through the Great Wall at its weakest point, they swept down on to the Yellow River plain and were only bought off by a huge present of silk, wine and grain. It was not until the reign of the Han dynasty emperor Wu-ti (140–87 B.C.) that the Chinese re-established their supremacy over the northern barbarians and even expanded their empire far beyond the Great Wall into Korea, and westwards towards central Asia.

The utility of the Great Wall as a means of defense has often been seriously questioned. Again and again throughout Chinese history the equestrian hordes of the Mongolian plains succeeded in detecting unguarded or weakly defended places, and poured through them on to the north China plain to wreak untold havoc. These comparatively primitive tribes of the inhospitable northern steppes found in the rich cities and well-cultivated homesteads south of the Wall an irresistible inducement to plunder. Their descent into China could sometimes be checked, but never permanently stopped. Only by keeping the Wall in constant repair and by garrisoning its whole length with well-seasoned and loyal troops could the government hope to keep out the intruders. In the days of the greatest of the Han, T'ang and Ming emperors the Wall provided a sure bastion against the invaders, but through long periods of internal weakness it proved entirely ineffective.

For some four centuries after the fall of the Han dynasty the whole of north China was governed by

barbarians. Throughout the fifth and the first half of the sixth centuries A.D. the Avars, a Mongol people variously called the Jou-jan or Juan-juan, maintained an empire north of the Great Wall extending from the borders of Korea to Lake Balkash, and they continually threatened north China. In 607 the Great Wall was again fortified, but at a prodigal cost: it is estimated that a million men worked for ten days during the summer of that year—and that half of them died. Later, in the Sung dynasty, the great Genghis Khan and his Mongol hordes were halted for two years by fanatical Chinese resistance; they did not break through the Wall until A.D. 1209.

The Great Wall not only helped to weld the Chinese people into a great nation, but it also helped to unify the peoples of the steppes into a political and military power. The building of the Wall marks a milestone, not only in the political history of China, but in that of Asia as a whole. It may have had a considerable effect in turning the Huns westwards to overrun Europe and thus change the course of European history. From the time that the Huns established a political hegemony over the region north of the Great Wall from Korea to central Asia, one power-structure after another rose to control that vast area. Yet none of them remained untouched by the cultural and civilizing influence of China. So strong was the cultural stability which developed in China that even when (for nearly four hundred years) north China was at the mercy of northern tribesmen, those non-Chinese conquerors gradually accepted Chinese culture and customs, and merged into the

civilization of those whom they had conquered. The same thing happened when the Mongols conquered China and founded their own dynasty. Chinese culture was immeasurably enriched by this admixture with peoples from beyond the Great Wall, but the basic structure of Chinese administration and life-style remained intact. In fact, neither the Mongols nor the Manchus could hope to be able to rule the vast Chinese empire without relying heavily on the Confucian scholar class.

After the Manchus took over the empire in A.D. 1644 the Great Wall ceased to be of military significance. Had the Chinese general Wu San-kuei defended the mighty fortress of Shan-hai-kuan at the eastern end of the Great Wall, a purely Chinese dynasty might have established itself in place of the effete Ming. Instead, he surrendered the fortress to the Manchu armies, who rapidly occupied the whole of north China and established their capital at Peking.

The empire of the Manchus was no longer bounded on the north by the Great Wall; Manchuria, Mongolia, Sinkiang and Tibet all remained outside it. New and entirely different enemies from over the seas began to engage the attention of the Chinese government, and the Wall, ungarrisoned and neglected, gradually fell into disrepair. Materials were even scavenged from it to construct the imperial tombs of the new dynasty. Today what remains of the Great Wall stands as an eternal witness to the dream of the First Emperor and great empire-builder, Shih-huang-ti.

D. HOWARD SMITH

Typical north China scenery in the neighborhood of Sian, with agricultural terraces on the slopes of the hills. It is through landscape such as this that the Great Wall runs for much of its length.

A window in a watchtower of the Great Wall.

The Great Wall of China did not always keep the invader out, but it did help to establish the geographical identity of the Chinese empire. The exact delineation of the boundaries of the empire gave its administration a positive geographical basis. The main subject of our next four chapters is Rome, and we shall be tracing some of the vicissitudes of her rise from small city-state to mistress of the Mediterranean world and Europe. The ultimate extension of Rome's power gave her a vast empire and, as with the empire of Shih-huang-ti, her territory was given a positive limit by permanent frontiers. The Great Wall of China has a smaller but still monumentally impressive parallel in Hadrian's Wall, built in the first years of the second century A.D. across the northern part of England, to keep out unconquered tribes from the north. The whole of the Roman Empire was ringed with systems of fortifications when natural barriers were not present, as the great forts of Germany and the *limes* (frontier system) of North Africa indicate. Our next chapter describes a remarkable episode. It is the story of an enemy of Rome who invaded Italy and conquered what one would have supposed was an insuperable natural barrier—the Alps.

## Hannibal

The enemy was the Carthaginian leader Hannibal. His epic journey across from North Africa up through Spain, across southern France, *over* the Alps and into Italy is in the tradition of Alexander's vast journeys across deserts and mountains to conquer half the world. Hannibal himself was a

true product of the Hellenistic age that Alexander's conquests had ushered in. It was an age of the professional war-leader. The outcome of military struggles largely determined the political development of the Mediterranean world at this time, and the leader of a powerful army could carve out a kingdom for himself. Military power had assumed greater importance since Salamis—the size of the confrontation, the empire of Persia against the Greeks, was significant. In the East, Hellenistic princes made and unmade states. In the West, meanwhile, relatively modest campaigns in Italy were gradually bringing to power a small city-state. By 270 B.C. Rome had consolidated her position as the dominant power in central Italy. Before we look at the course of events that led to conflict with the North African empire of the Carthaginians, it is worth seeing how the city of Rome, now on the brink of a Mediterranean expansion that would lead to world domination, had grown up.

## Origins of Rome

The Greeks, as we have seen, possessed very little information about their origins, though the Homeric epics had preserved for them some indications of a historic past. The Romans knew even less about their beginnings as a state, and for them legend provided the traditional account of Rome's early history. According to legend, Rome was founded in 735 B.C. by Romulus, son of Mars, on the hill known as the Palatine above the Tiber River. Rome's original constitution was monarchic; seven kings ruled over Rome until the last, Tarquinius Superbus, was

driven out and a republic set up. The last three kings were Etruscan. According to archaeology and modern historical analysis, Rome was founded sometime in the eighth century B.C.; the oldest settlement, which was on the Palatine, merged with other settlements on the group of seven hills above the Tiber, and the hill called the Capitol was subsequently fortified. Rome's local power grew, and she gained the leadership of neighboring Latin towns, forming a league.

Jupiter, supreme Roman god

## The Etruscans

The rise of the Etruscans to power in central and northern Italy

Fratricidal strife; Etruscan fresco

precipitated a clash with Rome. Rome lost the struggle and an Etruscan ruling house took over. Under this leadership Rome grew and prospered, learning the skills of civilization from the Etruscans as they had learned them from the Greeks. But at the beginning of the sixth century, the Etruscan domination was ended by a rebellion engineered by the more powerful families in Rome, and a republic was set up.

Etruscan couple; from a sarcophagus

## Roman society

Rome's population was made up of various families or clans (*gentes*). Certain families were more important than others, and their heads functioned as a council of elders, called the Senate. In the days of the monarchy this council was the source of advice for the king, who was also chosen from among the ranks of the senators, or *patres* (fathers), as they were then called. The more important and richer families, the patricians, were distinguished from the lesser families, the plebeians. After the expulsion of the Etruscan Tarquin, two magistrates were henceforth elected instead of a king—they were later to be known as consuls. The word for king, *rex*, became a hated symbol of excessive power and it was never again used officially. When, centuries later, the Roman republic was transformed into the Empire under Octavius, as we shall see in a later chapter, the emperors, even though they were sole rulers at first, never used the term, but called themselves *imperator* (general, or one who exercises supreme power, *imperium*).

## Patricians and plebeians

The decision-making body of early Rome was theoretically the *comitia*, or popular assembly, but in practice the Senate exercised power over it. In contrast, at Athens the popular assembly eventually curbed the power of the great nobles, as we have seen; Rome was thus never a democracy in the way that Athens was, but basically an oligarchy, increasingly dominated by powerful individuals. But unlike many Greek cities, Rome did achieve internal stability, and developed her constitution (and, perhaps almost as important, respect

According to tradition Romulus and his brother were reared by a wolf for it), without civil wars and the forcible imposition of rule by one group or another. The patricians and plebeians engaged in a long-drawn-out struggle for power, which was not simply rich against poor, for the ranks of the plebeians eventually contained influential families. The plebeians managed to obtain recognition of their own officials, the tribunes, who were then incorporated into the constitution of the Roman state. The calm conduct of what was a very real struggle is evident in the so-called

Roman patrician

"secession of the plebs," when the plebs withdrew their labor until their demands were met, thus showing by passive means their relevance to the Roman state.

## Roman citizenship

In contrast to the Greek city-states, Rome's expansion did not stop at temporary domination over neighboring states. The Greeks, always respecting the idea of the autonomy of the city-state, did not conceive of a larger unity except in the form of a hegemony, or league, as we have seen. The Romans conquered peoples and cities in Italy, but their hegemony brought with it the chance of assimilation. Rome's "allies" achieved certain of the rights of Roman citizenship, and eventually all of Italy gained full Roman citizenship. The people of Rome, as in other city-states, had political expression through citizenship, but what distinguished Rome from city-states like Athens for example, was the emergence of the idea that citizenship could be extended wholesale to other peoples. This larger concept of citizenship paved the way for the absorption of foreign peoples and the resulting political unity that was to be the mainstay of the Empire of Rome. Alexander's conquests had set loose the idea of a community of Greek culture that embraced the

whole inhabited world, the *oikoumene*; the *oikoumene* was to be given a political framework within the conquests of Rome which provided for the continuity of Greek, or rather Greco-Roman, civilization around the Mediterranean.

## Pyrrhus of Epirus

We now take up the story of Rome when she was as yet only a force inside Italy. In 270 B.C. Rome became involved in the quarrels of the Greek cities in the south of Italy. Her strong position in Italy gave her the potential role of arbiter, if not protector. In a dispute between Thurii and Tarentum, Thurii appealed to Rome for help, and it was given. Rome had

Elephants of King Pyrrhus

entered the sphere of Greek politics. The Tarentines, who saw Rome as a threat to their supremacy in southern Italy, enlisted the help of Pyrrhus, King of Epirus. Pyrrhus was a *condottiere* in the Hellenistic style, looking for a profitable cause to fight for, since his attempts to grab territory in Greece while the successors of Alexander were squabbling for power had been unsuccessful. Rome's first confrontation with the professional skill of Hellenistic mercenaries did not go well at first, and after a defeat at Heraclea, the Romans were forced back deep into Latium. The possible threat to Rome itself galvanized the Romans into uncompromising action: Pyrrhus was seen as a real

King Pyrrhus of Epirus

danger to Rome herself. He might play the war game for profit as did most of the Hellenistic war leaders, but Rome was in deadly earnest. Their stubborn efforts inflicted so many casualties on Pyrrhus that, although technically victor, he decided to withdraw from Italy (hence the proverbial Pyrrhic victory). He sailed off to Sicily to try his luck fighting for the Greek cities there against the Carthaginians. After a second try against the Romans in Italy, again without any real success, he returned to Greece where he was killed in a brawl at Argos.

## Conflict with Carthage

Behind such campaigning, the realities of politics brought Rome and Carthage to a head-on collision. Carthaginian power had only just been kept at bay by the Greeks in Sicily for centuries. Rome's interests, and her involvement with the Greek cities of Magna Graecia, meant that two spheres of influence were beginning to overlap. Conflict came when Rome embarked on armed intervention in Sicily. The struggle with Carthage that followed was to last intermittently for more than half a century (264–202 B.C.), with the three Punic Wars—"Punic" from the Latin *poeni, poenicus* meaning Phoenician. For Carthage was the greatest offspring of Phoenician colonization in the western Mediterranean. Her great strength was her navy, and Rome was forced to become a sea-power almost overnight in order to have even a chance against the might of Carthage. Carthage was,

Phoenician ship

unlike most Phoenician colonies, also a great land power, whose vast territories in North Africa, stretching as far west as the Straits of Gibraltar, added to her possessions in Sicily and Sardinia, made her one of the foremost powers in the Mediterranean.

Carthaginian sarcophagus

## The First and Second Punic Wars

The first war with Carthage ended with the ceding of Sicily to Rome, the first of Rome's overseas acquisitions and the beginning of her Empire. The Second Punic War brought to lasting fame the Carthaginian whose remarkable journey across the Alps is our next milestone. Hannibal was a great war leader, but he is distinguished from other Hellenistic captains of war by his sense of mission. It may not be acceptable to talk of destiny today, but to Hannibal and to the Romans it must have been a more valid concept. The destinies of Rome and Carthage were seen as intertwined in the Homeric past by the poet Virgil, who composed his epic poem *The Aeneid* in the reign of the Emperor Augustus. In this backward projection of history, the hero of the poem, Aeneas, a Trojan prince, leaves the ruins of defeated Troy and journeys to Italy to establish a new Troy—Rome—on the seven hills. On the way he stops off on the coast of North Africa, where he loves and leaves Dido, Queen of Carthage, who is building her great new capital. The deserted Queen swears perpetual vengeance against Aeneas' descendants and commits suicide. Hannibal is said to have sworn revenge on Rome on the altar of Melqart, and in the chapter that follows we shall see how his mission of revenge fared against the armies of Rome.

Aeneas sacrificing

# Hannibal Challenges Rome 217 B.C.

*Two powers confronted each other to dispute mastery of the Mediterranean—Rome and Carthage.*
*The Carthaginians were interested in colonial expansion as an extension of their trading interests,*
*but were prepared to protect those interests if necessary. Rome's view was essentially different.*
*In fact some Romans believed that the fates of the two nations were inextricably linked, and that*
*they were doomed to a duel to the death. Because Carthage's sphere of influence extended over a*
*great deal of the western Mediterranean, Rome had to become a naval power virtually overnight.*
*But Carthage too was arming for the confrontation, and under the leadership of the general*
*Hamilcar moved the theatre of war to Spain. It remained for his son Hannibal—one of the greatest*
*military geniuses of all time—to challenge the Romans on their homeground by crossing both the*
*Pyrenees and the Alps. In the ancient world such a feat seemed impossible. Only Hannibal would*
*have dared embark on such a venture.*

In the spring of 218 B.C., an army of 100,000 men gathered in a town in eastern Spain, now Cartagena, under the command of a young general, Hannibal Barca. These soldiers had been recruited from all the warlike tribes of Spain and North Africa. The officers were Carthaginians, descended from the ancient Phoenician people who had left the Lebanon six or eight centuries earlier and had colonized first the coasts, then the interiors of present-day Tunisia and Andalusia. In the next two years these men were to accomplish one of the most astonishing feats of history. They were to travel more than 1,200 miles through hostile or savage countries, crossing one of the biggest rivers in Europe and two of the highest mountain chains. At the end of this formidable journey they were virtually to annihilate the finest armies of the time and to threaten the very survival of Rome's power in the heart of her own territory.

Hannibal's aim was to avenge the defeat that Rome had inflicted on Carthage twenty-three years earlier, at the end of the First Punic War, a struggle that had lasted for nearly a quarter of a century. (The Punic Wars were so called after the Roman name for Carthaginians: Poeni, i.e., Phoenicians.) His fantastic venture so astounded both his contemporaries and posterity that its romantic aspect has overshadowed the rational, one might almost say scientific, manner in which the undertaking was planned and executed. The facts, however, emerge from the account given by the Greek historian Polybius, one of the soundest intellects of antiquity despite his Roman bias. Thanks to him, we realize that Hannibal's campaign was not the whim of a rash young leader; it was prepared and led by one of the greatest political figures of all time. In spite of ultimate failure, it influenced decisively the evolution of Mediterranean civilization.

By the end of the fourth century B.C. Carthage had accumulated great wealth from its vast trading empire. Its kings had brought terror to the Greeks in Sicily, conquered Sardinia and sent exploratory expeditions along the river banks of tropical Africa and the boundaries of Europe. Carthaginian dominance over the western Mediterranean was well established. Then the great landowners rose to destroy the monarchy and for a time Carthage had sought to live at peace. Concentrating on trade, she had allowed the militant Roman republic to establish power over the whole of Italy without making any move, and had even refused to help her old allies the Etruscans, in spite of centuries-old treaties of mutual aid. The peasant soldiers of Latium had no apparent reason to interfere with Carthaginian merchants, and Rome's still-primitive economy could not rival the highly developed scientific agricultural system of the vast African estates.

But some of the Roman senators had formed fruitful associations with the merchants of Campania, who had pointed out to them the enormous profits that would accrue from the conquest of Sicily, the granary of the western Mediterranean, a great cultural center—and an island partially under Carthage's control. In 263 B.C. a Roman force had occupied Messina, thereby securing control of the straits between Sicily and Italy. Carthage could not tolerate this encroachment in an area that she considered as belonging to her "governorship" of Sicily, and the First Punic War broke out.

During the first years of the conflict the military superiority of the Romans on land was evident, and the Roman fleets held their own against the celebrated Carthaginian navy. The Carthaginians were able to retain only a few bases in Sicily, and that much was salvaged only because of their superiority in siege warfare. But in 256 B.C. the Romans, led by Regulus, were halted on one of their forays into Africa. The conflict had reached a stalemate. This prolonged warfare, however, was disastrous for a

This head, from a Carthaginian coin, is possibly a likeness of the great Carthaginian leader, Hannibal.

*Opposite* The elephants Hannibal took on his campaign across the Alps are probably its best-remembered feature; from a Carthaginian coin.

country with a mercantile economy, such as Carthage. Exhausted and discouraged, in 241 B.C. the Carthaginian government finally renounced all claims over Sicily.

Following the end of the war, a grave social crisis was precipitated in Carthage by the mutiny of the mercenaries who had formed almost the entire part of the Punic army. The government fell and was replaced by a popular party, which handed power to Hamilcar Barca, Hannibal's father. This young general, already famous as head of commando units against the Romans, succeeded in controlling the mercenaries. Hamilcar recognized the basic weaknesses of the Punic government—weaknesses that had contributed to the loss of the war as well as to the revolt of the mercenaries. The problem was that government was in the hands of a self-centered plutocracy, with the ruling families vying with one another for power. While Hamilcar had little interest in internal politics, he modified the constitution to the extent necessary for him to carry out his plan of revenge against Rome.

Hamilcar did not in fact accept any possibility of compromise with the belligerent Italian republic. The Roman Senate had not attempted to subjugate Carthage even during the mutiny of the mercenaries, perhaps for fear of widespread revolution. But toward the end of Carthage's internal crisis Rome had annexed Sardinia, cynically and without regard for justice.

Hamilcar had three main aims: to have a free hand politically, without being obliged to account all the time to the rulers of Carthage; to be solely responsible for the country's economy and free to use its resources to influence both internal and foreign opinion; and to recruit an army that was efficient, well trained and completely loyal to him personally. He achieved all three aims in less than ten years, thanks to his conquest of southern Spain, which he organized into a virtually independent kingdom on the model of those that Alexander's successors had created in Asia. The mountain chains of Andalusia concealed the richest mines in the Mediterranean world. These provided enough revenue to pay Rome the war reparations fixed by treaty, to afford resources for Hamilcar's electoral campaigns in Carthage and to hire Greek technicians and propagandists necessary for his great plan. The warlike Celtiberian tribes provided courageous soldiers whose fervent loyalty to their leaders offset the disadvantages of their rapacious behavior. All this took place on the fringe of the civilized world, beyond the regions regularly inspected by the Roman intelligence service.

Hamilcar was killed in a campaign in 229 B.C. The system of succession that he had devised required that one of his close relatives should succeed him. His eldest son Hannibal was still too young, and power passed into the hands of his son-in-law, Hasdrubal. He continued to organize the Spanish kingdom, but he seems to have sought to delay any further conflict with Rome.

The Greeks of Massilia (now Marseille) and of Emporiae in Catalonia, old enemies of the Phoenicians, had finally persuaded the Romans of the danger that the Barca empire represented. Hasdrubal signed a treaty that set the boundary of his domain at the river Ebro, or possibly the Júcar. But Hasdrubal was assassinated, and in 220 B.C. Hannibal succeeded to power.

Hannibal at once adopted a more uncompromising, aggressive policy. To make it quite clear that he ruled Spain and that his enemies could expect no help from Rome, he attacked and destroyed

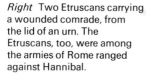
*Right* Two Etruscans carrying a wounded comrade, from the lid of an urn. The Etruscans, too, were among the armies of Rome ranged against Hannibal.

the Spanish town of Saguntum, which had a treaty of alliance with the Roman republic. The Senate, which had done nothing to save the people of Saguntum, demanded the punishment of the Carthaginian "butcher." The Carthaginian government replied that the Barca state in Spain was autonomous and that Rome had recognized this when negotiating with Hasdrubal. The Roman ambassador could only point out the inevitability of war.

The Second Punic War was welcomed by Hannibal; and his moral responsibility for it was largely justified by the brutality and cynicism of Roman policy toward Carthage. The only question was whether the young Carthaginian leader had a reasonable chance of winning. Hannibal was convinced he had. Educated by Greeks, he had broadened his outlook to embrace the whole Mediterranean world and even the uncivilized countries beyond. No other statesmen except perhaps Alexander and Pyrrhus of Epirus had attained so international an outlook; and the quality of the information at the disposal of the Carthaginians made Hannibal well qualified to assess the geographical and political situation.

Hannibal had carefully considered the structure of the political organization that we call, rather loosely, the Italian confederation. It had been created by linking the military power of Rome with the economic and commercial strength of Campania. Both parties had derived considerable benefits; for the legions constituted the strongest armed force in the Mediterranean, and the merchants and manufacturers of Campania dominated the whole market from Gibraltar to the Adriatic. However, its very success was a source of rivalry between the partners. For one thing, all important

Bronze cuirass belonging to one of Hannibal's soldiers.

policy was decided in Rome, and statesmen of Capua did not take kindly to having their ambitions restricted to a municipal scale. In addition, the constitution of Capua favored the development of what we would now call left-wing ideas whose supporters—in particular a certain Pacuvius Calavius—foresaw the breakup of the union. It is more than likely that these potential secessionists had made a deal with the Carthaginians before the outbreak of the Second Punic War.

If she were to be deprived of southern Italy, Rome would at once lose all her naval power—unequaled in the Mediterranean—and Carthage could have regained Sicily and Sardinia without striking a blow. But no one in any Italian town would dare oppose Rome so long as the legions controlled the country. Therefore a force had to be found that was capable of neutralizing the Roman army. Hannibal thought he might find this force in Gaul. For a long period the Celts had provided mercenaries for the Carthaginians, but no one as yet had the idea of treating these barbarians as a political force and concluding diplomatic agreements with them. One of the greatest errors of the Carthaginian government during the First Punic War had been its ignorance of the profitable use it might make of the Gauls in the Po Valley. In fact the Gauls had remained at peace throughout the war and had subsequently been subjugated by the Romans. Hannibal was determined that the same mistake should not be made again. He sent envoys throughout the Celtic territory, who brought back extremely useful information.

Until this time the Gauls had occupied the center, the east and the north of France, Holland and western and southern Germany. The Rhine ran through the middle of their territory. For several decades, however, the Celts east of the Rhine had been forced by the Germans to fall back toward the west and the south, driving before them tribes who had previously been settled in the west. This

*Opposite* Iberian warrior, from a sandstone relief found at Ossuna. Hannibal's army included many Iberians, recruited from Andalusia, which his father Hamilcar had subdued a few years before the invasion of Italy.

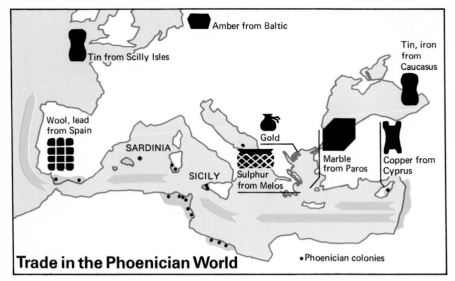

Trade in the Phoenician World

- Amber from Baltic
- Tin from Scilly Isles
- Tin, iron from Caucasus
- Wool, lead from Spain
- Gold
- SARDINIA
- SICILY
- Sulphur from Melos
- Marble from Paros
- Copper from Cyprus
- • Phoenician colonies

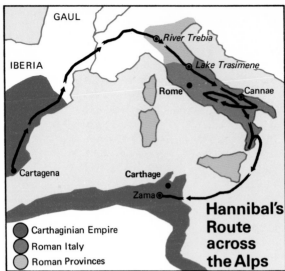

GAUL

IBERIA

River Trebia

Lake Trasimene

Rome

Cannae

Cartagena

Carthage

Zama

- Carthaginian Empire
- Roman Italy
- Roman Provinces

**Hannibal's Route across the Alps**

large migration had taken place around 230 B.C.; it was then that the Gauls settled and founded their towns, Paris among them. The repercussions of this great upheaval were felt to the limits of the Celtic world. In 225 B.C. the Romans found themselves face to face with bands of Germans mixed with Cisalpine Gauls.

For Hannibal this situation offered a double opportunity. For one, there was the possibility of recruiting seasoned auxiliaries from the numerous tribes who had been uprooted. Of even greater importance, the major difficulty facing a Carthaginian expedition from Spain to Italy was overcome. The Mediterranean coasts of Languedoc and Provence had until then been occupied by Iberian and Ligurian tribes who were partly Hellenized as a result of three centuries of trading with the Greeks. The politicians of Massilia could easily have raised from among them numerous opponents to Hannibal's passage. However, at about 230 B.C. the whole area between the Pyrenees and the Rhone had been subjugated by a Celtic tribe,

The prow of a Carthaginian warship; from a Carthaginian stele.

the Arecomican Volsci. Hannibal had only to reach agreement with them to gain not only the right of peaceful passage but also long-term occupation of certain garrisons. By maintaining these, Hannibal could retain his lines of communication with Spain and could receive reinforcements, as was to be the case in 208 B.C. At the same time he could prevent Roman armies from invading Spain by land.

In the light of such considerations it becomes clear that Hannibal's decision to invade Italy by land was not just a bold act of desperation. In fact, he had no other means of surprising an enemy whose defenses were otherwise impregnable. The only important problem that confronted the expedition was that of supply; and Napoleon himself remarked that such obstacles must never stand in the way of strategy. In this case the invading army compensated for its weakness by the factor of surprise. And Hannibal, only too well aware of the importance of propaganda, knew how to exploit the impression his extraordinary venture would make on public opinion. He could not foresee, of course, that this impression was to last for more than twenty centuries. Even today, most people remember Hannibal chiefly because he brought his elephants across the Alps.

We do not know with certainty the route Hannibal took across the Alps. It seems most likely that he crossed the valley of the Isère, through Maurienne and Mont Cenis. This route allows for one of the few authenticated traditions: that Hannibal passed through the Allobroges' territory. However, proof remains impossible.

The destruction of Roman military power and the dissolution of the Italian confederation were accomplished as Hannibal had planned, and with remarkable speed. The battle of Cannae on August 2, 216 B.C., following upon those at Tessin and Trasimeno, deprived Rome of a third of its forces, and that third comprised the youngest and most vigorous elements. Then the large towns of Campania and the Greek cities of Capua, Tarentum and Syracuse defected from Rome, and the Punic fleet was able to come into action.

Suddenly, however, the fortunes of war changed. The reasons for this reversal are much more complex than the reasons for Hannibal's success. Hannibal himself can be absolved from the accusation usually leveled against him, that he lacked decisiveness in failing to make a frontal attack on Rome after the battle of Cannae. In fact the capital's strategic position was so strong, and its perimeter so well equipped with the latest Greek defensive weapons, that a siege would have been extremely hazardous for an army already reduced and encamped in a hostile country. A heavy responsibility, however, must surely rest on the Carthaginian admirals and the leaders of the various rebellions against Rome who failed to coordinate their efforts and thus allowed the Romans to extinguish each outbreak in turn.

Hannibal himself made two bad errors of judgment: he underestimated the capacity for resistance of Rome itself, strongly ensconced as it was on plains surrounded by the mountains of Latium and the Sabine territory; and he overestimated the stability of the Barca kingdom in Spain, which collapsed like a pack of cards in the face of the small army of the Roman general Scipio. On this last point there is no doubt that Hasdrubal had seen the problem more clearly and had recognized the necessity of strengthening the Spanish state before embarking on so hazardous an expedition. In any event, Hannibal was forced to return to Carthage, and at Zama in 202 he was decisively beaten by Scipio. By the terms of the peace treaty of 201, Carthage lost its navy and its empire.

Hannibal was a victim of his Greek education. The successes of Alexander had accustomed men of that time to imagine that history was made and unmade by a few outstanding men helped by a handful of adventurers, and that economic, social and cultural factors or the popular mood could be discounted. The Barcas had hastily imposed a quite artificial political structure on the multitude of small and disparate social groups that inhabited the Spanish peninsula. The Roman state, on the other hand, had grown slowly by a natural process. Those who came to belong to Rome were not even completely aware of having been Romanized, but the process had altered their attitudes and created among them indissoluble bonds. Hannibal's sudden challenge could not interrupt Roman development, but it both modified and furthered the confederation by shattering the framework within which it had operated and allowing Rome to expand throughout Italy and the Mediterranean.

Thus Hannibal must be considered one of the chief instigators of the great revolution that transformed Mediterranean civilization and gave birth to the modern world. It is interesting to note that this view of Hannibal is substantially the same as that held by the Roman historians themselves, who saw the Carthaginians as a divine instrument sent to try the Roman people, purging them through suffering and thus making them more worthy of their divine mission to govern the world.

GILBERT CHARLES-PICARD

Scipio, the Roman general who was chiefly responsible for the defeat of Hannibal.

The ruins of Carthage, in present-day Tunisia.

The expansion of Carthage was brought to a grinding halt when the genius of the Roman general Scipio enabled the Romans to defeat the Carthaginians decisively on their own ground, at Zama in North Africa. Hannibal lived out the rest of his life a haunted exile, forever planning to challenge the might of Rome again, whether on behalf of Carthage or one of the Hellenistic kingdoms.

Rome was now undoubtedly mistress of the western Mediterranean. The dangers that she had experienced at the hands of a Greek leader, Pyrrhus, were not forgotten, so she also determined to keep a watchful eye on the East. She set about systematically forestalling the rise of any potentially dangerous rival in Greece, taking the side of the weaker party against the stronger in political quarrels, to maintain a certain balance of power. Philip v, King of Macedonia, the chief aggressor in Greece, was driven out and a protectorate was set up. Greece was again aided against an "aggressor" when the Syrian Antiochus III, the Great, invaded. He was hounded into Asia Minor by a Roman army, and heavily defeated. Roman influence then rapidly spread over Asia Minor. Pergamum became a client-kingdom, and discord was promoted in Syria so that no strong centralized control remained. In Egypt, the Ptolemaic kingdom was given Roman "protection," and this loose form of protectorate lasted until Egypt became an integral part of the Roman Empire after Actium, the subject of one of our subsequent chapters.

### The rise of Rome

From the ashes of Alexander's empire, the foundations of a new empire were rising, as Rome gradually filled the power vacuum left by the disintegrating Hellenistic states. For the first time, the whole Mediterranean area was to be dominated by one state.

Just as the collapse of the Athenian empire had caused Thucydides to ponder on the vicissitudes of political power, so contemporary historians were roused to speculate on the seemingly meteoric rise of Rome to world status. With the perspective of time, we can see the fundamental

Greek warrior

internal instability of the Hellenistic states, with their wandering armies and treasure-seeking princes, as one of the main causes; contemporary historians gave a schematic explanation of Rome's success that is not entirely unrelated. They attributed Rome's rise to the soundness of her constitution. In the neat fashion of Greek political theory, the Greek diplomat and historian Polybius (who had first-hand experience of Rome's expansion in Greece) emphasized its "mixed" character.

With the semi-royal powers of the highest office, the consulship, combined with the oligarchic component of the senate and the democratic component of the people's assembly, Rome had eliminated the potential for strife between oligarchs and democrats, or the dominance of single ruler-kings, tyrants or demagogues. This idealized analysis of Rome's constitution is certainly highly optimistic—as we shall see at Actium, where the Roman state was almost torn apart by a handful of individuals—but it does reflect a measure of truth about Rome's internal stability at this time, and the permanence of her political institutions that allowed her to operate a consistent foreign policy.

### Rome's expansion

The immediate question that springs to mind when surveying the hundred-year rise of a small city-state to a position as the leading power in the Mediterranean world is how far, and from when, a conscious policy of expansion was pursued. This has been a favorite question with historians for generations. What one can observe is that the establishment of loose protectorates, rather than permanent administration, would tend to indi-

Grain pits at Ostia

cate that Rome was initially filling a power vacuum for her own protection as much as anything. The advantages of achieving political stability by full-scale annexation could be outweighed by the disadvantages of the cost that it entailed in men and resources. Diplomacy was more feasible for Rome in the latter part of the second century B.C. But where there was an immediate economic "pay-off" Rome might annex territory on a permanent basis. Sicily became a "province"—i.e. under the direct and permanent administration of Rome—after the First Punic War. It was of strategic

value certainly, but its rich grain-lands soon played a vital part in Rome's grain supply.

Ships in harbor

### The Roman army

The desperate fight against Hannibal had hastened the development of the Roman military machine. It would not be long before this efficient new weapon would be used, not for the occasional skirmish or police-work to back up diplomatic policy, but with a ruthlessness foreign to the war games of the Hellenistic rulers. Roman peace-keeping in Greece took a more aggressive turn. Macedonian influence was effectively broken at the battle of Pydna in 168 B.C., but the Achaean League in central Greece was still causing trouble. The Romans decided to crush Greek resistance once and for all: the consul L. Mummius obliterated the city of Corinth in 146 B.C. This was indeed a bad year for Rome's enemies. The rising tide of opinion in the Roman Senate, which for years had been advocating the destruction of Carthage as the only solution to the danger of Carthaginian expansion, finally won. The Roman general Scipio Aemilianus was given a mandate to destroy the city. He razed it to the ground, so that hardly a trace remained, and is said to have wept when he had finished.

Frieze from the Great Altar of Pergamum

Sarcophagi from Carthage

Italian landscape; a Roman fresco

A by-product of this period of expansion and conquest was the flow of spoils and money from the conquests into Rome. The treasury, which had been drastically depleted by the major war-effort against Hannibal, showed a significant surplus by about 187 B.C. One of the chief economic effects of this influx of wealth was an increase in investment in Italy, much of it going into the purchase of the most solid investment available, land. This was also where the senatorial classes could best spend their wealth, as they were barred from commercial activity. With this growing interest in land came a desire to intensify agricultural production, to take advantage of growing urban markets. This meant there was a need for more labor.

## The slave question

The demand for labor was immediate, and there was a much faster and more predictable solution to such a demand than encouraging population growth or attracting the movement of free workers. Slaves could be imported to Italy when and where they were needed.

Traditionally in the Mediterranean world, conquest frequently involved the enslavement of defeated soldiers and local populations. It was a question of business: a captured enemy was worth something, a dead one was not. The idea of a human being as a commodity to be exploited, which is virtually what a slave was, may seem extraordinary and abhorrent today, but in the ancient world, slavery was an accepted institution. Even the most democratic of states, fifth-century Athens, had a large slave population. However,

Rome in the Republican period began to exploit the convention of enslaving conquered peoples on a greater scale than had occurred before. A revolt in Sardinia in 176 B.C. was crushed by a Roman general whose boast was that he had captured or killed some 80,000 people. Most of the captives would have found their way onto the slave market. In 167 B.C., some 150,000 inhabitants of Epirus in Greece were enslaved—the glut in slave labor that such an act must have contributed to can only make one fear for the cheapness of human life under such conditions.

The importation of large numbers of slaves to work on the land in Italy necessitated strict, not to say brutal, control of them. Slaves were worked in gangs, often chained together. The men were often segregated from the women. The Roman writer Cato records the grim reality of such slavery: he maintained that it was cheaper to work slaves to death and replace them, rather than to get less out of them by humane treatment. Slaves

Gladiator fighting beasts

could also be used as raw material for gladiatorial shows, trained and cosetted and fed until the few brief moments in the arena where they died for Rome's pleasure. Spartacus, the subject of our next chapter, was a gladiator.

Not every slave was at the very depths of exploitation. Through the accident of war, highly educated and cultured people might find themselves enslaved. This was particularly true of the Greeks who came into conflict with Rome, and was still the case at the end of the Medieval period. After the fall of the last bastion of Greek culture, the city of Constantinople (the subject of one of our chapters in Volume III), several Turkish businessmen found themselves the somewhat embarrassed owners of

Greek freedmen; formerly slaves of P. Licinius

cultured and indeed noble Greeks, and were perplexed by their courteous deference and superior education. Meanwhile, the children of Roman aristocrats learned the refinements of Hellenic culture from erudite Greek slaves. Roman Senators, barred from commercial activities, made great use of slaves as their deputies in business. Since slaves could not legally own property, the results of their economic activity flowed back into the purses of their masters. A talented slave could also earn enough to buy his freedom eventually. The ties of personal loyalty that bound such slaves to their masters (if sometimes through fear of punishment) made them useful also as instruments of imperial administration under the Roman Empire, and a slave frequently appeared as the Emperor's personal deputy.

Thus slavery, as a legal condition that was the by-product of

Roman market

conquest, could span a whole range of social classes, according to the historical accident which had made individuals slaves. But as a general economic system operated by the Roman Republic, it involved for the most part the exploitation of the lower classes. The use of slaves *en masse*, as herdsmen, cultivators or gladiators, constituted them as a well-defined social group, and this group-identity of large numbers of hideously-treated people brought about a rebellion within the Roman state which assumed almost catastrophic proportions.

Cloth-merchant's shop

# The Slaves' Revolt

*As Rome's armies marched victorious across the known world and her fleets patrolled the Mediter-ranean, hundreds and thousands of slaves were shipped back to Italy as cheap and expendable labor for the vast estates of the rich. Many worked in chain gangs under the lash of brutal task-masters or were sent as shepherds to the wilder parts of the country. Others were put into gladia-torial establishments, where a cruel and bloody death was an almost certain fate. In such conditions revolt seemed inevitable, and after an unsuccessful attempt in Sicily in 135 B.C. a new revolt, under the leadership of the Thracian, Spartacus, exploded in 73 B.C. An army of 40,000 under Crassus was needed to restore order, and 6,000 slaves were crucified as a warning to their fellows. Despite its immediate failure, the revolt hinted that the days of the Roman Republic were now numbered.*

Coin showing the sale of a slave.

One day in June 73 B.C., seventy-four gladiators broke out of their training establishment at Capua in southern Italy. They armed themselves with weapons stored for training and arena fighting, cut their way through the city and marched across country to Mt. Vesuvius. There near the top they made camp, and soon slaves from the towns and farms joined them. The leaders were the Thracian Spartacus and two Gauls, Crixus and Oenomaus, and their force included a strong contingent of Gauls and Thrac-ians. From the outset Spartacus dominated: it was he who had doubtless organized the breakout from Capua.

The alarmed authorities sent G. Claudius Glaber, a praetor of the year, who tried vainly to surround and dislodge the rebels. But the embold-ened slaves came down the slopes and roamed about the south, scattering detachment after detachment of troops. Soon they were masters of the whole south and their ranks were swollen with runaway slaves. Indeed by the spring of 72 they made up two armies, one under Spartacus, the other under Crixus.

In such a large-scale revolt the slaves were in a strong position only while they held together; as soon as they dispersed they were liable to capture or massacre. But unless they could take over the whole of a defensible and self-sufficient area, their only hope was to get back to their own lands. Spartacus knew that his only course was to maintain a massive force until he was safe from attack by Roman armies, then to break out. Once out of the peninsula, he and his men might find refuge in mountainous regions or march out of the Empire altogether. But these plans were impeded by Crixus and his men, who were lured by the plunder available in the rich cities of the south.

The Roman Senate recognized the need for quick, effective action. The two consuls L. Gellius Publicola and Gn. Lentulus Clodianus were each given an army. Crixus was cornered and routed near Monte Gargano, but Spartacus was too good a general to be so easily caught. No longer embar-rassed by Crixus, he decided to march north across the Alps. Somewhere in Picenum two battles were fought. Spartacus defeated Lentulus, then turned and smashed Gellius' army. The Senate suspended both generals, as Spartacus again moved north.

By then there were sharp debates in Spartacus' camp. Should they divide into small bands and steal away over the Alps, or hold together in a force that could break the legions? The men resolved to stay united, while still seeking an escape from the trap of Italy. They turned south. Spartacus is said to have contemplated an attack on Rome, although he knew such a venture could not succeed. In Sicily, however, more slaves would join him and he might found a separate state.

The Senate now appointed M. Licinius Crassus, praetor, as field commander. Crassus, a rich, unscrupulous man, had no prestige as a general, and he decided to minimize risks. Gathering the remnants of four legions, he added six more, then set out to bar Spartacus from the Strait of Messina. In the battles that followed, the weight of disci-plined troops told: Spartacus was driven down to Rhegium but failed to cross into Sicily. How many men the cautious Crassus had mustered was shown by the extensive fieldworks he then began: a 37-mile-long wall right across the rugged land of Italy's toe, behind which he planned to hem in the rebels and starve them out. But, concentrating his men at one point, Spartacus easily broke through. At last a really capable general, Gn. Pompeius, appeared on the Roman side. Pompey had returned from subduing Spain, and popular pressure made the Senate commission him to go to the aid of Crassus. Spartacus was hoping to seize the port of Brundusium and leave Italy; but his plan was spoiled by the arrival of M. Lucullus with a victorious army from Asia Minor.

*Above* Two gladiators in
combat, with a third standing
by ; a relief from Tevere.
These two gladiators are
similarly armed, but
sometimes men with different
kinds of armor or weapons
were matched—for example,
the *retiarius,* with net, dagger,
and three-pronged lance,
versus a fighter with orthodox
sword and shield.

The amphitheatre at Naples,
where many gladiators
must have died. The wall
surrounding the sunken
arena was to protect the
spectators, especially when
wild beasts were fighting.
In the distance is Vesuvius,
where the first rebel slaves
made their camp.

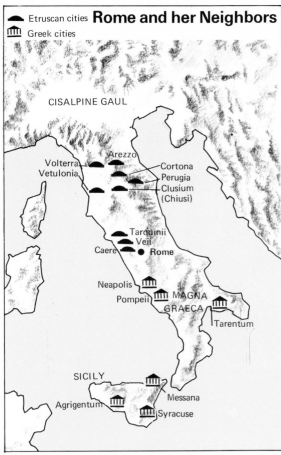

**Rome and her Neighbors**

🛏 Etruscan cities
🏛 Greek cities

CISALPINE GAUL

Volterra
Vetulonia
Arezzo
Cortona
Perugia
Clusium
(Chiusi)

Tarquinii
Veii
Caere · **Rome**

Neapolis 🏛
Pompeii 🏛 MAGNA
GRAECA
Tarentum

SICILY
Messana
Agrigentum 🏛 🏛 Syracuse

Slaves working with a huge windlass; detail of a relief from the Tomb of the Haterii.

In their difficult situation, dissensions inevitably broke out among the rebels. Two Gauls formed a force of their own, and Spartacus had to spend more time and thought on rescuing them from the results of their rashness than in building his own campaign. When the two Gauls were defeated in the mountains between Paestum and Venusia, Spartacus turned south again. A slight success roused his men to demand battle in hope of a decisive triumph. Now, however, Spartacus finally was beaten; he was killed in battle, and the revolt was crushed. Six months after his appointment, Crassus was able to carry out the masters' revenge on the slaves who had defied them. Six thousand captives were crucified all along the Appian Way from Capua to Rome—the usual punishment for offending slaves. Pompey arrived only in time to annoy Crassus by helping to round up fugitives.

It was fitting that the last great slave revolt was precipitated and led by men who refused to be gladiators; for it was in the bloody combats of the arena that the most cruel and debasing aspects of the Roman world were concentrated. The fights derived from Etruscan funeral games; but they were taken over and brutally expanded by the Romans.

Though the generalship of Spartacus made his the most serious revolt, there had been earlier large-scale uprisings. The Mediterranean world was undergoing an acute crisis as the system formed by Alexander the Great was collapsing and

Rome was striving to unite East and West in a single empire. As far back as early in the third century B.C. there had been a slave rebellion on the island of Chios, and in 279 came a movement to force the wealthy to give up their property; but the Macedonians, as champions of the *status quo,* intervened. Similar conflicts in Greece led at times to attempts to free slaves for service as soldiers. In 132 came an uprising at Pergamum with a plan for setting up a "City of the Sun," on an egalitarian basis inspired by Stoic thought; but this time Rome intervened.

In Italy, not until the second century, with its vast massing of war captives as slaves, did things become serious. The first warnings came from the wilder regions of the south, in Apulia, where slave herdsmen were gathered. By the nature of their work such men could not be closely superintended; their areas became centers of brigandage.

Then the storm broke, in Sicily. The dates are obscure. We may assume that the revolt proper crystallized from endemic brigandage. Sicily had become a place where slaves could hope to disappear and live by robbery; in about 140 a praetor is said to have sent back 917 fugitive slaves to their mainland masters. The island also attracted criminals and enemies of the Roman order. Jews and Chaldeans, evicted from Rome, seem to have gone there, as did guerrillas from Spain. As bands of desperadoes collected, the countryside became unsafe for unescorted travelers or free villagers.

In addition to fugitives and desperadoes and mutinous shepherds, there were large numbers of slaves massed in Sicily for work in the fields; for Sicilian agriculture had grown dependent on slaves. Landlords gave up using free labor and bought slaves, cheap and expendable on account of the wars. To the wretchedness of the latter's living conditions was added the brutality of overseers ready to flog the chain gangs. Often, when war prisoners were bought in bulk, men of the same tribe were gathered together and such groups were liable to breed concerted resistance.

A man who became a focus of slave hopes was Eunus, known at Enna as a magician and prophet. He claimed to see the gods and to have been told the future. Sometimes he breathed fire: historians say he did it by hiding in his mouth a pierced walnut full of burning sulphur and tinder.

At last in 135 a full-scale revolt broke and Enna was stormed. Damophilus, a particularly bad master, was tried in the theatre and spoke in his own defense, but was cut down by two leaders without a formal verdict. The assembly proclaimed Eunus king, and he took the name of Antiochus, calling his people Syrians. The workshops or dormitories of the slave gangs were broken open. We are told that prisoners of the rebels who had shown themselves humane were spared. On the whole it seems that the slaves behaved with modera-

tion; the small freeholders were the ones who were for revenge on the landlords.

Meanwhile western Sicily was also in turmoil. Under the leadership of a herdsman, Cleon, the slaves took Agrigentum. But, contrary to Roman hopes, the two bands did not clash, indeed they may have acted in concert. Cleon accepted Eunus as king and marched with his brother and some five thousand hillmen to Enna. A praetor sent from Rome levied some eight thousand Sicilians but was routed by the slaves. Eunus-Antiochus issued his own coins, with the goddess Demeter on one side, a corn ear on the other. Tauromenium, where the Roman commander had let the walls fall into disrepair, was taken. Lack of supplies forced the slaves to abandon their siege of Syracuse, but they captured a hill fortress, Morgantia.

In 134 one of the consuls took over the Sicilian command but he failed to crush the revolt. Slaves everywhere were stirred by the news of the successful rebellion. In Rome a plot by some 150 was suppressed; severe measures had to be taken against unrest at Minturnae and Sinuessa. In Sicily much confused fighting went on. In 133 a new consul took over; sling-bullets with his name, found at Enna, suggest that he made an assault there. But it was not until 132 that the Romans recaptured Tauromenium and then Enna was besieged; Cleon fell; Achaeus had already

Stele of Gaius Septimius, one of many grave-reliefs or statues that depict middle-class slave-masters whose lives were devoted to money-making. They are executed with a remarkable realism and insight into character which has been called Italian Verism.

Master and slaves; detail from a relief in the Tomb of the Haterii.

Slaves working in the fields, from a mosaic from Bardo in Tunisia. This is one of a series of mosaics depicting the various kinds of farms and villas along the North African coast; these mosaics deal with particular sites and were made to express the pride of the landowner in his estates.

disappeared; Eunus was caught in a cave. Perhaps because of his sacral claims, he was not executed, but was merely shut in a cell to rot. Flying columns of reprisal combed the island, and it is said that some twenty thousand slaves were crucified. Throughout their campaigns the rebels had made no effort to leave Sicily; they had hoped to build there an independent state, and their coins expressed dreams of a fertile earth and a full life.

For a generation things were fairly calm. Then in 104 the shock of the German invasions reawoke unrest. There were slave risings in Nuceria, then in Capua, then near Capua, when a Roman *eques* (of the middle class), ruined by love affairs, armed his slaves. The plebeian general Marius, badly needing men against the Germans, forced the Senate to decree the release of all citizens of allied states held as slaves in the provinces. The Sicilian landowners were infuriated; and after freeing some four hundred men, the governor Nerva refused to comply further. A small revolt in the west was broken by treachery. Then on the south coast the slaves defeated a Roman force, mustered six thousand men, and formed a regular army. Salvius, chosen as leader, took the title of king and threatened Morgantia. The town was saved, but Nerva failed to carry out his promise to free the loyal slaves there, and the latter left to join Salvius. Meanwhile another revolt came in the west under Athenion, who, though defeated,

joined Salvius and remained a considerable threat.

So far, only Roman garrison troops had been involved in Sicily; but the Senate now sent an army of seventeen thousand under the new governor, Lucullus. It included men from as far afield as Thessaly and Bithynia. The slaves, though still outnumbering the Romans, were in the end beaten by the discipline and organization of the legions. Athenion escaped capture by pretending to be dead. But then delays by Lucullus gave the survivors time to regain courage. Lucullus was beaten off, displaced, and finally exiled. Then in 101 the German menace in the north was ended. Manius Aquilius, an energetic and experienced campaigner, was sent to Sicily. Salvius was dead and Athenion was in sole command, but now he too was killed and Aquilius remorselessly rooted out the fugitives. Prisoners, sent to Rome, killed one another rather than be driven into the arena to amuse the mob by fighting wild beasts. There were no more rebellions in Sicily.

But on the mainland unrest grew. By 73 B.C. there were many elements to encourage slaves in thinking an opportune moment had come. For more than half a century the Roman state had been rent by violent inner conflicts. Between 132 and 82, seven consuls, a praetor, and four tribunes of the plebs were assassinated or died fighting other Romans. In 90 came the Social War, a revolt of other Italians demanding fuller rights; in 82 there was civil war that ended in Sulla's dictatorship, with its many proscriptions and legal murders; Sulla's death in 78 brought more political conflicts in Rome.

At the same time there were threats from without. Around the turn of the century came the big German invasions; in Spain sustained resistance was led by Sertorius (murdered in 72); and Pompey on his way to fight there in 77 had to quell a large rising in Transalpine Gaul. At sea there were the wars against the pirates; and in the east, Rome was challenged by Mithridates (not defeated until 66). Further, the free peasantry who had supplied the manpower for the legions was being reduced by war and the encroaching estates of the big landlords, a situation that underlay all the ceaseless social and political conflicts in Rome itself. At such a time slaves might well have hoped to break out of the system and win the wilder parts of Gaul, Thrace, and beyond.

Yet despite the apparently favorable conditions, Spartacus' revolt also failed. A strong and determined body of slaves could begin well, but they had little chance of long resistance to regular troops backed by all the resources of the cities. Their only hope was to move quickly into remote areas; staying in Italy ensured their final defeat.

Did the slaves who rebelled over the years have any social program beyond the desire to become free men? It is argued that in Sicily, by choosing kings, they showed the wish to build the same sort of society that existed elsewhere in their world. But Eunus was a prophetic character; and the

slaves may have used the term "king" to mean no more than leader.

Eunus' coins with their image of farming prosperity suggest an ideal of an earthly paradise that must have inspired his followers, just as his prophecies must have stirred them. The Romans clearly feared his propaganda. In 133 the Senate sent an embassy to placate the goddess Ceres (Demeter) of Enna; and walls were built round the precincts of the temple of Jupiter Aetnaeus, apparently to deprive the slaves of a source of religious enthusiasm.

In the second Sicilian revolt the slaves fought under the aegis of the Palici, Sicilian deities whose shrine had been founded by an early Sicilian patriot. We know from many sources that the lower classes everywhere were stirred at this time by dreams of world-end and world-renovation; and such dreams must have been voiced in Sicily and in the camps of Spartacus. But, no doubt, while some slaves responded to them, others thought only of escape and revenge.

While the slave revolts had few direct political consequences, their social and economic effects were of great importance. Sicily proved that to work the land with large slave gangs was dangerous and more and more landlords turned to tenant farmers rather than slaves for the cultivation of their estates. Columella, writing under Nero, recommended the use of slaves on the home farm, where they could be well supervised. The younger Pliny, a generation later, had much to say of troubles with defaulting tenants and mentioned that he never used slave gangs in chains. The third-century lawyers show the same sort of mixed farming. We get a picture of skilled slaves working on the home farm (attached to a residential villa) at jobs like vine-dressing, with arable farming given over to free tenants.

The slave revolts thus certainly played a large part in the supplanting of the free peasant farmer by the free tenant liable to turn into a share cropper and sink in status. They proved the perils of attempts to till land by slave gangs. And it is perhaps noteworthy that no attempts were made to build up big workshop units of slaves in the crafts and manufactures; it may be significant that in 134 there was much trouble, as we noted, at Minturnae, an industrial town. In the late Empire, with growing insecurity, there was a fall in slave prices, but no effort was made to revive gang work, and the social and economic position of the slaves began to approach that of tenants, who in turn found their lot worsened. Thus the way was opened to developments that slowly transformed the ancient world into the feudal economy of the Middle Ages.

JACK LINDSAY

The amphitheatre at Pompeii; a contemporary painting showing the kind of disorder liable to break out among the excited crowds.

*Below* Roman coin from the late Republican period.

117

Roman sacrificial procession

The happy judgment of the historian Polybius on the strength of the Roman constitution, because of its mixture of popular, oligarchic and monarchical elements, might certainly appear as an optimistic theorization after the revolt of Spartacus. The Roman state had been shaken by a bitter and violent social disturbance that had only been resolved by two individuals whose power, though technically constitutional, was far too great for the Senate to feel comfortable. Crassus, the multimillionaire, and Pompey, the popular general had succeeded where the regularly appointed consuls had failed, and the "extraordinary commands" with which they had been vested were a *de iure* recognition of the fact that the Roman state was now on the brink of being run by powerful individuals. The existence of such extraordinary commands, continuing until Octavian resolved the power struggle by his victory at Actium (the subject of our next chapter) and set about establishing the Roman Empire, with one individual in permanent possession of autocratic powers, indicates that the needs of the Roman state could no longer be met by using the established constitutional procedure. In the earlier days of the Republic generals had been given special authority in the face of a serious military threat, but the Senate had carefully limited their authority and had been strong enough to keep control. If we look back at the period of Rome's expansion into the Mediterranean we shall see that the Senate had in fact grown in strength, but that its increasing influence in government also brought with it the potential for individuals to influence affairs.

## The Roman Senate

During Rome's period of wars and expansion, from the time of the Punic wars onwards, the Senate, composed as it was of men whose experience and status gave them the ability to judge and make vital decisions in times of acute danger and stress, assumed greater direct responsibility in policy deci-

Roman senators

sions. Since the early days of Rome, the Senate had changed from being a council of men appointed by the consuls (as the successors of the kings) to being a governing body filled by ex-magistrates. The consuls would take their place in the Senate when their term of office was finished: hence a close attachment between these two "elements" of the Roman constitution. Thus the running of the state was concentrated in the hands of an oligarchy—the assembly of the Roman people still voted for magistrates, but had little real choice or influence in matters of government.

Within the Senate, cliques and

Scipio Africanus

power groups tended to form, and aimed at dominating the conduct of government. The great hero against the Carthaginians, Scipio Africanus, was eventually forced to retire from public life because of the success of a coalition of senators hostile to him and his

circle of relations and friends. This coalition indicates the tendency of the Senate to be dominated by groups of the most powerful of the Roman families, a kind of inner circle of old and influential families, the *nobiles* (those families who could claim a consul as an ancestor). The stage was thus set for the emergence of strong individuals, particularly if they had the glamour and popular support which attended a successful general, as Scipio had.

## The new army

But, so long as the army of Rome was composed of men from Italy who enlisted for a particular campaign, and were subsequently disbanded,

Plaque of Hermes and Hercules

the loyalty of troops to an individual general was limited. However, Rome found herself almost constantly involved in peace-keeping or in actual wars, and this meant a constant demand for troops. The solution from the military point of view was the creation of a professional standing army, and this was achieved at the end of the second century B.C., under the leadership of a solid

Marius, the Roman general

Italian soldier, who had risen from the ranks to command the armies of Rome, Marius. Once a campaign was over, the troops did not disband and return to their villages and towns as before; they now stayed together as a profes-

Roman soldiers building a fort

sional fighting unit, in need of employment as soldiers, and looking to their leader for guidance. The curse of the Hellenistic age had caught up with Rome: generals and their armies would henceforth face each other on Roman soil, to determine who might control the state. The problem of what to do with a standing army was not even approached until Rome truly became an Empire under Augustus, when he arranged for most of the troops to be stationed on or near frontiers. But it was never solved. The authority of individual emperors, backed up by a willing Senate, kept the problem at bay for the most part in the early Empire. But in the third century A.D. the Empire was to go through a severe crisis, one of whose main causes was the rapid turn-over of emperors made and unmade by the army.

## Political reform

The challenge of individual politicians to the collective authority of the Senate did not at first come from within its own ranks, nor yet from generals. The tribunate, originally created by popular pressure to give voice to the demands of the people's assembly and to provide a counterbalance to aristocratic power, provided the vehicle of protest—and almost of revolution, for two brothers, the Gracchi. Tiberius Gracchus attacked serious flaws in the Roman government from his

Roman soldiers marching

Coin of Julius Caesar

Julius Caesar

position as tribune of the people in 133 B.C., calling—among other things—for agricultural reforms to aid the peasantry. In attempting to achieve ratification of his proposals, he managed to get his fellow tribunes deposed, and was labeled by the senatorial opposition as a demagogue seeking autocratic powers. The fear of autocracy (one thinks of the traditional hatred for kingship) among the Romans provoked a violent reaction: Tiberius was killed. So too was his younger brother Gaius Gracchus, who had taken up his dead brother's cause and was campaigning on behalf of the people and on behalf of the equestrian class of citizens (the businessmen of Rome, below the senators in rank), whose interests were not represented politically.

Such violence in politics struck a new and warning note; so did the great wave of popular support which had temporarily carried the Gracchi forward into a position of dominance. The state could be swayed by individuals, and the whole direction of Roman government, despite its apparently solid framework, could be altered. The passionate respect which the Romans of the time had for their constitution, reflecting no doubt their genuine sense of stability, was to limit any attempts at real change. Marius, the Italian soldier-become-general, with the aid of help from an ancient and respectable senatorial family, the Metelli, and the support of the people and his troops, eventually dominated the Roman state. His overthrow was accomplished by a man who was a conservative. who was backed by the Senate, and who set himself up as dictator to patch up the flaws in the Roman constitution. This senatorial candidate, Sulla, produced a solid if backward-looking program of reform before stepping down to

let the constitution work without the guiding hand of an autocrat. But, for all the semblance of a senatorial revival, and an apparent return to the days when Rome was run along constitutional lines, politics was still at the mercy of individuals, and no issue could really be decided without an army. This was clear when, some twenty years after the reforms of Sulla, the victorious Pompey returned from his campaigning in the East. He had pacified the rebellious territories there, and laid the foundations for their administration as Roman provinces (permanent annexation was replacing diplomacy almost everywhere within the Roman orbit). But his extraordinary command had been voted to him by the people, and since he was not a senatorial candidate, the Senate refused to ratify his arrangements. He could exert no pressure on them because he had disbanded his army, perhaps foolishly under the circumstances. It took pressure from another individual *with* an army, Julius Caesar, to get Pompey's work ratified.

## Julius Caesar

Thus the late Republic drew to its end with military power paramount. The years before the battle of Actium, which was finally to resolve the crises of the Republic, were dominated by soldier-politicians like Pompey and Julius Caesar, and then by Antony and Octavian. Their support came not just from their armies (officially legions representing the Senate and people of Rome, but in practice private armies), but intermittently

from the people of Rome, whose influence was temporarily—even if not effectively—increased by the political auctioneering that took place. The Senate itself was divided according to the inclinations and interests of its individual members. As a group it gravitated towards support of Pompey against his former ally Caesar, when Caesar in his campaigns and administration of the new provinces in Gaul showed himself to be too successful and clever for the Senate's liking. Caesar proved his superiority by crushing Pompey and his legions in a civil war in Italy itself. He controlled the Roman state for four years, until he was murdered in 44 B.C. for, so his opponents claimed, setting himself up as a

Augustus as a young man

"king" over the Republic. His nephew Octavian inherited his political support, and as we shall now see, finally put an end to the political competitions that were exhausting the resources and vitality of the Roman state.

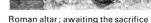
Roman altar; awaiting the sacrifice

# The Battle of Actium

31 B.C.

*The assassination of Julius Caesar in 44 B.C. initiated thirteen years of bloodshed, during which the people who had plotted his death were hunted down and those who remained in positions of power disputed that power among themselves. Finally the struggle resolved itself into a duel between Octavian, Caesar's grand-nephew and heir, and Marc Antony, his most able lieutenant, in alliance with Cleopatra, Queen of Egypt. In the final confrontation at the naval battle of Actium, Marc Antony and Cleopatra were routed and Octavian became ruler of the world as the Emperor Augustus. Egypt's last bid for world empire had been thwarted. But more important, the work begun by Julius Caesar was continued, and the transition from the anarchy of the end of the Roman Republic to the glory of the Empire was completed.*

Late in the summer of 31 B.C., the two largest fleets the world had ever seen confronted each other off the northwestern shores of Greece. The four or five hundred warships of Marc Antony, including sixty belonging to Queen Cleopatra of Egypt, faced outward into the Ionian Sea. Against this navy stood another of approximately equal size, which had come with the young Octavian, the future Augustus, from Italy. War had been declared against the foreigner Cleopatra and, by implication, against Antony, her husband in Egyptian though not in Roman law. The crews on each side numbered well over a hundred thousand men.

Behind Antony's ships, on the opposite banks of the narrow channel leading into the Gulf of Ambracia, were posted the two rival armies, each more than eighty thousand strong. Octavian's troops had come from Italy and landed at a port in Epirus, from which they had marched down and seized the northern promontory at the entrance to the Gulf. Only six hundred yards away, across the channel, they could see the troops of Antony stationed on the southern promontory, the peninsula of Actium.

For some years past, the cold, deliberate Octavian had ruled all the Roman possessions west of the Ionian and Adriatic seas—Italy, Gaul, Spain, and much of North Africa. Meanwhile, the more flamboyant Antony—in infatuated alliance with Cleopatra, whose Egypt was nominally independent of Rome—governed the lands that lay eastwards, as far as the Roman frontier on the Euphrates and including the rich territories of Asia Minor. But the conflicting ambitions and personalities of the two men had made a clash inevitable.

To meet Octavian's expected thrusts, Antony had moved his land forces up to positions along the western coasts of Greece, deploying his fleet before them, with his strongest contingents concentrated

at Actium. Cleopatra, who saw in the confrontation her great hope of winning the entire Roman world, made the enormous treasures of Egypt available to Antony, thereby providing the bulk of his funds. She persuaded him to fight at sea, not, as some of his generals advised, on land. Moreover, she insisted on taking part in the engagement herself, though the presence of this exotic siren—the target of much hostile propaganda from Octavian—undermined the morale of many of Antony's senior officers. Taking advantage of this situation, Octavian's admiral Agrippa, a superb tactician, had succeeded in weakening Antony's position well before the major battle, by persuading several of his important officers to desert the key points for which they were responsible along the Greek seaboard. Antony's supply lines to Egypt and the east were thus not only threatened but partially cut. Time was against him, and he decided to offer the challenge.

The engagement that followed was one of the decisive encounters in history. Many details have been lost or obscured in a subsequent flood of fragmentary, contradictory accounts, but patient detective work has made it possible to gain some idea of what happened.

Octavian's purpose at Actium is reasonably clear: destruction of the enemy, the conquest of the eastern provinces and seizure of Egypt's revenues. Antony's aims are more obscure. No doubt he, too, hoped to destroy his foes, but, being too good a strategist not to realize that his position had deteriorated, he decided upon an alternative plan. If defeated, he would break through Octavian's line and sail south, and then east into the Aegean. In such an event, his failure to crush Octavian would at least leave him in a position from which he could control his eastern possessions and protect Egypt, the land of his love—and of his financial backing.

In preparation for such a contingency, Antony

Apollo of Actium; a Roman coin issued by Augustus, for whose victory in the battle the god Apollo was held to have been responsible.

*Opposite* Cleopatra, the queen of Egypt whose fatal attraction for Marc Antony helped to cause the civil war with Octavian, and Antony's decisive defeat at Actium. From a coin of Cleopatra.

121

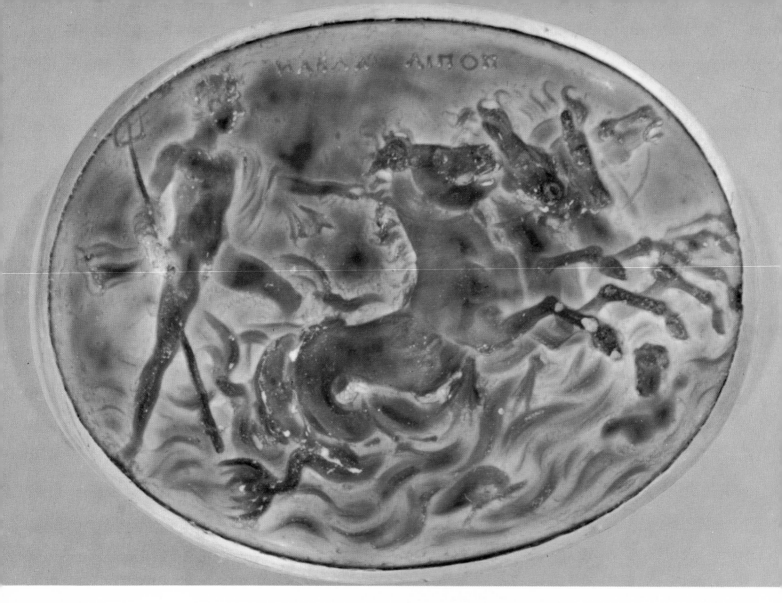

Neptune, god of the sea; from a Greco-Roman sard. Neptune was one of the gods whom Virgil, in the *Aeneid*, arrays against Antony at Actium.

gave two unusual orders: the war chest was to be moved from land and lodged on Cleopatra's transport ships, and the entire fleet was to take its sails on board. The secret transfer of the treasury may not have attracted undue attention, but the shipping of the sails had a most disquieting effect on the men. It seemed to them that Antony was already contemplating flight and, although they were no doubt told that the sails were intended solely for victorious pursuit, they could scarcely have been convinced.

After several days of rough weather, September 2 brought calm, and Antony's fleet moved out of harbor. While Cleopatra's well-equipped squadron was kept in the rear—to act as a reserve and to prevent desertions—Antony, at the far right of the front line, directly faced the opposing admiral, Agrippa. Each commander hoped to be able to outflank and turn the other in the afternoon, when a northwest wind usually begins to blow in the Ionian Sea.

The wind shifted and battle was joined. As it raged furiously, Antony witnessed a blood-chilling development: suddenly, three of his six squadrons broke off action and started back to harbor. There is little doubt that this was treachery—the loyalty of the men had been undermined in advance by the enemy to whom they were now deserting. To Antony himself, and to Cleopatra in the second line, the withdrawal posed an immediate and disastrous threat. Now Cleopatra's flagship, with its gold-encrusted stern and purple sails, was seen to get up speed and set out for the open sea, followed by the rest of her squadron. Those who hated the queen interpreted this move, then and later, as cowardice and betrayal.

It is more likely, though, that Cleopatra acted in accordance with a plan prearranged with Antony in the eventuality of defeat. In any case he, too, made the fateful decision that flight was now the only course. His flagship was so heavily engaged that its extrication was impossible, but he managed to transfer to another vessel and, followed by forty or more ships of his squadron, joined Cleopatra in the open sea. As they fled southward toward Egypt, the rest of Antony's ships fought on. Leaderless and without hope, they were all eventually destroyed or captured. Within a week, the army, which had watched these disasters from the shore, capitulated.

Meanwhile, hastening from the scene on Cleopatra's flagship, Antony sat in silence and gazed out to sea. His dream of world rule was over, and so was hers.

122

According to Virgil, who was a passionate supporter of the victorious side, the battle had been foretold in mythological times, when the god Vulcan had engraved the principal scenes upon the shield given to Aeneas, the founder of Rome's fortunes:

On one side Augustus Caesar, high up on the poop,
is leading
The Italians into battle, the Senate and the People
with him,
His home-gods and the great gods: two flames
shoot up from his helmet
In jubilant light, and his father's star dawns
over its crest.
Elsewhere in the scene is Agrippa—the gods and
the winds fight for him—
Prominent, leading his column: the naval crown
with its miniature
Ship's beaks, a proud decoration of war, shines on
his head.
On the other side, with barbaric wealth and motley
equipment,
Is Antony, fresh from his triumphs in the East, by
the shores of the Indian
Ocean: Egypt, the powers of the Orient and
uttermost Bactra
Sail with him, also—a shameful thing—his
*Egyptian* wife . . .
Viewing this, Apollo of Actium draws his bow
From aloft: it creates a panic; all the Egyptians, all
The Indians, Arabians and Sabaeans now turn tail.

Although there were, in fact, no Indians in Antony's forces, Virgil and many others saw the battle in terms of the millennial struggle between East and West, with Actium commemorating the resistance of Greece to Persia four and a half centuries before.

The defeated pair did not stop until they came to Egypt. Octavian followed, reaching the outskirts of Alexandria the next summer. In a last desperate attempt to save the city of his queen, Antony resisted Octavian's advance. But in the face of superior numbers, the last of Antony's dwindling troops deserted to the enemy. Returning to the city and hearing a false report of Cleopatra's death, Antony committed suicide. Unopposed, Octavian entered Alexandria, where Cleopatra attempted to

The Emperor Augustus; a Greco-Roman gem.

The triumph of Octavian over Antony represented a victory for the Greco-Roman world over the rulers of the Orient. Two Asiatic prisoners are depicted here on the foot of the sarcophagus of the Pharaoh Horemheb (*c.* 1300 B.C.) The Egyptians, who held a semi-independent status under Rome before Actium, had themselves been conscious of defending their ancient civilization against barbarians from the east.

win him over—as she had so successfully won his great-uncle Caesar, and Antony. But Octavian was not to be wooed, and he actually planned to display his exotic captive in triumph to the Roman crowds. To thwart him and to avoid humiliation, Cleopatra had a snake brought to her and, arrayed in royal robes, put it to her breast. She died of its bite, but in her death there was some victory, for the venom of an asp, according to Egyptian religion, imparted immortality.

Augustan poets generally had no love for Cleopatra, but Horace at least could not withhold his admiration:

In calm deliberate death too proud
To freight Liburnian galleys and be shown
In Triumph, fallen from her throne:
The mockery of a Roman crowd.

And so Egypt fell into the hands of the ruler of Rome. The kingdom founded by Alexander's general Ptolemy had come to its final end, and the last of the great successor kingdoms of Alexander was no more. First Macedonia had gone, then Pergamum (which had become independent of the Seleucid empire of Syria and the east), then the Seleucids themselves, and now, finally, Egypt. For many years past, it is true, Egypt had not been fully independent of Rome. Cleopatra's father, Ptolemy Auletes, was obliged to call for Roman aid to regain the throne from which the Alexandrians had chased him. But Roman aid came high, and one of those who had to be paid, and paid enormous sums, was Julius Caesar. It was principally in order to collect that money that he went to Egypt and fought the Alexandrian War in 48–47 B.C. He also had the enjoyable experience of meeting Cleopatra, whom he established as ruler of the country. Whether he would have allowed her an empire, however, is doubtful. At any rate, he died while she was in Rome, and Cleopatra returned to Egypt declaring that her child

The prow of a Roman warship, showing warriors probably about to disembark. The crocodile symbol of Egypt indicates that this must be a ship that fought at Actium.

Caesarion was Caesar's, though this claim was, and is, disputed.

Later, supported by the love and troops of Antony, she indeed became an empress. Unprecedentedly placing the head of this foreign woman on his coins, Antony described Cleopatra as "Queen of kings and of her sons who are kings." The defeat at Actium brought the whole dream to an end. Despite some interruptions, Egypt had been a united and independent country for the better part of three thousand years. Now it belonged to Rome.

It was a strange empire that Octavian now ruled. Kings were traditionally unpopular in Rome, and the fate of Caesar had shown that dictators were not wanted either. Yet Octavian guessed that the Romans, eager for peaceful order, would be willing to accept autocracy if Republican institutions were revived. In 27 B.C. he solemnly renounced all extraordinary powers and officially transferred the State to the free disposal of the

Three coins of Antony: *Top* his head on an issue of the Greek east; *below left* one of his warships; *below right* the standard of one of his legions; part of a series issued just before the battle of Actium.

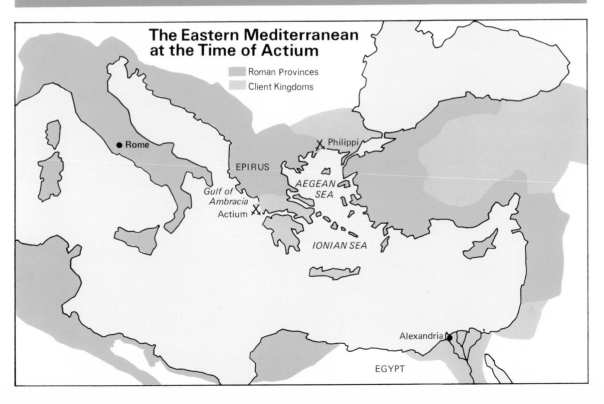

The Eastern Mediterranean at the Time of Actium

Roman Provinces
Client Kingdoms

Rome

Philippi X

EPIRUS

AEGEAN SEA

Gulf of Ambracia

Actium XX

IONIAN SEA

Alexandria

EGYPT

*Right* The Nile in flood; a Greco-Roman mosaic at Praeneste (Palestrina).

*Below* Small Egyptian mosaics, probably from a decorative mosaic in a rich man's house.

Senate and the people of Rome. Nevertheless, he reserved various means of maintaining control. In the huge group that constituted his special provinces—the greater part of Gaul, Spain, and Syria, as well as the whole of Egypt—he ruled, through subordinates, as supreme governor. He also held, for life, the ancient, democratic-sounding power of the Tribunes, the traditional supporters of the common people's rights. He chose to be designated "princeps," took the venerable name Augustus, and induced first the western, and then the eastern, territories to swear an oath of personal allegiance; an oath which meant more to ordinary citizens than the constitutional fictions that soothed the governing class.

The key to empire was the army. After the battle of Actium, the number of legions (including Antony's, which Augustus inherited) amounted to sixty. The maintenance of so many troops was not only extravagant but perilous to authority, so Augustus reduced the legions to twenty-eight—approximately 150,000 men. Nearly all these professionals were Italians or westerners; a further 150,000 auxiliaries were from less civilized parts of the Empire and usually served in their country of origin.

The army was not the only branch of administration that Augustus transformed to cope with imperial complexities. The Senate was reduced from nine hundred to six hundred members, and the consuls—annually elected chief magistrates—took on important new juridical duties. These duties, performed in collaboration with the ruler, gradually eclipsed the existing law courts. Thus, the old governmental and legal systems that Tacitus described as "incapacitated by violence, favoritism—and (most of all) bribery" were at last reformed. Augustus was helped, of course, in maintaining this great new multiracial system by the senators who governed major provinces in accordance with his wishes.

Egypt, however, was in the peculiar position of having as governor not a senator but a knight. The Order of the Knights had risen to wealth as Rome became an imperial power, and yet, being outside the Senate, had hitherto held no governmental power. Under Augustus the Order was reorganized to provide the beginnings of an Imperial Civil Service. Knights were posted as agents or procurators with such financial duties as tax collection. They could become commanders of the Vigiles, a metropolitan police force and fire brigade of seven thousand ex-slaves; they could serve as generals commanding the Praetorian Guard; and they were entrusted with Rome's vital corn supply.

It was perhaps for this last reason that Augustus put knights in control of the immense wealth he had won at Actium. For Egypt, despite a steady political decline, was an enormously rich country, and its main asset was corn. The Ptolemies had organized a centralized economy which ensured that most of the country's resources remained in their own hands. So determined was Augustus

that no one should share the profits he had won that he went to the exceptional length of forbidding any Roman senator to visit Egypt without his permission.

It was not the first time that Rome's financial situation had been transformed by the acquisition of immensely rich territories. Pergamum in western Asia Minor had become a province in 133 B.C., and Syria was won seventy years later by Pompey from the last feeble descendants of Alexander's general Seleucus. Now there was Egypt. Rome itself had become very largely a subsidised city fed from its overseas provinces, and Roman rulers could never for long forget about corn, since their popularity and success depended upon it. Moreover, successive Roman politicians of the previous century had gradually adopted the Hellenistic concept that a great deal of corn must be distributed to the people below the market price—or even free.

Thus Egypt at once became an indispensable bulwark of the Empire. In the centuries that followed, the economic dependence of Rome on supplies from its largest dominions eventually led to the establishment of rival centers of power outside the capital, and there were those who deplored the parasitic condition of the city. Yet, if there were disadvantages to the system, the whole of industry, commerce and communications prospered under Augustus, and the Pax Romana brought new security and freedom of intercourse throughout the Empire. Now for the first time the last bit of Mediterranean shore was under Roman control; to them it had indeed become *Mare Nostrum*, Our Sea.

MICHAEL GRANT

Roman coin issued to commemorate the defeat of Antony and Cleopatra. It is inscribed with the Egyptian crocodile and the words AEGYPT CAPTA—Egypt captured.

*Below* Part of a Roman villa at Utica, in Tunisia.

A few weeks after January 1 in the year 29 B.C. the doors of the temple of Janus in Rome were closed. This traditional act symbolized that the Roman state was at peace. The closing of the doors on this occasion

Temple of Janus

was greeted with more than the usual joy and relief that marked the termination of war. Since the murder of Julius Caesar in the Forum in the year 44 B.C., Rome had been plunged, with little intermission, in civil war. From that long agony the state had finally been delivered by Octavian's victory at Actium and the subsequent deaths of Antony and Cleopatra. The Senate and people of Rome were, in consequence, deeply grateful to the man who had brought them this relief, and they were disposed to accept his leadership.

## Octavian supreme

Octavian knew this and recognized the strength of his present position. But he was also astute

Augustus with the goddess Roma

and cautious, as well as being a statesman profoundly concerned with the future well-being of Rome. He perceived what were the realities of power, and what were its trappings; and he was careful never to confuse the two.

His uncle, Julius Caesar, of a more flamboyant nature than his own, in the moment of his power had offended Republican principles and had fallen beneath the knives of ardent Republicans. The civil war had taken a heavy toll of these Roman oligarchs; but even in the year 29 Rome was still officially, and by a long and revered tradition, a republic. It would be imprudent to disregard the fact.

## Weaknesses of Republican Structure

The civil war, and the struggle between Pompey and Caesar that had preceded it, had revealed the weakness of the Republican constitution. It could not cope with the new power situation that Rome's acquisition of empire had brought. The conquest and control of lands, some of them rich and famous, inevitably meant that the commanders concerned won great fame and acquired immense power. The large armies that they commanded tended to give them personal allegiance. They looked to them for reward rather than to the Senate of distant Rome.

The opportunities afforded by such commands naturally tempted the ambitious. The struggle to obtain them was fierce and expensive. Once obtained, the successful competitor exploited his opportunities to the fullest and sought to extend his term of office. Back in Rome, his enemies prepared for his recall, with accusations of maladministration. And his friends fought to strengthen his position. The perils of such a situation had been demonstrated by the careers of both Pompey and Caesar, and presaged by the earlier struggle between Sulla and Marius. The ambition of Marc Antony, united with that of Cleopatra, had threatened the very sovereignty of Rome itself.

## Transfer of Power

The problem that confronted Octavian after Actium was that of a reconstruction of the state that would preserve the semblance of its traditional Republican form yet obviate its manifest weaknesses by investing the reality of power in himself. This he secured by contriving to have various crucial offices assigned to him by the Senate. At the same time he strove to appear as the champion *par*

*excellence* of the Republic's laws and constitution. Thus in 27 B.C. he dramatically resigned all the offices which he had acquired since 43 B.C. In exchange, the Senate granted him the *imperium* or command over all the armed forces for the next ten years. This also gave him control over those provinces in which armies were located.

## Augustus

The Senate also bestowed on him the title of "Augustus." It is difficult to define the exact meaning of this title, by which Octavian has subsequently become known. According to the historian Dio, it signified "as being something more than human." Suetonius reports that there was also a suggestion that he should take the name of Romulus as the second founder of Rome. But this was rejected because Romulus had been a king and Octavian would never be connected with this office or title. Indeed, Octavian was most careful to use no exceptional title for himself. He preferred to call himself *princeps*, in the sense of being the leading citizen of the state. He also kept the military title of *imperator*, which was justified by his command of the Roman armies. In time, as "Emperor," the title became the peculiar designation of the head of the Roman Empire.

## Social and religious reforms

Augustus set in motion a number of measures designed to restore the social, moral and economic well-being of the state. In particular, by a series of marriage-laws he sought to increase the true Roman stock which, for a variety of reasons, had been steadily dwindling. He tried also to revive the antique Roman

virtues and improve the moral tone of society by reanimating Rome's ancient religion.

Priesthoods, such as those of the *Flamen Dialis* and the *Fratres*

Roman Archigallus; a bas-relief

*Arvales*, were reconstituted. New temples were built, including one to Apollo on the Palatine (a tribute to the Apollo of Actium, believed to have given Augustus the victory), and to Mars Ultor, as the avenger of Caesar's assassination. Augustus himself assumed the title of *Pontifex Maximus* (high or chief priest); the title was inherited by successive emperors and finally adopted by the Pope of Rome. It is generally thought that Virgil and Horace supported Augustus in his religious policy through their poetry. Such measures inevitably have the air of a precious antiquarianism. For, although they were punctiliously performed, the vitality of the ancient rites was now beyond recall.

## Emperor worship

There was, however, a development in the state-religion at this

Rites of Isis, introduced to Rome from Egypt

Jupiter; from a Roman altar

Coin of Augustus Caesar

The Emperor taking leave of his army after a victory

upheavals of the civil war had prepared the way for a certain change of view. Julius Caesar had been deified after his death, and in the year 29 B.C. a temple had been solemnly dedicated in Rome to him as "Divus Julius." In consequence of this deification Octavian as the heir of Julius had received the title of "Divi filius." His later title of Augustus reinforced the tendency to regard him as having more than human status. However, the association of deification and kingship was probably

time which was destined to have important repercussions later, particularly for emergent Christianity. It had long been the custom in the ancient Near East for divine honors to be paid to kings and rulers: e.g. the Egyptian Pharaoh had been worshiped as the incarnate son of the sun-god Rē. Alexander the Great had regarded himself as divine; and many eastern peoples readily agreed to acclaim as a god one of such stupendous genius and success. In turn, the later Hellenistic rulers expected and were accorded divine honors.

## Julius Caesar deified

To Republican Rome such ideas were naturally abhorrent. But the

Temple of Vesta

enough to prevent the veneration paid to him from turning into actual worship in Rome and Italy during his life.

## Divus Augustus

But it was otherwise in the provinces. Temples were dedicated to Roma and Augustus in Pergamum and Nicomedia. In 12 B.C. Drusus consecrated an altar at Lugdunum in Gaul to Roma and Augustus. The association of the genius of the city and the Emperor is significant; for the cult of the two came to constitute a declaration of political loyalty. On September 17, A.D. 14, shortly after his death, the Senate decreed that Augustus should take his place among the gods of the state as "Divus Augustus." His golden image was placed on a couch in the temple of Mars to receive divine honors.

## Architect of the Roman Empire

Augustus has been called the "architect of the Roman Empire," and there is abundant justification for the title. As he is reputed to have said of his building activity: "I found Rome of brick, I leave it of marble," so he might have said: "I found the Roman state a Republican ruin, I leave it a

strong monarchical Empire." Although eschewing the title and trappings of kingship, Augustus had gathered all effective power into his own hands. And, out of the chaos he had inherited, he fashioned the imperial Rome that was to dominate the ancient world for the next four centuries, and the imagination of Europe for long centuries after. But the hands into which such absolute power had been gathered were strong, and the mind which controlled and directed that power was far-seeing and firm.

## The Army's power

However, Augustus could not ensure that he would be succeeded by emperors equally sagacious and strong. Moreover, although he succeeded in controlling the power of the army, the fate of Rome always rested ultimately on the army—not only for its defense against the barbarian peoples beyond its frontiers, but also for its own internal stability and well-being. Thus the future of the Empire, and with it the civilization of the ancient world, depended upon two problematic factors: the ability of the Emperor and the efficient loyalty of the army.

## Decline and fall

The subsequent history of the Roman Empire is that of the operation and interaction of these

two factors. And its main theme is the growing awareness of the army, or those who commanded its most powerful contingents, that they could both make and destroy emperors. The internecine warfare that resulted, punctuated only by short intervals of peace, gradually sapped both the economic and military strength of the Empire.

The collapse was gradual but inevitable. Rome itself was twice sacked by barbarian armies before the resignation of the Emperor Romulus Augustulus in 476 brought the Western Empire to an end. However, the division of the Empire by Constantine, and the

Battle between Romans and Dacians

founding of Constantinople in 330 as the capital of the Eastern Empire, ensured the continuance of the Roman *imperium* in the eastern Mediterranean lands for another thousand years—indeed until the fall of Constantinople to the Ottoman Turks in 1453.

We will now see how the problem of assimilating conquered peoples became too big for Rome, and how a major disaster limited future expansion of the Empire.

# Arminius, Liberator of Germany

*By 9 B.C. it seemed that Augustus' ambition to extend Roman territory to the Elbe had almost been achieved. But the Romans overestimated the extent to which they had successfully assimilated their new province. Encouraged by revolts in the Empire, German aspirations to freedom and prowess in arms both found their champion in Arminius, a German by birth but also a Roman citizen. Arminius' knowledge of the terrain made a German victory a strong possibility, and his annihilation of the legions sent to maintain order shook the Empire to its core. Rome was forced to abandon any idea of a province beyond the Rhine, and the implications for the future of Europe were incalculable.*

A barbarian holds out a child to the Emperor Augustus, symbolizing Roman responsibility for the dominions of the Empire.

Augustus pushed the frontiers of Roman dominion outward in almost every direction. But during the forty-five years of his sole rule he was forced to fight constant and simultaneous campaigns to maintain the lines he wished to draw on the map of Europe. The frontier between the subject province of Gaul and barbarian Germany was to prove especially troublesome, and the whole might of Rome eventually was to be challenged by one barbarian leader, Arminius, of the Cherusci tribe. But Arminius, whom Tacitus called the liberator of Germany, was not the first German to threaten Rome.

Around the end of the second century B.C., two barbarian tribes, the Cimbri and the Teutons, had gradually migrated southward from the neighborhood of Jutland until they reached the northern frontier of Rome. After pushing the Roman armies as far south as Orange, in the Gallo-Roman province of Narbonensis, they proceeded toward Italy itself. They were stopped, however, by one of Rome's outstanding generals, Marius, who defeated them at Aix-en-Provence in 102 B.C. and obliterated them at Vercelli the following year.

Germanic pugnacity engraved itself upon the Roman mind and tongue: a man of ferocious character was called "Cimber," and the "furor Teutonicus" was spoken of long after the tribe had disappeared. Although there was nothing yet approaching a German nation, Rome remained highly conscious of this mass of Germanic peoples in northern Europe. The line of demarcation between the Celts in Gaul and the Germanic tribes to the east was vague, and though the Celts tended to concentrate west of the Rhine, there was still a lot of German blood and influence in that region.

Then in 58 B.C. Julius Caesar entered the picture. The territory of which he was governor included not only the Adriatic coast and what is now north Italy but also the province of Narbonensis. Caesar picked a quarrel with Ariovistus, a German leader influential in Gaul. He then proceeded to annex all Gaul, establishing the Rhine as the frontier between Roman and non-Roman lands. And so Caesar crystallized the idea of a subject Gaul west of the Rhine and a free Germany east.

Half a century later, Augustus gradually pushed Rome's eastern European frontier to the Danube. But a frontier consisting of the Rhine and the Danube made a very long and devious line, including a right angle along their upper courses. An Elbe-Danube line would be a great deal shorter, communications would be easier, and potentially hostile tribesmen would be safely enclosed within the Empire. So Augustus' younger stepson, Drusus, crossed the Rhine to fight four successive campaigns in Germany. He reached the Weser and finally, in 9 B.C., the Elbe. The Romans built fortresses, and the entire area from the Rhine to the Elbe was regarded as a new Roman province.

The Germans were, for the most part, semi-civilized pastoral nomads. Tacitus, in his *Germania*, vividly describes these people with their wild, blue eyes, reddish hair, and hulking bodies—politically unstable tribesmen who loved a fight but disdained work. The Romans hated their new province, "bristling with woods or festering with swamps," but Roman influence gradually seeped in, and modern excavations show that a good deal of trade was conducted.

One Roman governor after another fought laborious campaigns to consolidate the new conquests and frontiers. The greatest weakness lay in the fact that the shorter Elbe-Danube frontier could not be completed until Bohemia (now western Czechoslovakia) was conquered too. This became obvious when an astute German chief, Maroboduus, led his entire Marcomannic tribe on a migration from occupied southwestern Germany into free Bohemia and established authority over the German tribes of Saxony and Silesia. The Roman government decided that it was imperative to put a stop to the expansion of Maroboduus.

The Gemma Augustea, or Vienna Cameo, showing Augustus seated with the goddess Roma; to one side, the victorious Tiberius steps from his chariot. In the lower register, captive Germans are held by the hair, while Roman soldiers erect a trophy of victory.

*Below* A barbarian surrenders his standard to the Emperor Augustus; the reverse of a coin issued by Augustus.

*Left* Part of the reliefs on the Altar of Peace, dedicated by Augustus in 9 B.C. The veiled figure in the center of this section of the relief is probably Augustus' great general Agrippa.

*Right* Varus, who led the disastrous expedition that was destroyed by the German leader, Arminius; from a coin issued in North Africa, at the time when Varus was governor there.

In A.D. 6, therefore, twelve legions were launched in a massive three-pronged invasion under the supreme command of Augustus' elder stepson and heir apparent, Tiberius. But a huge revolt broke out in northern Yugoslavia, putting an end to the campaign against Maroboduus. Nevertheless, the tribal chieftain very sensibly came to terms with Rome and was recognized as a king and friend of the Roman people. Meanwhile, the Yugoslavian revolt, described as Rome's gravest foreign threat since Hannibal, took three years to suppress.

The new province of Germany watched these events with rising excitement. The Romans were not, after all, infallible; they had been compelled to spare Maroboduus. Prolonged resistance to their power was not beyond the bounds of possibility. These were the circumstances when a new Roman governor, Publius Quintilius Varus, reached Germany. Husband of Augustus' grandniece, Varus was among the Emperor's closest friends and had a hard-won reputation for firmness and order. When he arrived in Germany, however, he miscalculated the situation. He regarded the country as already subjugated and believed he could impose civilian methods of control such as were possible in the rich, well-organized provinces he had hitherto governed. The third-century Greek historian Dio Cassius describes the situation:

"The Romans held portions of the country, not entire regions but such districts as happened to have been subdued . . . The soldiers wintered there, and cities were being founded. Gradually the barbarians adapted themselves to Roman ways, getting accustomed to holding markets, and assembling peacefully.

"But they had not forgotten their ancestral ways, their inborn nature, their old proud way of life, their freedom based on arms. As long as they were unlearning their ancient customs gradually and as it were by degrees, they did not protest against these changes in their mode of life, for they were growing different without being aware of it. But when Quintilius Varus was appointed governor of the area and in the course of his official duties attempted to take these people in hand, striving to change them, issuing orders as though they had already been subdued and exacting money as from a subject nation, their patience was exhausted."

Earlier, in A.D. 4, Tiberius, at that time governor of Germany, had given an important West Germanic tribe, the Cherusci, the privileged position of a federated state within the Empire. Members of their ruling class, among them the young prince Arminius, were made Roman citizens. Arminius entered the imperial service as an officer in its auxiliary military forces, gaining the status of a Roman knight.

The Cherusci, whose territory reached almost to the Elbe, played a leading part in the arrangements of Varus. Like his predecessors, Varus proposed to winter on the Rhine and spend the summer at advanced posts far inside the recently conquered province. And so in A.D. 9 he established a summer camp for his three legions (6,000 men each) in Cheruscan territory. Two legions were left behind on the Rhine. His own advance headquarters were on the west bank of the Weser. Varus befriended the Cheruscan chiefs, including Arminius, little realizing that Arminius was even then plotting against him.

Some of the chiefs tried to warn the governor of this impending treachery, but Varus was persuaded to lend the conspirators legionary detachments, which they said they needed to guard certain posts and escort supplies for the Roman army. More-over, when the time came for Varus to withdraw to the Rhine for the winter, the plotters persuaded him to change his route. He had intended to march back to his winter camp at Vetera by the military road, but the fictitious report of a local rising induced him to make a northwesterly detour through difficult wooded country. The conspirators saw the main army off from their summer camp on the Weser. As Varus took his leave, they asked for and received permission to rejoin their tribes—ostensibly to recruit men to help put down the revolt that they had invented.

The Roman column moved slowly. It was encumbered by a heavy baggage train and large numbers of women, children and servants. As it proceeded through the rough country, felling trees and making paths and causeways, a shower of missiles suddenly descended. There could be no doubt of what had happened. The Germans were attacking. The legionaries were hampered by the wind, rain and mud that had always made them dislike Germany. They were too short of auxiliaries—cavalry, archers and slingers—to strike back effectively. All they could do was press on and hope to reach the nearest fortress, Aliso, which lay somewhere on or near the Lippe River, perhaps two-thirds of the way from the Weser back to the Rhine.

Discipline asserted itself sufficiently for a camp to be pitched for the night on high ground. Wagons and baggage were burned or jettisoned and next morning the march was resumed. The legions started off in better order over open country, but this left them vulnerable to German attacks, and they were again compelled to take refuge in the woods, where they spent a most disagreeable day struggling through obstacles. They suffered heavy losses, some of them self-inflicted because of the difficulty of distinguishing enemy from friend. That night they managed to huddle together in another makeshift camp, with a totally inadequate rampart.

When morning came, it was still raining, there was a biting wind and they could see that the Germans had received reinforcements. The commander of the Roman cavalry lost his nerve and rode off with his regiment in the vain hope of reaching the Rhine. Varus was suffering from wounds and fully realized what the Germans would do to him if they caught him alive. To avoid this fate, he killed himself. Some members of his staff followed his example, and the two generals who were left in charge did not long survive. One mistakenly offered capitulation, which turned into a massacre; the other fell fighting as the Germans broke into the encampment. Except for a few legionaries who escaped under cover of darkness, the entire Roman force, some 20,000 men, was either captured or slaughtered.

Six years later another Roman commander in the area, Germanicus, formed the idea—according to his uncle Tiberius a very demoralizing one—of taking his troops to visit the site. The occasion provided Tacitus with one of his highlights:

Sword of honor with decorated scabbard, probably one of many made for presentation to officers who served under Germanicus in A.D. 17. The upper panel of the scabbard (detail *left*) shows Tiberius welcoming Germanicus on his return.

"Now they were near the Teutoburgian Wood, in which the remains of Varus and his three legions were said to be lying unburied. Germanicus conceived a desire to pay his last respects to these men and their general. Every soldier with him was overcome with pity when he thought of his relations and friends—and reflected on the hazards of war and of human life. Caecina was sent ahead to reconnoiter the dark woods and build bridges and causeways on the treacherous surface of the sodden marshland. Then the army made its way over the tragic sites.

"The scene lived up to its horrible associations. Varus' extensive first camp, with its broad extent and headquarters marked out, testified to the whole army's labors. Then a half-ruined breastwork and shallow ditch showed where the last pathetic remnant had gathered. On the open ground were whitening bones, scattered where men had fled, heaped up where they had stood and fought back. Fragments of spears and of horses' limbs lay there —also human heads, fastened to tree-trunks. In groves nearby were the outlandish altars at which the Germans had massacred the Roman colonels and senior company commanders.

"Survivors of the catastrophe, who had escaped from the battle or from captivity, pointed out where the generals had fallen, and where the Eagles were captured. They showed where Varus received his first wound, and where he died by his own unhappy hand. And they told of the platform from which Arminius had spoken, and of his arrogant insults to the Eagles and standards—and of all the gibbets and pits for the prisoners."

Exactly where the Roman army was annihilated is uncertain—though not for lack of attempts to locate the site. Early in the sixteenth century, when

133

the story was becoming celebrated, the Lippischer Wald was renamed the Teutoburger Wald, and a monument to Arminius now stands on the supposed site of the battle.

As had been feared, the triumphant Germans swept on toward the Rhine. All the advance forts to the east of the river, except Aliso, fell without resistance. Aliso's commander and a force of archers succeeded in holding out until their stores were exhausted. Then on a dark night, the garrison slipped out—women, children and all—and managed to make its way to the winter camp at Vetera on the Rhine. There they found the province's two remaining legions, which Varus' nephew Lucius Asprenas had hastily brought north from Mainz.

The disaster upset Augustus more than anything in his long life, and he took every counter measure that he could think of. He dismissed all the Germans and Gauls in his personal bodyguard. Determined efforts were made to replace the lost legions, but few recruits of military age were available. Finally a force consisting mainly of retired soldiers and former slaves (who were not normally admitted to the legions) was entrusted to Tiberius, who had rushed back from Dalmatia. He led them to the Rhine to join the remaining two legions and defend the entire line of the border.

The Germans did not, however, manage to approach the Rhine. Deterred by Asprenas and delayed before the ramparts of Aliso, they lost any chance of mounting a surprise attack. Moreover,

an attempt by Arminius to convert his rebellion into a national German revolt came to nothing. Such a revolt was contingent upon the support of Maroboduus, whom Arminius tried to intimidate in a gruesome manner. His men had come upon some of the Romans cremating the body of Varus in the Teutoburg Forest. They seized what was left of the corpse and mutilated it. They cut off the head and sent it to Maroboduus, appealing to him to join the insurrection. But he saw no advantage in harnessing himself to the ambition of Arminius. It seemed wiser to stand by his treaty with Rome. The head of Varus was forwarded to Augustus, who performed the funeral rites.

Five years later Augustus died. Shortly before his death he sent his brilliant young grandnephew, later called Germanicus, to take command on the Rhine. When Tiberius came to the throne in A.D. 14, Germanicus fought three massive and expensive campaigns against the Cherusci. A longstanding quarrel between Arminius and his pro-Roman father-in-law Segestes flared anew, with Germanicus siding with Segestes. Arminius' wife fell into Roman hands, and although Arminius himself was urged by his brother to collaborate with Rome, he refused. And so a great battle between Arminius and the Romans was fought at Idistaviso, probably near Minden. Germanicus claimed the victory, despite the fact that his legions and auxiliaries had been forced to retreat. But the Germans were far from subjugated.

In A.D. 19 Arminius picked a quarrel with Maroboduus, the German who had snubbed him, and a battle ensued. Although the outcome was indecisive, Maroboduus lost much of his power, and soon afterward his Bohemian kingdom lost its independence. But Arminius' end was also at hand, as Tacitus describes:

"I find from the writings of contemporary senators, that a letter was read in the Roman senate from a chieftain of the Chatti, Adgandestrius by name, offering to kill Arminius if poison were sent him for the job. The reported answer was that Romans take vengeance on their enemies, not by underhand tricks, but by open force of arms.

"However, the Roman evacuation of Germany and the fall of Maroboduus had induced Arminius to aim at kingship. But his freedom-loving compatriots forcibly resisted. The fortunes of the fight fluctuated, but finally Arminius succumbed to treachery from his relations.

"He was unmistakably the liberator of Germany. Challenger of Rome—not in its infancy, like kings and commanders before him, but at the height of its power—he had fought undecided battles, and never lost a war. He had ruled for twelve of his thirty-seven years. To this day the tribes sing of him. Yet Greek historians ignore him, reserving their admiration for Greece. We Romans, too, underestimate him, since in our devotion to antiquity we neglect modern history."

Tacitus was justified in calling Arminius the man who had freed Germany. He was not, however, a national chief. "He was only," wrote one historian, "the leader of a faction even among his tribesmen, not a champion of the German nation, for no such thing existed. The very name was of recent date, an alien appellation; there was among the Germans little consciousness of a common origin, of a common interest none at all."

Still, it was thanks to his extraordinary skill and courage that the Romans were excluded, from then on, from Germany across the Rhine. With the exception of a coastal strip and a tract on the upper Rhine and Danube, the province was abandoned. Rome was forced to recognize that annexation was impossible or inadvisable and to treat trans-Rhenane Germany as a client-state, dependent economically, but nothing more.

Had Arminius not frustrated Augustus in his aim to establish an Elbe-Bohemia-Danube frontier, almost the whole of the present Federal Republic of Germany and the Czech area of Czechoslovakia would have been parts of the Roman Empire. Might-have-beens are notoriously unprofitable, but it is likely that in the end these territories, under Roman rule, would have become as docile and Latinized as Gaul. Any idea of the Rhine as a frontier would have been irrelevant and forgotten. The whole concept of Germany would have been unimaginably different, and so, therefore, would every subsequent century of European history.

MICHAEL GRANT

Triumphal Roman arch at Orange, in southern France, probably built by the Emperor Tiberius to commemorate his suppression of a Gallic revolt.

The slaughter of Varus' legions abruptly halted the northward expansion of Rome's power. It also marked the end of the expansion of the Roman Empire as a whole. The Emperor Trajan was to annex the new province of Dacia at the end of the first century A.D., but the period of giant growth which had taken Rome from being a small city-state in the middle of Italy to her position as mistress of the civilized world was effectively ended. The victory of German arms over the might of the invincible legions was also an augury for the later years of the Empire when Rome employed Germans as top military commanders as her armed strength lost its potency.

The victory of Arminius must have brought home the lesson that consolidation was now the most urgent task facing Augustus. The armies of conquest were henceforth armies of territorial defense, deployed at strategic intervals around the vast periphery of the Empire. Within its frontiers, territories conquered by the sword were turned into provinces of the Empire. The establishment of towns with all the accompanying apparatus of Greco-Roman institutions and civilization meant that within a century the uncouth cousins of Arminius could be as Roman as anyone in Rome itself. Roman citizenship was not available automatically to the inhabitants of a province. It was granted to individuals and urban centers thought worthy of the honor and likely to provide a foundation for the actual Romanization of an

Tombstone of Roman centurion

area. The Romans accepted local distinctions—a man from Syria would still be a Syrian even if he were also a Roman citizen. Local characteristics were not usually suppressed, but they were often dropped in favor of appearing more Roman. At least, they were not suppressed while they offered no threat to the power or basic tenets of Roman rule. The assimilation of a measure of Roman culture, and lip-service to the fact of Roman power, were the two things required of provincials. It was clearly easier in some ways to assimilate primitive barbarian Germans. Once their political and military resistance had been broken, the way lay open to the benefits of civilization. They had no strongly rooted cultural traditions and values of their own to conflict.

## Rome's problems in the East

The problem that the new Empire faced in its southern provinces was of a different order. On the southern fringes of the Mediterranean, civilizations had existed thousands of years before Rome had appeared on the scene, as we have already seen. Rome was no doubt seen by the Greeks and Jews and other people of ancient stock as just another in a long line of conquerors. Alexander had marched about, subduing many people who were in some cases rather more Greek than he was. Then there had been the Carthaginians, and now the Romans. The imposition of Roman power was just another political domination, not the joyous arrival of a chance to be civilized.

The Emperor Trajan

Arminius may not have been a nationalist leader, but his conflict with Rome involved the clash of two distinct political and racial groups. In a sense, Roman civilization was anti-nationalist in that Romanness overrode any national or local identity. It was only specifically anti-nationalist when faced with nationalism that refused to accept the few basic principles of Roman rule and when any group offered a real threat to Roman rule.

## The Jewish people

The Jewish people offered just such a threat. Their religion was decidedly ethnic and exclusive, and rigidly fixed in its orthodoxy. There was no chance that syncretism could accommodate the demands made by official emperor-worship. These very conditions were to bring about the fall of the Temple and the destruction of the Jewish nation, as we shall see. But they were also to determine the development of Christianity, whose dramatic beginning is the subject of our next chapter, for the Christians inherited the Jewish antipathy to emperor-worship, and thus brought upon themselves the fate of martyrs when faced with a test of their loyalty to the Empire.

But for Romans, the life and death of Jesus was not at all significant. In the context of the history of Rome that we have so far explored, Jesus was just another rebellious troublemaker. Thousands of slaves had been crucified in like manner after the revolt of Spartacus. His death was merely one more item in the list of repressions that Rome found necessary to consolidate her power. Let us now look at the background to the emergence of Jesus as a religious leader.

## Herod the Great

Jewish history during the four decades preceding the birth of Jesus of Nazareth is notable for the reign of Herod the Great. Herod was descended from the Idumaeans, an Arab people dwelling to the south of Judaea. They had been forcibly converted to Judaism by the Jewish king John Hyrcanus (134–104 B.C.). Herod's father Antipater had been chief minister of the High Priest Hyrcanus II

German couple; from a tombstone

Jupiter (Zeus): a Greco-Roman plaque

Master and pupils; Roman relief

Mummy shroud from Roman Egypt

(75–40 B.C.); his good relations with the Romans had made him the virtual ruler of Judaea.

Herod was appointed governor of Galilee by his father, and quickly distinguished himself by his efficient and vigorous rule. But he soon needed all his ability to survive the turmoil into which Judaea was plunged in consequence of the Roman civil wars, the attacks of Jewish enemies, a Parthian invasion, and the intrigues of Cleopatra of Egypt. From an amazing series of adventures, which were graphically described by the Jewish historian Josephus, Herod eventually emerged in 31 B.C. as King of the Jews. He enjoyed the friendship of Augustus, who admired his ability and appreciated his usefulness. Since Judaea constituted a vital strategic link in the defense of Syria and Egypt, it was important to the Romans that it should be securely held. Augustus found in Herod a client-king whose loyalty he could trust and whose government would be strong and efficient.

## Herod's Temple

Herod was undoubtedly the most capable king who ever ruled Judaea. He improved its prosperity, rebuilt many of its cities, made a superb seaport at Caesarea, and encouraged trade. His foreign policy greatly benefited the Jews of the Diaspora. He also rebuilt the Temple at Jerusalem on a most magnificent scale—the wonder which it evoked has been preserved in the *Gospel of Mark*.

Yet, for all his achievement, Herod was hated by the Jews for his Idumaean descent and his

pagan tastes. They hated him also for dark tragedies that clouded his domestic life. His suspicious nature caused him to order the deaths of the leading members of the Hasmonaean family, to whom he was related by marriage but whose position he had usurped. Among those who thus died was his wife Mariamne, whom he dearly loved, and their sons—but in these tragedies Herod's sister Salome had played a sinister part.

## Herod's policy

Herod's pagan tastes were really the expression of his Hellenizing policy, which had far-sighted motives. Herod professed the Jewish faith, which he signally patronized by his munificent rebuilding of the Temple. But he

Coin of Herod the Great

knew the innate fanaticism of Judaism, and foresaw the dangers of its ultimate conflict with Rome. He promoted the Greco-Roman

Tombstone of Roman legionary

Egyptian mummy shroud showing the dead person attended by gods

way of life by the building of temples dedicated to Augustus, and theaters, amphitheaters and stadiums. His purpose was probably to acquaint the Jews with this wider culture, without constraining them to adopt it. But it was in vain. When he died in the year 4 B.C. the Jews seemed even more fanatically disposed, encouraged perhaps by their pride in the very Temple which Herod had built for them. They failed to appreciate the fact that Herod's reign had

preserved them for three decades from the grim realities of direct Roman rule. That rule they were soon to experience with baleful consequences. The events of the next few years would ultimately be of significance for the whole world: the Roman Empire, which put to death a religious dissident, would eventually be taken over by the religion that he had founded, as the first chapter in Volume II will show. But first we will look at the beginnings of that religion.

Roman tax-collector

# Jesus of Nazareth, Saviour-God of a New Religion

A.D. **30**

*For Romans alive about A.D. 30 the life and death of Jesus was of no significance whatsoever. In the context of Roman history, Jesus was just another rebellious troublemaker. After the revolt of Spartacus thousands of slaves had been crucified in the same way as Jesus. His death was merely one more item in the list of repressions that Rome found necessary to carry out in order to consolidate her power. And yet in the end the religion founded by Jesus would take over the Roman Empire itself, and eventually make its way all over the world. The consequences for the subsequent history of civilization were incalculable.*

Writing early in the second century, the Roman historian Tacitus told his readers how Nero had been suspected of burning Rome in A.D. 64. To free himself from suspicion, the infamous Emperor "fastened the guilt and inflicted the most exquisite tortures on a class hated for their vices, whom the people called Christians. Christus, from whom the name derived, suffered the extreme penalty during the reign of Tiberius on the order of the procurator Pontius Pilate. The pernicious superstition, suppressed for the moment, broke out again, not only in Judaea, the source of the evil, but in Rome itself . . . Accordingly, acknowledged members of the sect were first arrested; then, upon their evidence, an immense multitude was convicted, not so much of the crime of firing the city, as of hatred of mankind."

This significant passage from the *Annales* of Tacitus shows what an educated Roman knew and thought about Christianity some eighty years after its birth. To him it was a dangerous subversive movement whose founder had been executed for sedition by the Roman governor of Judaea; but that had only temporarily checked the movement, and it had spread from Judaea to the underworld of Rome. Nero had found that the Christians were convenient scapegoats for the fire; for people already believed that Christians hated mankind.

We need not accept as accurate this damning estimate of primitive Christianity. Yet it is important historical evidence because it is the earliest non-Christian source; all our other information comes from Christian writings that were inspired by theological, and not historical, interests. This fact constitutes a fundamental problem for the historian of Christian origins, for it is his task to understand how Christianity began as a historical movement. The Christian Gospels purport to give factual accounts of the life of Jesus; but these writings are based on the assumption that Jesus

was not just a man, but that he was the Son of God, sent by God into this world to save mankind. This assumption involved some very complex theology; it had nothing to do with historical fact.

These theological ideas, nevertheless, are of historical importance, because they form the basis of Christianity—and the birth of Christianity is certainly one of the most important milestones of history. The historian, therefore, must explain how such ideas originated, and trace how they developed into the religion we know as Christianity. But he must also explain who Jesus was, and what he taught and did as an historical person. There have been thinkers who have denied that Jesus ever existed and have regarded him as a mythical figure. This view is no longer held by responsible scholars. But there is much conflict of opinion about what can reasonably be accepted as historical fact about both the person and career of Jesus.

Ironically, the most certain fact that we know about Jesus is that he was crucified by the Romans for sedition against their government in Judaea. The Roman governor who ordered his execution was Pontius Pilate, who held the office of Governor of Judaea from A.D. 26 to 36. We can be certain of this one fact because the Roman execution of Jesus is recorded not only by the Roman historian Tacitus, but also by the authors of the four Gospels, who might have wished to suppress such damaging evidence. That Jesus had been crucified for sedition was indeed an embarrassing fact. For Christians it meant that their master had been regarded as a rebel against Rome, and that they were likely to be incriminated as well.

The early Christians would probably have preferred to keep quiet about the execution of Jesus, but the fact was too well known to conceal. Instead, they attempted to show that Jesus was really innocent of sedition. A large part of each of the four Gospels is devoted to the trial and crucifixion of Jesus. The Gospel of Mark, earliest of the

An inscription, found at Caesarea in 1961, containing the names of the Emperor Tiberius and Pontius Pilate; the latter is designated "Praefectus of Judaea."

*Opposite* The Crucifixion, depicted on a Gnostic gem probably made in the third century A.D. It is one of the earliest representations of the Crucifixion, the Church having at first tended to emphasize the glory of Jesus rather than his shameful death.

Coin of Tiberius, A.D. 14–37, the "tribute penny."

four, sets the theme for the others by endeavoring to show that the death of Jesus had been plotted by Jewish leaders who hated him. These leaders, Mark points out, condemned Jesus to death for blasphemy in their own court, the Sanhedrin; but they lacked the authority to execute him. Consequently, they handed Jesus over to Pilate, charging him with sedition against Rome. Pilate was not convinced by the charge and sought to release Jesus. His efforts, however, were frustrated by the Jewish leaders, who stirred up the mob to demand the crucifixion of Jesus. Pilate was forced to accede and so, at last, ordered the execution. Hence, according to the Gospels, Jesus was really the victim of the malevolence of the Jewish leaders and the weak character of Pontius Pilate.

The most certain fact we know about Jesus thus entails a problem: Christian evidence admits that Jesus was executed for sedition against Rome; but it also maintains that he was innocent. Can this claim be accepted? This question is basic to all understanding of Jesus as an historical person.

If Jesus were really a rebel against the Roman government in Judaea, he would have been very different from the gentle person Christian doctrine holds him to be. But, at the same time, he would be more intelligible historically, for among the Jews of his time there was a fierce hatred of Roman rule. That rule was an affront to their religion since they fervently believed that they were the Elect People of their god Yahweh and

should not be subject to a heathen lord. To them Judaea was Yahweh's holy land, and its produce should not be given in tribute to the Roman Caesar. Many Jews, in fact, refused to submit to Rome and died as martyrs for Israel's freedom. The usual Roman penalty for rebellion was crucifixion. Hence the problem: did Jesus also die as a martyr for Israel's freedom? Or was he obedient to Rome, as the Gospels make out, and was his crucifixion due to the Jewish leaders?

Long and complex research has been devoted to these problems. All we can do here is outline some possible answers.

The Gospel accounts of the trial of Jesus reveal a strong apologetic motivation. The early Christian authors were obviously concerned with transferring the responsibility for the crucifixion of Jesus from the Romans to the Jews. Their purpose in so doing was a result of the situation in which the Christians found themselves after A.D. 70. That year marked the end of a four-year-long Jewish revolt against Rome, and anti-Jewish feeling had grown intense among the Romans. The Gentile Christians, consequently, found themselves in a dangerous and perplexing situation. The Jewish origins of their religion were well known; so, too, was the awkward fact that Jesus had been executed by the Romans as a rebel. To the Roman authorities and people, all Christians were suspected of being sympathetic to Jewish nationalism and to Messianic fanaticism.

The Gospel of Mark deals with this dangerous situation as it affected the Christians of Rome about A.D. 71. But Mark's attempt to turn Pilate into a witness to the innocence of Jesus and make the Jews solely responsible for his death breaks down under critical analysis. This is also the case when the accounts of the trial of Jesus in the other Gospels are examined. We must conclude, therefore, that the Romans crucified Jesus as a rebel because they deemed him to be one.

This conclusion, necessarily summarized here, is confirmed by an abundance of cumulative evidence from various sources.

Something of the career of Jesus as a historical person can be reconstructed from a critical appraisal of the Gospels. A native of Nazareth in Galilee, Jesus was at first associated with John the Baptist. John announced, in the tradition of Hebrew prophecy, the imminence of the kingdom of God and sought to prepare the Jews for this fateful event by a baptism of repentance. Jesus, perhaps after the arrest of John by Herod Antipas, carried on the mission. He achieved a measure of success in Galilee but soon encountered opposition from the Jewish authorities. Jesus then became convinced that it was these authorities who were delaying Israel's preparation for the kingdom of God.

By his followers and by many of the people, Jesus was recognized as the Messiah, God's chosen agent for the redemption of Israel. And he also undoubtedly so regarded himself. At this stage in his ministry, Jesus was probably more concerned with the opposition of the Jewish authorities than

he was with the Romans, for Galilee was then ruled by a Jewish prince, Herod Antipas. Jesus came into direct contact with the Romans only when he visited Jerusalem, which was in Judaea. The Jewish authorities in Galilee, however, were closely associated with the Roman rule of Judaea, for Jerusalem was the religious center for all Jews. The High Priest at Jerusalem was actually appointed by the Roman governor to control "native" affairs and maintain good order among his people. Consequently, both the High Priest and the Sadducean aristocracy, of which he was a member, were suspicious of any popular movement likely to disturb the peace. And the movement led by Jesus appeared to be just such a disturbance.

The priestly aristocracy, headed by the High Priest, controlled the Temple of Yahweh at Jerusalem; their position gave them great authority as well as a rich income. Seeing them as the chief obstacle to Israel's conversion, Jesus finally decided to challenge their control of the Temple. Accordingly, with his disciples and Galilean followers he staged a Messianic entry into Jerusalem at the feast of the Passover. Gathering support, he attacked the trading activities of the Temple. These activities were a profitable source of revenue to the priestly aristocrats, and Jesus' attack was obviously a far more serious affair than the Gospels represent it to have been. It is even possible that Jesus intended to seize the Temple and reform the priesthood, as the Zealots were later to do in A.D. 66. The outcome of

Jesus' bold move is difficult to assess. It would seem that he did not achieve complete success; but his supporters remained too numerous for the Jewish leaders to arrest him publicly.

After this so-called "Cleansing of the Temple," Jesus stayed on in Jerusalem, although he withdrew from the city each night. He seems to have been uncertain of his next move. The question that the historian must now face is whether the action of Jesus in the Temple had been connected with a Zealot operation. We learn from the Gospels that at this Passover there had also been an armed rising against the Romans, apparently led by Barabbas, which seems to have involved the Zealots. That two uprisings, one against the Jewish authorities and one against the Romans, should have occurred in Jerusalem at the Passover is certainly remarkable. The coincidence suggests that there may have been some connection between the two events.

Jesus continued his stay in Jerusalem until the night of the Passover feast, which he ate with his disciples within the city. By then he probably realized that his attempt to challenge the authorities had failed and that it would be wiser to withdraw to Galilee.

Christian tradition records that, in Gethsemane that night, Jesus experienced an agony of indecision. However, the initiative suddenly passed from him to his enemies. One of his apostles, Judas Iskariot, had defected and betrayed his rendezvous to the

*Above* Ivory plaque showing scenes of the arrest and trial of Jesus; from a reliquary of the fourth century A.D.

*Below* The crypt of the Convent of the Sisters of Zion on the site of King Herod's Antonia Fortress, which was probably the site of Jesus' trial.

## The Earliest Churches

Rome
Ephesus
Athenae
Damascus
Cyrene Hierosolyma (Jerusalem)
Alexandria

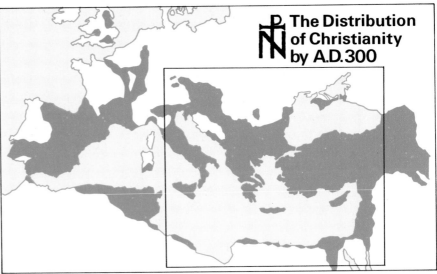

## The Distribution of Christianity by A.D.300

*Below* Pagan caricature of a crucifixion, from a wall of the Palatine Palace, probably dating from the third century A.D. It shows a slave (?) praying to a crucified figure with an ass' head, and the inscription reads "Alexemenus worships his god."

Jewish leaders. Taking no chances, they sent a heavily armed band to arrest Jesus. After an armed struggle in the darkness, the disciples fled and Jesus was taken. During the rest of that night the Jewish authorities interrogated him about his aims and his disciples, so that they could draw up a charge preparatory to handing him over to the Romans. In so doing, the High Priest was discharging his duty to the Roman government.

The High Priest charged Jesus with sedition, particularly for his claim to be the Messianic King of Israel. It is possible that he also accused Jesus of being the real leader of the recent rising against the Romans, thus exonerating Barabbas who was under Roman arrest. In other words, it is likely that Jesus was charged with heading a two-pronged attack: on the Jewish authorities in the Temple, and on the Romans in the Antonia Fortress and Upper City. What is certain is that Pilate condemned Jesus. The *titulus* which he ordered to be placed on the cross above the crucified Jesus, is evidence of the political nature of the charge: "This is Jesus the King of the Jews."

The crucifixion of Jesus as a rebel by the Romans was not an extraordinary event in the light of contemporary Jewish history. Thousands of other Jews similarly perished, either as leaders or supporters of revolt. But from this point onwards Christian tradition makes even more problematic the search for historical fact about Jesus. It was the usual practice for the bodies of executed criminals to be buried in a common grave. According to the Gospels, this did not happen to the body of Jesus. Instead, a disciple named Joseph of Arimathaea obtained the body from Pilate and buried it in a rock-hewn tomb of his own. Three days later, the tomb was found to be empty. Subsequently a series of visions, in which the crucified Jesus appeared to various disciples, convinced his followers that Jesus had risen from the dead. The visions were, significantly, limited to the disciples of Jesus; no one outside their fellowship is recorded

to have had a similar experience. According to Christian tradition, these appearances of the Risen Jesus continued for forty days.

It is difficult to evaluate these traditions of the Resurrection of Jesus. Although the physical reality of the Risen Jesus is stressed, it is never asserted that he resumed his life on earth; instead he is said to have ascended to heaven. But, whatever the truth of the traditions about the Risen Jesus, there can be no doubt that from the disciples' faith in it, Christianity was born.

When the original disciples of Jesus became convinced that he had risen from the dead, their faith in his Messiahship revived. But, in the light of their new conviction, they had to adjust their own Jewish ideas. According to contemporary belief, the Messiah would overthrow the nation's oppressors and "restore the kingdom of Israel." But Jesus had been executed by Israel's oppressors: how could he, then, be the Messiah? The disciples soon found a solution in Holy Scripture. The prophet Isaiah had spoken about a suffering Servant of Yahweh, and the disciples applied this prophecy to Jesus. Because of Israel's sins, Jesus had died as a martyr; but God had raised him up. He would soon return, with supernatural power, to fulfill his Messianic role and redeem Israel.

So the Christianity of the original disciples was essentially a Jewish faith. They probably never contemplated that it would lead to a new religion distinct and separate from Judaism.

The transformation of Christianity from a Jewish Messianic sect into a universal salvation-religion, centered on Jesus, was due to Paul of Tarsus. Paul had not been an original disciple of Jesus. In fact, he had at first fiercely rejected Jewish Christianity because it preached a "crucified Messiah"—a scandalous thing to a pious Jew— and helped persecute members of the movement. Suddenly, however, Paul had a profound spiritual experience, which he attributed to the intervention of God. He became convinced that God had chosen him to reveal Jesus to the Gentiles, in a completely different guise from the one presented by the Jewish Christians. The Jewish Christians, in fact, had not even considered their faith in Jesus as being applicable to non-Jews.

Paul's new conception of Jesus drew its inspiration from Hellenistic ideas rather than from Judaism. The Gnostic philosophy, which was widely followed in Syria and Alexandria and farther east, held that all mankind was enslaved by demonic powers and taught how Gnosticism could save men from their subjection to the demonic vein, taught that God had sent Jesus into the world to save men from their subjection to the demonic rulers of the planets.

It was a very esoteric doctrine but one that Greco-Roman society of that time could understand and appreciate. Jesus was presented by Paul as a savior-god, who had died and risen again. Through the sacrament of baptism, Christians were ritually identified with Jesus in his death and

resurrection. In consequence, they were reborn to a new risen life *in Christo*.

Paul's new "gospel" was repudiated by the Jewish Christians of Jerusalem. They also rejected his claim to be an apostle, and sent out emissaries to his converts to present their own "gospel" as the true and original form of Christianity. Paul's teaching might easily have been finally discredited and lost, but in A.D. 70 the Mother Church of Christianity at Jerusalem itself perished in the destruction of the city by the Romans. Christianity was thus freed from its primitive involvement with Judaism and Paul's version of Christianity survived and set the pattern for the entire faith.

Before the destruction of Jerusalem, Christianity had already spread outside Palestine. It moved mainly northwestwards, through Syria and Asia Minor, to Greece and Italy, although it was also established at an early date in Egypt. Freed from its Jewish cradle, Christianity quickly adapted itself to the spiritual needs of Greco-Roman society and eventually even survived the downfall of the Roman Empire in the West. The subsequent conversion of the barbarian peoples, who were to form the new nations of Europe, gave the Christian Church immense influence and power. The civilization of medieval Europe was, indeed, essentially the product of Christianity, and the later predominance and diffusion of the European peoples throughout the world made Christianity a cultural force of universal influence.

The Christian system of chronology still proclaims, even in a secular world, the decisive nature of the birth of Jesus—though ironically, it sets the event at least four years too late. By the sixth century, Christians regarded the birth of Jesus as so significant a turning point in world history that they reckoned time from it—the *Anni Domini* (A.D.), the "years of the Lord," that continue to designate our present era.

S. G. F. BRANDON

Houses and churches made by early Christians in the caves of Goreme, in Turkey, with (*left*) the interior of one of the churches.

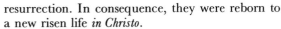

143

# Revolt in the East leads to the destructior

Herod the Great died in the spring of 4 B.C.; his death sparked off an explosion of the long pent-up feelings of his Jewish subjects. Revolts immediately broke out in different parts of the country under various leaders. The situation was made worse by a Roman procurator, Sabinus, who moved in with troops to secure Herod's very considerable property for the Emperor Augustus. At Jerusalem, crowded with pilgrims for the feast of the Passover, armed conflict soon broke out. The Romans were ordered to withdraw by the rebels, "and not to stand in the way of men who after a lapse of time were on the road to recovering their national independence."

This statement of Jewish aims, which is recorded by the Jewish historian Josephus, is significant. It embodied an ideal, inspired by traditions of the heroic days of David and the Maccabees, which was rooted in the peculiar nature of Jewish religion. Every Jew was brought up to believe—and the belief was reinforced daily by the study and practice of the Torah—that Yahweh, the god of Israel, had given his people the land of Canaan as their Holy Land, where they were faithfully to serve him. This belief implied a conception of the state as a theocracy; Yahweh owned it and was its sovereign lord, and his vice-regent on earth was the high priest. This conception in turn implied the freedom of the Jewish people to devote themselves to the maintenance of this theocracy.

## Judaea under Roman rule

The Jewish revolt, which was apparently uncoordinated, was eventually suppressed by Varus, the Roman governor of Syria, who

Roman soldiers; an oil lamp

Terracotta impression of 10th legion

intervened with two legions and ruthlessly crushed the rebels, two thousand of whom he crucified. What was to be the future government of Herod's kingdom was decided by Augustus, the Roman Emperor. He seems not to have regarded any of Herod's sons as being capable of succeeding their father in the sole rule of the kingdom. Consequently, he divided it: one son, Archelaus, was appointed ethnarch of Judaea and Samaria; another, Herod Antipas became tetrarch of Galilee; a third son, Philip, received other territories outside Palestine proper, also with the title of tetrarch. So far as Judaea and Samaria were concerned, this arrangement lasted only till A.D. 6. Archelaus, having proved an incompetent ruler, was deposed, and Augustus put his ethnarchy under Roman rule.

## The Prefect and the High Priest

To implement the decision, a Roman governor—called praefect or procurator—was appointed.

Under the new order, the Jewish High Priest was recognized by the Romans as the head and representative of the Jewish people. He was given control of domestic affairs and jurisdiction over his people in matters relating to Jewish law. The Jewish priestly aristocracy, since it was not popular with the people, naturally tended to be pro-Roman in its attitude. The maintenance of Roman rule guaranteed the continuation of its own favored position in the Jewish state.

## Roman tribute

One of the first actions taken by the Romans on incorporating Judaea into their Empire was to order a census for the purpose of assessing tribute. The Jews had been accustomed to pay tribute to Herod. They hated Herod; but he was a Jewish king, and their tribute went to the maintenance of a Jewish state. But the imposition of Roman tribute was another mat-

ter; it gravely affected their religious principles.

The fact that it did so was immediately made clear by a rabbi, Judas of Galilee, who was backed by Sadduq, a Pharisee. Judas told his fellow-countrymen that the payment of tribute to Rome would be an act of apostasy towards Yahweh. Obedient to Judas' exhortation and despite the contrary advice of Joazar, the High Priest, that they should submit to the tribute, many Jews rose in revolt. They were rigorously put down by the Romans, and Judas of Galilee and many others perished.

However, the teaching and example of Judas were not forgotten. Many of his followers took to the deserts of Judaea, to wage guerrilla warfare against the Romans. The members of this "resistance" movement, which was led by the sons of Judas of Galilee, were called Zealots, because of their zeal for the cause of Yahweh.

## Pontius Pilate

This unpropitious start to Roman rule in Judaea was followed by some twenty years of internal peace. This conclusion is drawn from the fact that Josephus mentions nothing during the period. Perhaps the ruthless suppression of the revolt in A.D. 6 had cowed the Jews. Whatever the cause, trouble started again in 26 when Pontius Pilate was appointed as governor.

Since the public ministry of Jesus and his crucifixion took place during Pilate's term of office (26–36), interest in the happenings of these years is naturally very great. Pilate's involvement with Jesus has already been discussed in the preceding chapter; attention, therefore, can here be given to other aspects of Pilate's government.

For Pilate's career we are completely dependent on the accounts of Josephus given in his *Jewish War* and *Jewish Antiquities*, and on a tractate written by Philo of Alexandria. The accounts of Josephus are intrinsically problematic, because out of the ten years of Pilate's term of office only three events are narrated. Philo's account also raises difficulties, since the incident which he describes is not mentioned by Josephus.

## Affair of the Standards

Josephus begins his account of Pilate with an incident that must have happened shortly after his arrival in Judaea. It had apparently been the custom of previous governors, out of deference to Jewish religious scruples concerning graven images, to arrange for troops on garrison duty at Jerusalem to remove the effigies of Roman gods from their standards before entering the holy city. Pilate canceled this arrangement. When the Jews of Jerusalem saw the images displayed on the

A defeated opponent submits to the Emperor; from the Arch of Constantine

# f Jerusalem and the scattering of its people

Jewish sarcophagus

standards, they were horrified. According to Josephus, they flocked in crowds to Caesarea, to beseech Pilate to countermand the order. Pilate was obdurate, and tried to frighten them into submission. Faced with their readiness to die for their religion, he at last relented. Josephus claims that Pilate was acting on his own malevolent decision in this matter. There is, however, much reason to think that the governor was obeying orders from Rome.

## The Aqueduct

The next clash, recorded by Josephus, occurred over the building of an aqueduct. Jerusalem needed more water, so Pilate had the aqueduct built and defrayed the cost from the Temple treasury. Since this money was sacrosanct, there was a great uproar, which Pilate suppressed with heavy Jewish casualties.

## The Gilded Shield

The incident related by Philo is curiously similar to that of the standards. This time Pilate placed some gilded shields, dedicated to the Emperor Tiberius, on the Herodian palace in Jerusalem, which the Romans used as their headquarters. The Jews immediately objected. Their reason is obscure. Since the shields bore no images, their offense probably lay in the inscription, which might have mentioned the divinity of the Emperor. After a fierce altercation and a Jewish appeal to Rome, Tiberius ordered the shields to be removed to the Temple of Augustus in Caesarea.

## Pilate and the Samaritans

According to Josephus, Pilate's career as governor was terminated by his savage action against the Samaritans. These people, whom the Jews regarded as heretics, met in arms at their sacred Mount Gerizim, stirred up by some Messianic prophet. Pilate, fearing a revolt, promptly intervened with force, and heavy Samaritan casualties resulted. The Samaritan leaders complained to Vitellius, the legate of Syria, who ordered Pilate to Rome for trial. However, before he reached there, Tiberius had died, and Pilate passes out of history into Christian legend.

These accounts of Pilate's relations with the Jews, even allowing for the manifest distortions of Josephus and Philo, are significant. They reveal the basic impossibility of the Jews living ever peaceably under Roman rule. Quite apart from Roman harshness, which many other peoples also resented, Jewish religion made submission intolerable.

## Caligula's threat

Jewish suspicions concerning Roman intentions against their religion were not, however, groundless. In A.D. 39 their worst fears were realized. The Emperor Caligula, who was probably mad, believed passionately in his own divinity. Knowing this, the gentile inhabitants of the Jewish city of Jamnia erected an altar to him, for the purpose of offering sacrifice to his divinity. The altar was promptly destroyed by the Jewish inhabitants. Caligula, enraged by

this affront to his divinity, ordered Petronius, the legate of Syria, to prepare a colossal gilt image of himself, in the guise of Zeus, for erection in the Temple at Jerusalem. The Jews were horrified at the projected sacrilege. Petronius procrastinated, fearing that the attempt to set up the statue in the Temple would be met by a fanatical revolt of the whole people. The situation was approaching a crisis when Caligula was murdered in Rome.

Coin of Caligula (obverse)

Roman standards; coin of Caligula

The Temple seemed thus to have been miraculously saved from most awful desecration—a desecration which paralleled that of the "Abomination of Desolation" erected by Antiochus Epiphanes in 167 B.C. The Jews were profoundly thankful for their deliverance. But the threat from which they had so narrowly escaped remained to haunt them with the fear that it might be renewed by another emperor.

## King Agrippa

After the death of Caligula, independence under a Jewish king unexpectedly came to Israel. This sudden change of fortune was due to the gratitude felt by the new Emperor Claudius towards the

The Emperor Claudius

Jewish prince Agrippa, who had helped him to secure the imperial throne. As a reward, Claudius appointed Agrippa King of the Jews. Although he was of Herodian descent, being a grandson of Herod the Great, Agrippa was a pious Jew. His devotion to Judaism won him the approval of his subjects. However, this happy situation lasted only four years, for Agrippa died in the year 44.

Agrippa's death was a bitter blow to the Jews. For Claudius, passing over Agrippa's son on account of his youth, placed Judaea back again under direct Roman rule. The brief interlude of national independence seems to have made the re-imposition of Roman rule even more intolerable. The revolt and fatal consequences form the subject of our last chapter.

The Ark of the Covenant; synagogue relief

Menorah from Jewish stone sarcophagus

# Destruction of Zion

*After the death of King Agrippa in A.D. 44, Judaea returned to direct Roman rule, and from that moment Jewish history seemed to take on an air of inevitability. According to orthodox Jewish belief the Holy Land belonged to God and God alone. The presence of a Roman Governor in Jerusalem was in itself an affront to God, and to pay tribute to the Emperor was to give to a non-believer what was God's by right. Tension and disorder steadily increased, stimulated by Roman maladministration, Messianic excitement and nationalist activity. The fatal explosion finally came in A.D. 66. With the resulting loss of their land and the Temple at Jerusalem, the Jews' religion ceased to be a religion that demanded the ritual of sacrifice and the people themselves were scattered abroad without a national home until the present century.*

Reverse of a coin of Vespasian, issued in A.D. 70 to commemorate the capture of Jerusalem. It is inscribed JUDAEA CAPTA, and shows a Jewish prisoner and the symbolic mourning figure of Judaea.

*Opposite top* General view of Jerusalem.
*Below* Jewish ossuary of first century A.D. with inscriptions in Greek. The practice of placing bones in ossuaries was against Jewish tradition, but around Jerusalem at this time it was used fairly widely.

In the summer of the year 66 the priests of the great Temple of Yahweh in Jerusalem refused to offer their customary daily sacrifices for the well-being of the Roman Emperor and people. These sacrifices were an accepted token of Israel's loyalty to Rome, and a refusal to continue making them was tantamount to a declaration of revolt. The priests concerned were members of the lower order of the Temple clergy, who subscribed to Zealotism. For sixty years or more, the Zealots had formed the "resistance" against the Romans in Judaea, and their ideas were shared by many other Jews who were not active members of their party.

Behind this refusal of the lower priests lay a complex situation. The higher clergy, who formed a priestly aristocracy, were presided over by the High Priest. This aristocracy supported the Roman government of Judaea because it ensured their own social and economic position; the maintenance of the "loyal" sacrifices was essential to good relations with the Romans. But the policy and attitude of these priestly aristocrats made them unpopular with the people and particularly with the lower clergy, who longed for the freedom of Israel. To control the members of the lower clergy, the High Priest had reduced or cut off their stipends. The fateful refusal to offer the sacrifices, however, was only taken when Eleazar, a young aristocrat and captain of the Temple, defected to the lower clergy. Eleazar's defection provided the malcontents with an able and vigorous leader, and it was he who persuaded them to revolt.

Fighting quickly broke out in Jerusalem. The High Priest and his party, reinforced by troops sent by the Jewish prince Agrippa II, sought to gain control of the Temple. They were fiercely opposed by the lower priests, who were joined by the *Sicarii*, the extreme action group of the Zealots. Meanwhile, Menahem, the surviving son of Judas of Galilee and now leader of the Zealots, had suddenly attacked and destroyed the Roman garrison at Masada, the great fortress by the Dead Sea. Equipping his followers from the armory there, Menahem quickly made his way to Jerusalem and at once took charge of the revolt. The forces of the High Priest and Agrippa were soon defeated, and many of the priestly aristocrats were murdered.

Menahem seems to have assumed royal powers, probably as the Messiah-King, but his reign was short. Eleazar, doubtless jealous of the new leader who had assumed command of the revolt that he had started, plotted to have him murdered in the Temple. Some of Menahem's followers, including a relative named Eleazar ben Jair, managed to escape the ensuing massacre and withdraw to Masada.

The death of Menahem left the revolt leaderless. He had been dynastic head of the Zealot movement and had been at once accepted as the charismatic leader of Israel's revolt against Rome. None of the other leaders of Zealot bands or rebel groups had the prestige or authority needed to command a national revolt. However, the Jews were committed to rebellion, and they continued to wipe out surviving Roman garrisons in Jerusalem and elsewhere. In retaliation the Gentile inhabitants of Caesarea, the Roman headquarters, rose against the Jews and slaughtered twenty thousand of them, according to the Jewish historian Josephus. This massacre provoked Jewish reprisals against many Gentile cities in Palestine and in Gaulanitis, east of the Sea of Galilee. In turn, Jews living as far afield as Syria and Egypt had to pay the penalty for their compatriots' actions.

The procurator of Judaea, Florus, seems to have done nothing effective to maintain Roman authority during the initial stages of the revolt. Josephus claims that Florus actually welcomed the revolt as an opportunity to cover up his own maladministration, which had far exceeded that of any previous governor. Whether or not that was

*Above* Sixth-century mosaic of Jerusalem from Madaba, south of Amman.
The Romans had rebuilt Jerusalem in A.D. 130, calling it Aelia Capitolina.

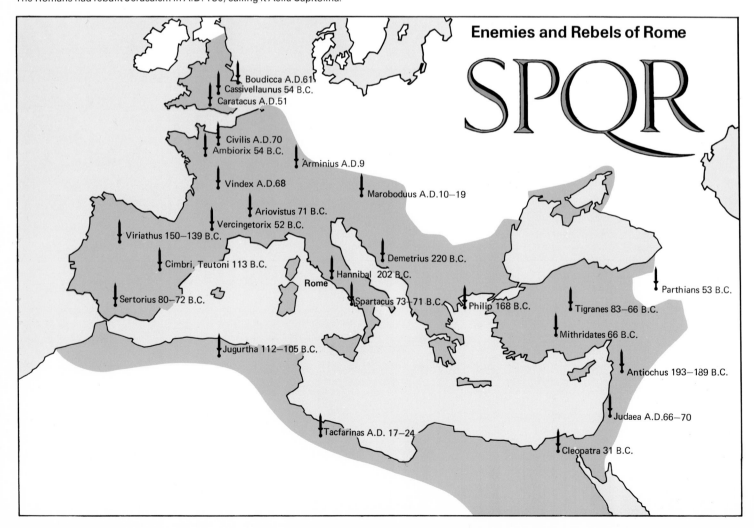

**Enemies and Rebels of Rome**

**SPQR**

Boudicca A.D.61
Cassivellaunus 54 B.C.
Caratacus A.D.51
Civilis A.D.70
Ambiorix 54 B.C.
Arminius A.D.9
Vindex A.D.68
Maroboduus A.D.10—19
Ariovistus 71 B.C.
Vercingetorix 52 B.C.
Viriathus 150—139 B.C.
Demetrius 220 B.C.
Cimbri, Teutoni 113 B.C.
Hannibal 202 B.C.
**Rome**
Parthians 53 B.C.
Sertorius 80—72 B.C.
Spartacus 73—71 B.C.
Philip 168 B.C.
Tigranes 83—66 B.C.
Mithridates 66 B.C.
Jugurtha 112—105 B.C.
Antiochus 193—189 B.C.
Judaea A.D.66—70
Tacfarinas A.D. 17—24
Cleopatra 31 B.C.

the reason for Florus' initial inaction, the situation in Judaea rapidly grew beyond his military resources to cope with it. It was now the duty of the legate of Syria, Florus' superior in the administration of the Roman Empire, to intervene and restore Roman sovereignty.

The Syrian legate, Cestius Gallus, took some three months to assemble his forces for the punitive expedition. His army consisted of one full-strength legion, the twelfth, with other specially selected legionary reinforcements, six cohorts of other infantry, four squadrons of cavalry and some fourteen thousand auxiliary troops. It was a formidable force, well calculated to deal with the disorganized and untrained Jewish rebels.

Entering the country from the north, the Roman army swept aside whatever opposition the rebels had managed to organize in the countryside and laid siege to Jerusalem itself. They soon penetrated the city's fortifications and made preparations for the final assault on the Temple walls. Occupying a commanding position superbly reinforced by massive walls, the Temple constituted the key-point in the defense of Jerusalem. It was, moreover, the most sacred spot in the Holy Land, and all Jews could be expected to fight fanatically in its defense.

The Jews did, indeed, fight with fanatical courage, but they were no match for Roman military science and professional discipline. They were actually beginning to despair of the outcome of the contest, when Cestius Gallus suddenly and unaccountably ordered the operation to stop and withdrew his troops to neighboring Mount Scopus. The next day the Jews saw the Roman army retiring northwards, evidently breaking off the siege. At first they feared a ruse, but when they realized that the Romans were indeed retreating, their joy and exultation knew no bounds—here truly was proof of the succor of Yahweh, their god. In his honor they had challenged the might of Imperial Rome, and, at the eleventh hour, he had miraculously intervened and put their dreaded foe to flight. The Jews quickly pursued the retreating Romans and caught them as they descended the narrow Beth-horon pass. Only by sacrificing his rearguard and abandoning his heavy equipment was Cestius Gallus able to extricate his forces and struggle back to safety in Syria.

Thus ended the first armed encounter between puny Israel and mighty Rome. The Jewish rebels had trusted to their god and not to their military resources; matched with Rome, their cause was hopeless. But they had won, defeating a legionary army. The very site of their victory, the Beth-horon pass, was portentous—there Joshua had defeated the Amorites, and Judas Maccabaeus had triumphed over the Seleucid army under Seron. Yahweh was the god of battles: he had given victory to their ancestors fighting against enormous odds, and so had he given victory to them. In the face of what appeared to be such a marvelous demonstration of divine approbation, even the cautious and hesitant were won over to a whole-hearted commitment to this struggle for Israel's freedom. Coins were specially struck, expressive of their exultation and faith. They bore inscriptions: "Jerusalem the Holy;" "Deliverance of Zion;" "Redemption of Zion."

The defeat of Cestius Gallus was a serious blow to the Romans, both to their prestige and to their imperial ambitions. Judaea was a vital link in the defense of their Near Eastern provinces and Egypt. There was, moreover, a large Jewish population in Mesopotamia that might rise in sympathy. And Rome's traditional enemies, the Parthians, were always ready to invade at a sign of Roman weakness. The Emperor Nero, whatever his other failings, made a wise choice of commander to restore Rome's dominion over rebel Judaea. He appointed Vespasian, a veteran who had proved his ability in hard campaigning in southwestern Britain. No chances could be taken next time, and Vespasian set about preparing a powerful army of three legions and a strong auxiliary force.

The exact situation in Jerusalem at this time is difficult to determine, because of the historian Josephus' apologetic concern about his own dubious part in the events that he describes. He is our chief source of information, but he is often elusive and obscure about matters in which he was personally involved. From the accounts, sometimes conflicting, in his *Jewish War* and in his *Autobiography*, it would seem that a moderate party endeavored to gain control in Jerusalem and co-ordinate the nation's forces for the greater struggle with Rome that was sure to come. Josephus claims

(1) Bronze coin of Agrippa, A.D. 50–100. (2) Shekel of Bar-Kokhba, A.D. 133. (3) Antioch assarion of Tiberius, A.D. 14–37. (4) Bronze coin of Herod the Great, 37–4 B.C. (5) Shekel of the first Jewish revolt, A.D. 66–70. (6) Dilepton of Mattathias Antigonus, 40–37 B.C.

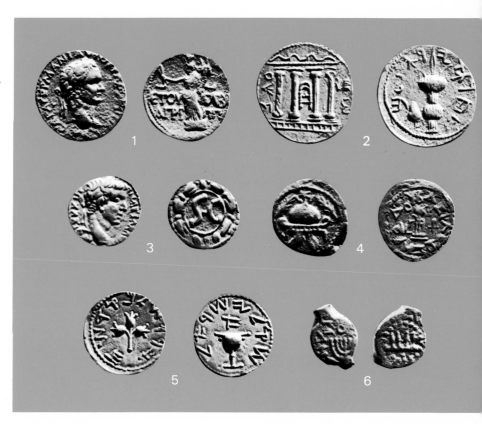

Roman civilization was well established in Palestine and the Middle East before the revolt of the Zealots. Great public buildings included the temple at Sebaste.

that he was appointed general in Galilee, to fortify its cities against a probable Roman advance from Syria, and he tells how assiduous and ingenious he was in carrying out his task. He also discourses at length on the iniquities of various rebel bands, and particularly on one of the Zealot leaders, John of Gischala. But, as the sequel suggests, there was undoubtedly another side of the story, and it is probable that John already suspected Josephus' loyalty to the Jewish cause.

By the spring of 67 Vespasian was ready to begin his campaign. But the new Roman commander was confronted with a very different situation from that which had faced Cestius Gallus the previous autumn. His route to the insurgent capital was now blocked by a number of fortified towns, which had first to be reduced before he could venture into the barren hills of Judaea for the final siege of Jerusalem. This was a difficult, protracted task, for it meant a succession of sieges of strongly held places. Unable to oppose the Roman legionaries successfully in the open field, the Jews nevertheless excelled at fighting among fortifications; in such operations their fanatical courage and individual resourcefulness matched the discipline and military science of the Romans. But it was a mode of warfare that took a terrible toll of life: not only was the defeated garrison eventually wiped out, but the inhabitants were generally massacred by the Romans, exasperated by long resistance and their own heavy losses.

During the campaign of 67, Vespasian captured a number of Judaean towns. Josephus gives a long account of the siege of one of them, Jotapata, where he was the Jewish commander. To escape death after the final assault on the town, Josephus surrendered to the Romans. Brought before Vespasian, he assumed the role of prophet and foretold that Vespasian would become Emperor of Rome. Whether Vespasian believed this audacious prophecy, we have no means of knowing other than from Josephus' own account. But he kept Josephus a prisoner at his own headquarters instead of sending him to Rome as he had first intended. In 68 Nero died, and from a resulting civil war Vespasian emerged in 69 as Emperor. Josephus' fortune was made. He first served as a liaison-officer on the staff of Titus, Vespasian's son and successor as commander in Judaea. After the successful siege of Jerusalem, Josephus returned to Rome with his imperial patrons and there he wrote his *Jewish Wars* to commemorate their victory over his own people.

The Roman reduction of Galilee seems to have resulted in an internecine struggle for leadership among the insurgents in Jerusalem. Josephus' account of it was inspired by apologetic motives; but it would appear that the moderate party, led by Ananus, a former High Priest, gradually lost control as Zealot groups from Galilee congregated at Jerusalem. The arrival in Jerusalem of John of Gischala gave the Zealots a

Aerial view from the south of the rock of Masada, the last stronghold of the Zealots. In the distance is the Dead Sea.

capable leader and, supported by a strong body of Idumaean rebels, they finally overwhelmed the moderates, and killed Ananus and other leading figures. The Zealots now had complete control of the Temple, and it is significant that they proceeded to elect a new High Priest by the ancient custom of drawing lots—doubtless an attempt to end the monopoly of the office long exercised by the priestly aristocracy. The Zealots also burned the public archives, containing the money-lender's bonds, an action taken, according to Josephus, to encourage the poor to rise against the rich.

The Roman campaign of 68 was devoted to reducing insurgent centers outside Jerusalem. It was probably during the operations in the area of Jericho that the monastic settlement of Qumran was destroyed. The members of the community had anticipated the attack by hiding their sacred scriptures in adjacent caves, where they remained forgotten until their chance discovery in 1947 and their subsequent fame as the Dead Sea Scrolls.

When Vespasian was elected Emperor, the campaign of 68 ended. It became necessary for him to leave Palestine, with a considerable force, to make good his title at Rome. As fighting ceased, only the strongholds of Herodium, Masada and Machaerus—outside of Jerusalem itself—remained in Jewish hands.

The suspension of the war in Judaea during 69, however, was of little avail to the Jews. According to Josephus, fierce struggles for mastery still continued among the insurgents in Jerusalem. He charges the rebel leaders with terrible enormities, of which the chief victims were the people of Jerusalem. That his account is distorted by personal interests is certain; it paid him to blame the Zealots to cover up his own betrayal. Indeed, the theme of his *Jewish War* is that of a peaceable people being dragged to disaster by brigands and fanatical desperadoes—namely, the Zealots. He is silent or elusive about the religious ideals of the Zealots; for they clearly had a faith, however fanatical, which he lacked. Josephus was always too mindful of the reality of Roman power to share in the Zealots' whole-hearted devotion to Yahweh.

In the spring of the year 70 the Romans were ready for their long-delayed vengeance on rebel Jerusalem. Vespasian appointed his elder son, Titus, to command the final operations. Titus assembled his army in Egypt and from there

The courtyard of the citadel at Jerusalem, built against the city's western wall on the site of Herod's palace, which was the last stronghold of the rebels in the city.

Titus, the son of the Emperor Vespasian, commanded the Roman expedition that captured Jerusalem from the Zealots.

marched into Judaea at the head of the most powerful force yet directed against the Jews. There were four legions, including the twelfth, which was intent on avenging its defeat in 66, and they were supported by a large auxiliary force.

The approach of the Romans shortly before the Passover at once united the Jewish factions within the city. John of Gischala and the Zealots held the Temple, and Simon ben Gioras organized the defense of the rest of the city. Jerusalem had three separate strongholds: the Temple; the fortress of Antonia, adjacent to it; and the palace of Herod, defended by massive towers, in the Upper City. Surrounded and subdivided by walls, the city had to be taken piecemeal. From the east it was overlooked by the Mount of Olives; but the steep intervening valley of the Kedron rendered it virtually impregnable on that side. The northern side was its weakest, despite efforts made to strengthen the defenses. And, accordingly, it was from the north that Titus began his attack.

The subsequent siege, one of the most terrible in history, is vividly described by Josephus, who was present on the staff of Titus. From the start the Jewish cause was hopeless. The city was crowded with refugees, as well as with troops, and famine soon became a more terrible scourge than the bombardment of the Roman *ballistae*. Josephus records a case of cannibalism—a mother killed her child and ate it. The Romans completely encircled the city with a wall of their own, built to prevent supplies from entering and refugees from escaping. Jerusalem was, indeed, "kept in on every side," as Jesus is recorded to have prophesied.

The Romans gradually broke their way through the outer and inner walls of the city, but the Jewish patriots fiercely contested every advance towards the Temple, focal point of their resistance. The fighting was extremely savage, and prisoners were cruelly treated by both sides. The reply made by John of Gischala to a Roman offer of

surrender on terms shows the spirit of the defenders. The Romans had waited until Jewish morale would be at its lowest; the last lamb had been offered in the Temple, and now the daily sacrifice to Yahweh had to stop. The Zealot commander nevertheless replied firmly that "he never would fear [its] capture, since the city was God's."

At last on August 29 the legionaries broke into the Temple. Its courts were crowded with refugees, hoping to the last for a miracle of divine intervention, and they were butchered by the ferocious legionaries. By accident, according to Josephus, the Temple was set ablaze by a Roman soldier who hurled a firebrand into an inner chamber. Despite the efforts of Titus to save the famous sanctuary, the legionaries could not be stopped in their lust for slaughter and destruction. Thousands of Jews perished in the Temple courts. Many priests retreated to the roofs, where they hurled ornamental spikes down on the Romans and finally plunged to their deaths in the flames of their burning sanctuary. When order was restored, the victorious legionaries erected their standards in the Temple courts and offered sacrifice to them, saluting Titus as Imperator. This act was a strange fulfillment of the prophecy the Jews had long feared—that the "Abomination of Desolation" would be set up in their Temple.

The capture of the Temple marked the virtual end of the revolt. Fierce fighting continued in the Upper City, but by September 26 all Jerusalem was in Roman hands. Most of the city had been reduced to a smoking ruin, and Titus ordered what was left standing to be razed, except the three great towers of the palace of Herod, which he preserved as a monument to the former strength of Jerusalem. Jewish losses during the siege had been enormous—Josephus puts the number at 1,100,000. The figure is surely a gross exaggeration; but the true figure must have been very large, for the siege was long, the famine severe and the

Part of the foundations of Herod's temple revealed near the Wailing Wall by recent excavation at Jerusalem.

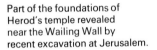

fighting fierce and at close quarters. The number of Jewish prisoners taken during the whole war is estimated by Josephus as 97,000, many of whom subsequently perished in the arenas of the Empire.

Titus returned to Rome. There, in 71, Vespasian and Titus celebrated their victory over rebel Judaea in an elaborately staged triumph. The victorious legionaries paraded through the streets of Rome with multitudes of Jewish prisoners displaying the rich booty, including the treasures of the Temple, followed by their proud commanders. The triumph culminated with the execution of Simon ben Gioras, as the chief rebel general, and a sacrifice of thanksgiving to Jupiter Capitolinus for the victory. On the Arch of Titus, in the Forum, two bas-reliefs still commemorate this triumph— the legionaries exulting as they carry the great Menorah of the Temple, the silver trumpets and the altar of shew-bread, while a winged Victory crowns Titus.

Even after the fall of Jerusalem, the Zealots did not give up the struggle. Some escaped into Egypt, where they tried to stir the Alexandrian Jews to revolt. They were rounded up, tortured in an endeavor to make them acknowledge "Caesar as lord" and executed. At Masada, by the Dead Sea, the Zealot garrison under Eleazar ben Jair held out until A.D. 73, when the Roman commander Silva laid siege to the fortress with the tenth legion. By incredible feats of military engineering in that waterless desert terrain, the Romans surrounded the great rocky plateau with a wall, obviously intent on preventing any escape. They also built a great ramp, to bring their battering-rams

within range of the fortress walls. But the Zealots fought back until they saw that further resistance was hopeless.

On the night before the final assault, the Jewish defenders killed their families and then themselves, preferring suicide to surrender. When the Romans broke in the next day, nine hundred and sixty dead bodies, among the smoking ruins of the fortress, testified to Zealot faith and fortitude.

The destruction of Jerusalem in A.D. 70 marked the definitive end of the Jewish national state until its rebirth in 1948. During the intervening nineteen centuries the Jews, scattered throughout the world, were a homeless and persecuted people. In 1967, in the Six Days' War, they finally completed their return to their ancient home by gaining possession of the Temple site. But, in the struggle to resurrect their national state, it has been to the Zealots of Masada that many have looked for inspiration. The excavation of that tragic site has been an act of national piety, which movingly links the new Israel with the old Israel that died there so heroically in A.D. 73.

S. G. F. BRANDON

Roman soldiers carrying loot—including the Menorah and altar of shewbread—from the sack of Jerusalem; a bas-relief from the Arch of Titus, at Rome.

153

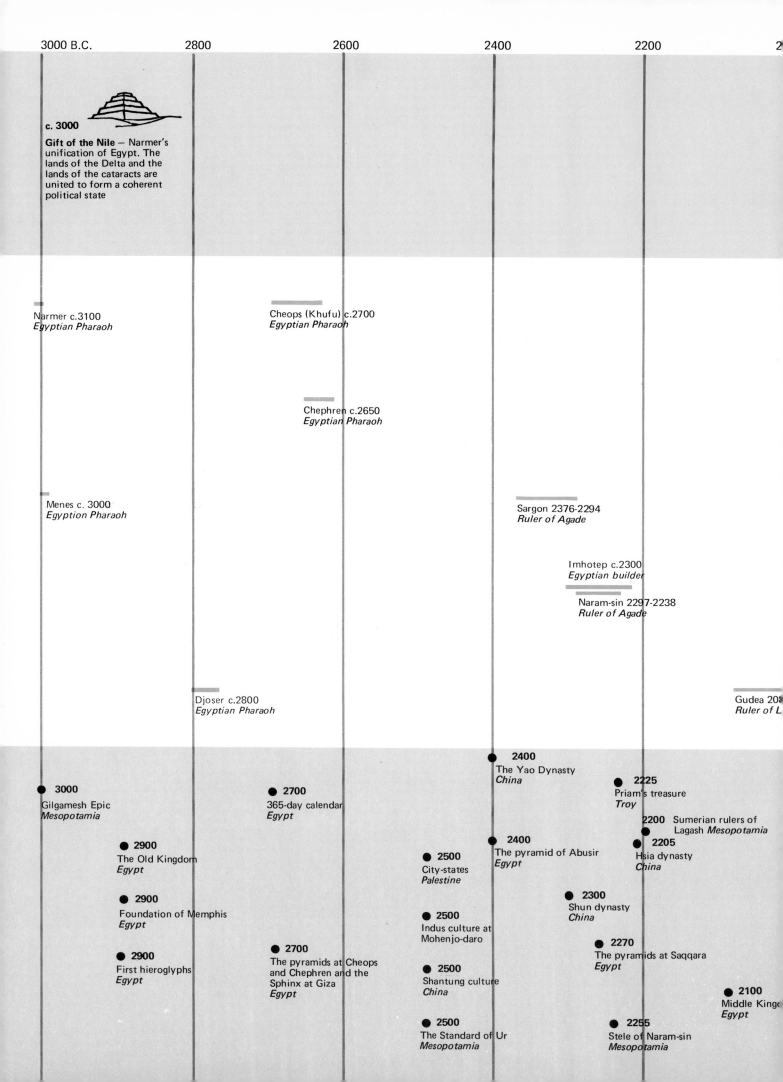

**c. 3000**

**Gift of the Nile** — Narmer's unification of Egypt. The lands of the Delta and the lands of the cataracts are united to form a coherent political state

Narmer c.3100
*Egyptian Pharaoh*

Cheops (Khufu) c.2700
*Egyptian Pharaoh*

Chephren c.2650
*Egyptian Pharaoh*

Menes c. 3000
*Egyption Pharaoh*

Sargon 2376-2294
*Ruler of Agade*

Imhotep c.2300
*Egyptian builder*

Naram-sin 2297-2238
*Ruler of Agade*

Djoser c.2800
*Egyptian Pharaoh*

Gudea 20
*Ruler of L*

● **2400**
The Yao Dynasty
*China*

● **3000**
Gilgamesh Epic
*Mesopotamia*

● **2700**
365-day calendar
*Egypt*

● **2225**
Priam's treasure
*Troy*

● **2200**  Sumerian rulers of
Lagash *Mesopotamia*

● **2900**
The Old Kingdom
*Egypt*

● **2400**
The pyramid of Abusir
*Egypt*

● **2500**
City-states
*Palestine*

● **2205**
Hsia dynasty
*China*

● **2900**
Foundation of Memphis
*Egypt*

● **2500**
Indus culture at
Mohenjo-daro

● **2300**
Shun dynasty
*China*

● **2270**
The pyramids at Saqqara
*Egypt*

● **2900**
First hieroglyphs
*Egypt*

● **2700**
The pyramids at Cheops
and Chephren and the
Sphinx at Giza
*Egypt*

● **2500**
Shantung culture
*China*

● **2100**
Middle Kingo
*Egypt*

● **2500**
The Standard of Ur
*Mesopotamia*

● **2255**
Stele of Naram-sin
*Mesopotamia*

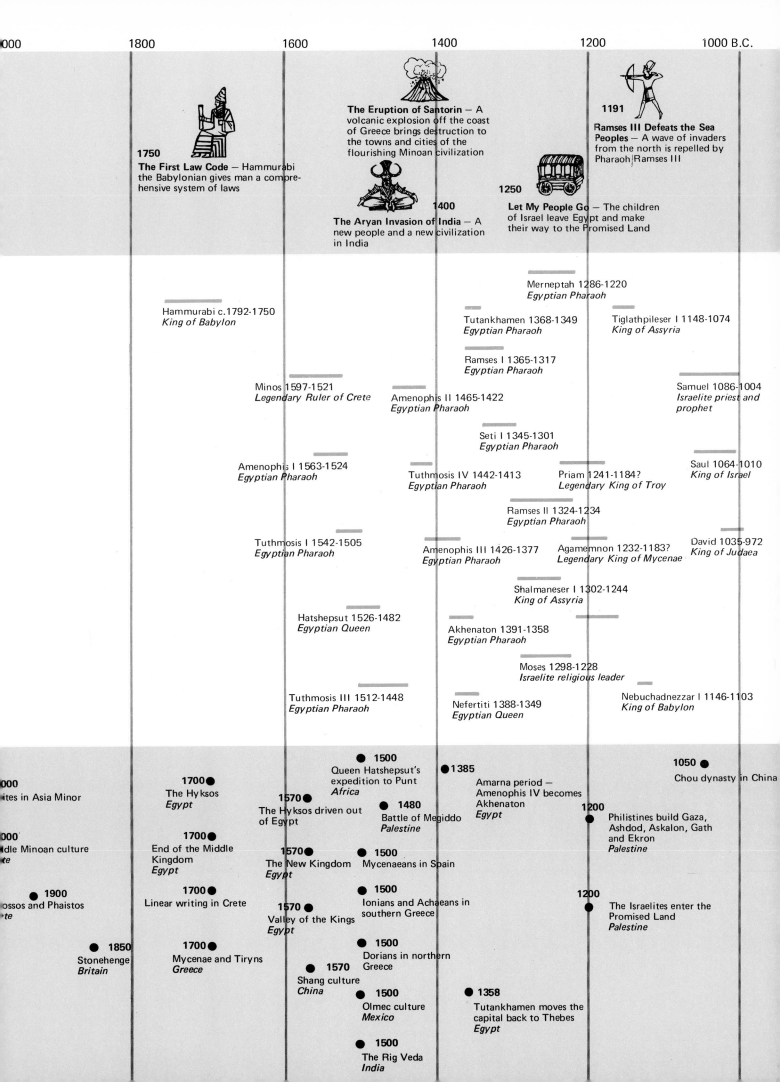

**2000** | **1800** | **1600** | **1400** | **1200** | **1000 B.C.**

**1750**

**The First Law Code** — Hammurabi the Babylonian gives man a comprehensive system of laws

**The Eruption of Santorin** — A volcanic explosion off the coast of Greece brings destruction to the towns and cities of the flourishing Minoan civilization

**1400**

**The Aryan Invasion of India** — A new people and a new civilization in India

**1250**

**Let My People Go** — The children of Israel leave Egypt and make their way to the Promised Land

**1191**

**Ramses III Defeats the Sea Peoples** — A wave of invaders from the north is repelled by Pharaoh Ramses III

Hammurabi c.1792-1750
*King of Babylon*

Merneptah 1286-1220
*Egyptian Pharaoh*

Tutankhamen 1368-1349
*Egyptian Pharaoh*

Tiglathpileser I 1148-1074
*King of Assyria*

Ramses I 1365-1317
*Egyptian Pharaoh*

Minos 1597-1521
*Legendary Ruler of Crete*

Amenophis II 1465-1422
*Egyptian Pharaoh*

Samuel 1086-1004
*Israelite priest and prophet*

Seti I 1345-1301
*Egyptian Pharaoh*

Amenophis I 1563-1524
*Egyptian Pharaoh*

Tuthmosis IV 1442-1413
*Egyptian Pharaoh*

Priam 1241-1184?
*Legendary King of Troy*

Saul 1064-1010
*King of Israel*

Ramses II 1324-1234
*Egyptian Pharaoh*

Tuthmosis I 1542-1505
*Egyptian Pharaoh*

Amenophis III 1426-1377
*Egyptian Pharaoh*

Agamemnon 1232-1183?
*Legendary King of Mycenae*

David 1035-972
*King of Judaea*

Shalmaneser I 1302-1244
*King of Assyria*

Hatshepsut 1526-1482
*Egyptian Queen*

Akhenaton 1391-1358
*Egyptian Pharaoh*

Moses 1298-1228
*Israelite religious leader*

Tuthmosis III 1512-1448
*Egyptian Pharaoh*

Nefertiti 1388-1349
*Egyptian Queen*

Nebuchadnezzar I 1146-1103
*King of Babylon*

● **1500**
Queen Hatshepsut's expedition to Punt
*Africa*

●**1385**

**1050** ●
Chou dynasty in China

**1700**●
The Hyksos
*Egypt*

**1570**●
The Hyksos driven out of Egypt

● **1480**
Battle of Megiddo
*Palestine*

Amarna period — Amenophis IV becomes Akhenaton
*Egypt*

**2000**
...ites in Asia Minor

**1200**
●
Philistines build Gaza, Ashdod, Askalon, Gath and Ekron
*Palestine*

**2000**
...ddle Minoan culture
...te

**1700**●
End of the Middle Kingdom
*Egypt*

**1570**●
The New Kingdom
*Egypt*

● **1500**
Mycenaeans in Spain

● **1900**
...ossos and Phaistos
...te

**1700**●
Linear writing in Crete

**1570**●
Valley of the Kings
*Egypt*

● **1500**
Ionians and Achaeans in southern Greece

**1200**
●
The Israelites enter the Promised Land
*Palestine*

● **1850**
Stonehenge
*Britain*

**1700**●
Mycenae and Tiryns
*Greece*

**1570**●
Shang culture
*China*

● **1500**
Dorians in northern Greece

● **1500**
Olmec culture
*Mexico*

● **1358**
Tutankhamen moves the capital back to Thebes
*Egypt*

● **1500**
The Rig Veda
*India*

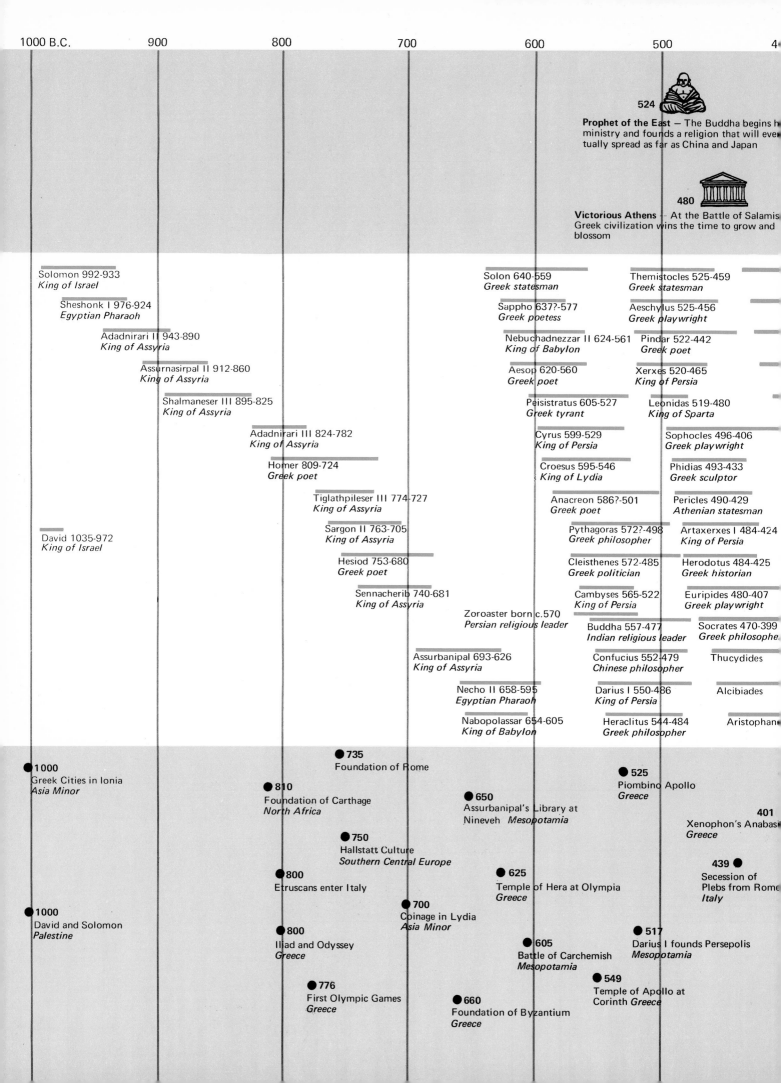

**1000 B.C.** | **900** | **800** | **700** | **600** | **500** | **4**

524

**Prophet of the East** — The Buddha begins his ministry and founds a religion that will eventually spread as far as China and Japan

480

**Victorious Athens** — At the Battle of Salamis Greek civilization wins the time to grow and blossom

Solomon 992-933
*King of Israel*

Sheshonk I 976-924
*Egyptian Pharaoh*

Adadnirari II 943-890
*King of Assyria*

Assurnasirpal II 912-860
*King of Assyria*

Shalmaneser III 895-825
*King of Assyria*

Adadnirari III 824-782
*King of Assyria*

Homer 809-724
*Greek poet*

Tiglathpileser III 774-727
*King of Assyria*

Sargon II 763-705
*King of Assyria*

Hesiod 753-680
*Greek poet*

Sennacherib 740-681
*King of Assyria*

David 1035-972
*King of Israel*

Solon 640-559
*Greek statesman*

Sappho 637?-577
*Greek poetess*

Nebuchadnezzar II 624-561
*King of Babylon*

Aesop 620-560
*Greek poet*

Peisistratus 605-527
*Greek tyrant*

Cyrus 599-529
*King of Persia*

Croesus 595-546
*King of Lydia*

Anacreon 586?-501
*Greek poet*

Pythagoras 572?-498
*Greek philosopher*

Cleisthenes 572-485
*Greek politician*

Cambyses 565-522
*King of Persia*

Zoroaster born c.570
*Persian religious leader*

Buddha 557-477
*Indian religious leader*

Assurbanipal 693-626
*King of Assyria*

Confucius 552-479
*Chinese philosopher*

Necho II 658-595
*Egyptian Pharaoh*

Nabopolassar 654-605
*King of Babylon*

Themistocles 525-459
*Greek statesman*

Aeschylus 525-456
*Greek playwright*

Pindar 522-442
*Greek poet*

Xerxes 520-465
*King of Persia*

Leonidas 519-480
*King of Sparta*

Sophocles 496-406
*Greek playwright*

Phidias 493-433
*Greek sculptor*

Pericles 490-429
*Athenian statesman*

Artaxerxes I 484-424
*King of Persia*

Herodotus 484-425
*Greek historian*

Euripides 480-407
*Greek playwright*

Socrates 470-399
*Greek philosopher*

Thucydides

Darius I 550-486
*King of Persia*

Alcibiades

Heraclitus 544-484
*Greek philosopher*

Aristophanes

● **735**
Foundation of Rome

● **1000**
Greek Cities in Ionia
*Asia Minor*

● **810**
Foundation of Carthage
*North Africa*

● **650**
Assurbanipal's Library at
Nineveh *Mesopotamia*

● **525**
Piombino Apollo
*Greece*

● **401**
Xenophon's Anabasis
*Greece*

● **750**
Hallstatt Culture
*Southern Central Europe*

● **800**
Etruscans enter Italy

● **625**
Temple of Hera at Olympia
*Greece*

● **439**
Secession of
Plebs from Rome
*Italy*

● **1000**
David and Solomon
*Palestine*

● **700**
Coinage in Lydia
*Asia Minor*

● **800**
Iliad and Odyssey
*Greece*

● **605**
Battle of Carchemish
*Mesopotamia*

● **517**
Darius I founds Persepolis
*Mesopotamia*

● **776**
First Olympic Games
*Greece*

● **549**
Temple of Apollo at
Corinth *Greece*

● **660**
Foundation of Byzantium
*Greece*

**323**

**The Death of Alexander the Great** — Alexander's death, when there was little left for him to conquer, robbed the world of one of its most favorable opportunities for cohesion

**Building The Great Wall of China** — The first universal Emperor Shih-huang-ti of the Ch'in Dynasty builds the Great Wall of China and establishes the boundaries of his empire **221**

**217**

**Hannibal Challenges Rome** — Hannibal crosses the Alps to launch the Second Punic War which ends in the eventual destruction of Carthage — Rome's great Mediterranean rival — thus clearing the way to Imperial Power

**The Slaves' Revolt** — Crassus crushes the revolt of the slaves, led by Spartacus. Hundreds are crucified and the Republic totters to its end

**The Battle of Actium** — The Battle of Actium confirms the supremacy of Augustus at the head of the Roman Empire and marks the end of Egypt as a force in world affairs **31**

**73**

**A.D.9 Arminius, Liberator of Germany** — Arminius defeats the Romans in the Battle of the Teutoburg Forest and so ends Augustus' plan to conquer all of Germany

**31 Jesus of Nazareth, Saviour God of a New Religion** — The Crucifixion of Jesus ensures a world role for Christianity in future centuries

**The Destruction of Zion** — The Temple at Jerusalem is destroyed along with the city, and the Jews are scattered throughout the known world **70**

---

Isocrates 436-338
*Greek orator*

Xenophon 430-353
*Greek historian*

Plato 427-347
*Greek philosopher*

Darius III ?-404
*King of Persia*

Diogenes 412-323
*Greek philosopher*

Praxiteles 403-335
*Greek sculptor*

Aristotle 384-322
*Greek philosopher*

Demosthenes 383-322
*Greek orator*

Philip II 382-336
*King of Macedonia*

Euclid 365-276
*Greek mathematician*

Callisthenes 360-327
*Greek poet*

Alexander 356-323
*Ruler of Macedonia and world conqueror*

59-398
*reek historian*

56-404
*reek politician*

46-385
*reek playwright*

Archimedes 284-212
*Greek thinker*

Hamilcar 282-229
*Carthaginian general*

Shih-huang-ti 259-209
*Emperor of China*

Hannibal 247-183
*Carthaginian general*

Scipio 235-183
*Roman general and statesman*

Cato 234-149
*Roman politician and man of letters*

Judas Maccabaeus 193-160
*Jewish patriot*

Wu-ti 157-87
*Emperor of China*

Marius 156-86 *Roman general and politician*

Sulla 138-78 *Roman general and politician*

Mithridates 132-63
*King of Pergamum*

Crassus 114-53 *Roman politician and general*

Spartacus 109?-71
*Leader of slave revolt*

Pompey 106-48 *Roman general and politician*

Cicero 106-43 *Roman politician and man of letters*

Pyrrhus 318-272
*King of Epirus*

Theocritus 301?-253
*Greek poet*

Asoka 299-227
*King of India*

Julius Caesar 100-44
*Roman statesman and general*

Marc Antony 83-30
*Roman politician*

Vercingetorix 80-46
*Gallic leader*

Herod the Great 72-4
*King of Judaea*

Virgil 70-19
*Roman poet*

Cleopatra 69-30
*Queen of Egypt*

Horace 65-8
*Roman poet*

Agrippa 63-12 *Roman statesman and general*

Augustus 63- A.D.14
(Octavian) *Founder of the Roman Empire*

Varus 48-A.D. 9
*Roman general*

Ovid 43- A.D. 17
*Roman poet*

Tiberius 42-A.D.37
*Roman Emperor*

Herod Antipas 27-A.D.40
*Ruler of Judaea*

Maroboduus 24?-A.D.37
*Leader of the Marcomanni*

Pontius Pilate 26?-A.D.36
*Roman Governor of Judaea*

Arminius 16-A.D.21
*German leader*

Germanicus 15-A.D.19
*Roman general*

Claudius 10-A.D.54
*Roman Emperor*

John the Baptist 7-A.D.29
*Jewish preacher*

Jesus Christ 6- A.D.30
*Jewish religious leader*

Vespasian A.D.9 - A.D.79
*Roman Emperor*

Pliny the Elder 23-79
*Roman writer*

Agrippa II 27-100
*Jewish prince*

Nerva 26-98
*Roman Emperor*

Nero 37-68
*Roman Emperor*

Josephus 37-95
*Jewish historian*

Titus 40-81
*Roman Emperor*

Plutarch 47-122
*Greek man of letters*

Tacitus 55-120
*Roman historian*

Suetonius 70-160
*Roman historian*

---

● **356**
Temple of Diana at Ephesus burned by Herostratos *Asia Minor*

**320** ●
Chandragupta First Paramount Ruler of India

● **286**
Foundation of Library at Alexandria *Egypt*

**272** ●
Kingdom of Asoka in Afghanistan and North India

● **264**
First Punic War between Rome and Carthage

Shih-huang-ti First ● **220**
Universal Emperor of *China*

● **245**
Lion Capital at Sarnath *India*

● **219**
Second Punic War between Rome and Carthage

● **202**
Foundation of Han Dynasty *China*

● **167**
First Maccabaean revolt *Palestine*

● **149**
Third Punic War between Rome and Carthage

● **197**
Rosetta Stone (discovered 1822) *Egypt*

● **111**
Jugurthine War *Italy*

● **100**
Qumran manuscripts — Dead Sea Scrolls *Palestine*

● **88**
First Mithridatic War

● **60**
First Triumvirate — Caesar, Pompey and Crassus — in Rome *Italy*

● **49**
Caesar crosses the Rubicon *Italy*

● **46**
Introduction of Julian Calendar *Italy*

● **43**
Second Triumvirate — Marc Antony, Octavian and Lepidus — in Rome *Italy*

● **17**
Maroboduus launches Marcomannic War *Southern Central Europe*

● **30**
Apicus' cookbook *Italy*

● **45**
St. Paul begins his missionary journeys

● **75**
Kushana Dynasty *Northern India*

● **79**
Pompeii and Herculaneum destroyed *Italy*

● **80**
Colosseum completed *Italy*

# Acknowledgments

The authors and publishers wish to thank the following museums and collections by whose kind permission the illustrations are reproduced. Page numbers appear in bold, photographic sources in italics:

**1** (1) Egyptian Museum, Cairo (2) British Museum, London (3) Archaeological Museum, Heraclion (4) *Josephine Powell*
**2** (1) British Museum (2) *Werner Forman* (3) Musée Guimet, Paris: *Agence Rapho*
**3** (1) British Museum (2) Museo Archaeologico Nazionale, Naples: *Scala* (3) Private Collection, Prague: *Werner Forman*
**4** (1) Musée des Antiquités, Rabat: *Service des Antiquités de Maroc* (2) Ny Carlsberg Glyptotek, Copenhagen (3) British Museum
**5** (1) Kunsthistorisches Museum, Vienna (3) Israel Museum, Jerusalem
**12** *Werner Forman*
**13** (1) Egyptian Museum: *Michael Holford*
**14** (1) Staatliche Museen, Berlin (East): *Werner Forman* (2) Ashmolean Museum, Oxford
**15** Egyptian Museum: *Hirmer Verlag*
**16** (1) British Museum (2) Louvre, Paris: *Réalités (J. Guillot)* (3) British Museum: *Michael Holford*
**17** (1) Egyptian Museum: *Hirmer Verlag* (2) *United Arab Republic Ministry of Information*
**18** Egyptian Museum: *Werner Forman*
**19** (1, 2) British Museum: *Michael Holford*
**20** (1) Louvre (2) Iraq Museum, Bagdad (3) British Museum (4) Iraq Museum
**21** (1) Iraq Museum (2) Oriental Institute, Chicago (3) National Museum of Pakistan, Karachi (4) British Museum (5) Iraq Museum
**22** Louvre: *Françoise Foliot*
**23** Louvre: *Françoise Foliot*
**24** British Museum: *Etienne Hubert*
**25** Louvre: *Françoise Foliot*
**26** (1) *Paul Popper* (2) British Museum
**27** (1, 2, 3) Louvre: *Etienne Hubert* (4) British Museum
**28** Louvre: *Françoise Foliot*
**29** British Museum: *Michael Holford*
**30** (1) British Museum: *C. Raeburn* (2, 3, 4) British Museum
**31** (1) National Museum, Aleppo: *Adrian Arthaud* (2) Staatliche Museen, Berlin (West) (3) British Museum (4) *Josephine Powell*
**32** *F. Cianetti*
**33** Archaeological Museum, Heraclion: *Leonard von Matt*
**34/35** *Hirmer Verlag*
**35** *Josephine Powell*
**36** (1) *Hirmer Verlag* (2) *Leonard von Matt*
**37** (1) *Leonard von Matt* (2) *F. Cianetti*
**38** National Museum, Athens: *Hirmer Verlag*
**39** National Museum, Athens: *Dimitrios Itarissiadis (© George Rainbird Limited)*

**40** (1) *Lehnert and Landrock* (2) Eygptian Museum: *John Freeman* (3) *Werner Forman* (4) *Hirmer Verlag*
**41** (1) British Museum (2) Egyptian Museum: *Michael Holford* (3, 4) *Werner Forman*
**42** *Josephine Powell*
**43** *Josephine Powell*
**44** (1) British Museum (2) *Sir Mortimer Wheeler*
**45** (1, 2, 3) *Sir Mortimer Wheeler*
**46** (1, 2) *Sir Mortimer Wheeler*
**47** (1, 2) *Norma Schwitter*
**48** (1) British Museum (2) *Egyptian State Tourist Administration* (3) British Museum (4) Ashmolean Museum, Oxford (5) Staatliche Museen, Berlin (West) (6) Louvre: *Marburg*
**49** (1) National Museum, Aleppo: *Maurice Chuzeville* (2) Louvre: *Giraudon* (3) British Museum (4) *Roger Percheron*
**50** *Réalités (J. L. Swiners)*
**51** *Roger Percheron*
**52** *Agence Rapho*
**53** (1) British Museum: *Michael Holford* (2, 3, 4) National Museum, Beirut: *Roger Percheron, C. Raeburn*
**54** *Adrian Arthaud*
**55** (1) Staatliche Museen, Berlin (East): *Werner Forman* (2) British Museum: *Michael Holford*
**56** (1) *Lehnert and Landrock* (2) Egyptian Museum: *Anderson* (3) *Norma Schwitter* (4) *Turkish Embassy* (5) *Hirmer Verlag* (6) *Josephine Powell*
**57** (1) *Hirmer Verlag* (2) Museo Capitolino, Rome: *David Harris* (3) *Paul Ronald Arthaud* (4, 5) *Josephine Powell*
**58** Egyptian Museum: *Werner Forman*
**59** *Werner Forman*
**60** (1, 2) *Werner Forman*
**61** *Werner Forman*
**63** (1) *Roger Percheron* (2) British Museum: *Michael Holford* (3) *Norma Schwitter*
**64** British Museum
**65** British Museum
**66** (1) Archaeological Museum, Ankara: *Josephine Powell* (2, 3, 4) British Museum
**67** (1) Staatliche Museen, Berlin (East) (2) Walters Art Gallery, Baltimore (3) British Museum (4) Archaeological Museum, Teheran: *Josephine Powell*
**68** Musée Guimet, Paris: *Werner Forman*
**69** Musée Guimet: *Werner Forman*
**70** (1, 2) British Museum: *Werner Forman*
**71** (1, 2) British Museum: *Werner Forman*
**72** (1) Musée Guimet: *Agence Rapho* (2) National Museum of Pakistan: *Norma Schwitter*
**73** *Douglas Dickins*
**74** (1) Acropolis Museum, Athens: *Hirmer Verlag* (2) Archaeological Museum, Heraclion (3, 4) British Museum (5) Deutches Archäologisches Institute, Athens
**75** (1) Museo Archaeologico, Florence: *Aliniari* (2) Vatican Museum, Rome: *Werner Forman, John Freeman*
**76** Museo Ostia, Rome: *James Austin*
**77** (1) *Roger Percheron* (2) British Museum: *Michael Holford*

**78** (1) Archaeological Museum, Teheran: *Roger Percheron* (2) British Museum
**79** (1) Archaeological Museum, Teheran (2) Museo Villa Giulia, Rome: *Alinari*
**80** (1) British Museum (2) *Hirmer Verlag*
**81** (1) Archaeological Museum, Delphi: *Werner Forman* (2) National Museum, Athens: *Hirmer Verlag*
**82** (1) *Greek National Tourist Office* (2) British Museum: *Michael Holford*
**83** British Museum: *Werner Forman*
**84** (1) Archaeological Museum, Sparta: *Mansell Collection* (2) *Hirmer Verlag* (3) British Museum (4) Rheinishes Landesmuseum, Trier: *Mansell Collection*
**85** (1) British Museum: *John Freeman* (2) Museo Archaeologico Nazionale: *Alinari* (3) *Hirmer Verlag* (4) Staatliche Museen, Berlin (East) (5) Acropolis Museum: *Alinari* (6) Ny Carlsberg Glyptotek
**86** Museo Archaeologico Nazionale: *Scala*
**87** British Museum: *Ian Graham*
**88** Archaeological Museum, Istanbul
**89** Archaeological Museum, Istanbul: *Roger Percheron*
**90** (1) *Werner Forman* (2) *Roger Percheron*
**91** *Roger Percheron*
**92** British Museum: *Michael Holford*
**93** (1) National Museum of Pakistan: *Norma Schwitter* (2) National Museum, Damascus: *Werner Forman*
**94** (1, 2, 3) *Abe Čapek*
**95** (1, 2, 3) *Abe Čapek*
**96** British Museum
**97** *Secas—B. Vilerbue*
**98** (1, 2) Private Collection, Prague: *Werner Forman*
**99** Private Collection, Prague: *Werner Forman*
**100** British Museum
**101** (1) *Werner Forman* (2) *Secas—B. Vilerbue*
**102** (1) Museo Capitolino: *Alinari* (2) Vatican Museum (3) *Alinari* (4) Museo Villa Giulia: *Alinari*
**103** (1) *Hirmer Verlag* (2) Museo Villa Guilia: *Gabinetto Fotografico Nazionale* (3) *Werner Forman* (4) *Alinari* (5) *John Freeman* (6) Museo Archaeologico Nazionale: *Anderson*
**104** Bibliothèque Nationale, Paris: *Picard*
**105** Bibliothèque Nationale: *Picard*
**106** Museo Villa Giulia: *Alinari*
**107** Museo Arqueológico, Madrid: *Picard*
**108** *Picard*
**109** (1) *James Austin* (2) *J. Allan Cash*
**110** (1, 2) Staatliche Museen, Berlin (West) (3) *Werner Forman* (4) *Courtauld Institute* (5) British Museum
**111** (1) *Alinari* (2) Uffizi, Florence (3) British Museum (4) *James Austin* (5) British Museum
**112** Ny Carlsberg Glyptotek
**113** (1) Museo delle Terme: *James Austin* (2) *Alinari*
**114** (1) Museo Lateranese, Rome:

*Alinari* (2) British Museum: *Werner Forman*
**115** (1) Ny Carlsberg Glyptotek (2) Museo Lateranese: *Alinari*
**116** Bardo Museum, Tunis: *Norma Schwitter*
**117** (1) *Scala* (2) British Museum: *Werner Forman*
**118** (1) Louvre: *Giraudon* (2, 3) *Alinari* (5) Vatican Museum
**119** (1) *Giraudon* (2) Louvre (3) Vatican Museum (4) British Museum (5) Vatican Museum
**120** British Museum: *Werner Forman*
**121** British Museum: *Werner Forman*
**122** Museum of Fine Arts, Boston
**123** (1) British Museum: *Werner Forman* (2) British Museum: *Michael Holford*
**124** Vatican Museum
**125** British Museum
**126** (1) Museo Archaeologico Nazionale: *Alinari* (2) British Museum: *Michael Holford*
**127** (1) British Museum: *Werner Forman*
**128** (1) British Museum: *John Freeman* (2) Kunsthistorisches Museum (3) *Alinari* (4) Vatican Museum
**129** (1) *Foto Unione* (2, 3) British Museum (4, 5) *Alinari*
**130** British Museum: *Werner Forman*
**131** (1) Kunsthistorisches Museum (2) *Alinari*
**132** (1) *Alinari* (2) British Museum
**133** (1, 2) British Museum
**134** (1) *Alinari* (2) British Museum: *Michael Holford*
**135** *Roger Percheron*
**136** (1) *Helga Schmidt-Glassner (© J. G. Cotta'sche Verlag)* (2) Niederoster-reichisches Landesmuseum, Vienna (3) Rheinishes Landesmuseum (4) *Warburg Institute* (5) Museo Treviri, Florence: *Alinari*
**137** (1, 2) British Museum (3) Staatliche Museen, Berlin (East)
**138** British Museum
**139** (1) Caesarea Museum, Kibbutz Sedot Ham: *David Harris*
**140** (1) *Jordan Ministry of Information* (2) British Museum
**141** (1) *Hirmer Verlag* (2) *Jordan Ministry of Information*
**144** (1, 2) Israel Museum: *David Harris* (3) *Alinari*
**145** (1) British Museum (2, 3) British Museum: *John Freeman* (4) Vatican Museum: *Alinari* (5, 6) Israel Museum: *David Harris*
**146** (1) Israel Museum: *David Harris* (2) *Roger Percheron*
**147** (1) *Roger Percheron* (2) Israel Museum: *David Harris*
**148** *Jordan Ministry of Tourism*
**149** British Museum
**150** (1, 2) *David Harris*
**151** *David Harris*
**152** (1) Museo Capitolino: *Anderson* (2) *David Harris*
**153** *Alinari*

# Index

ISBN: Clothbound edition 0-88225-058-2
ISBN: Deluxe edition 0-88225-059-0
Library of Congress Catalog Card No. 70—98159

© George Weidenfeld and Nicolson Ltd, 1970
First published 1970. Second edition 1973.

Printed and bound in Italy
by Arnoldo Mondadori Editore - Verona

217

73

31 B.C.

# I Ancient Empires

480

323

221 B.C.

**Newsweek Books**  New York

*Editor*  S.G.F. Brandon

1280

1191

524

# 1 Ancient Empires

3000          1750          1450          1400 B.C.